Elusive Jannah

Elusive Jannah

The Somali Diaspora and a Borderless Muslim Identity

CAWO M. ABDI

UNIVERSITY OF MINNESOTA PRESS
MINNEAPOLIS · LONDON

The publication of this book was supported by an Imagine Fund grant for the Arts, Design, and Humanities, an annual award from the University of Minnesota Provost's Office.

Copyright 2015 by the Regents of the University of Minnesota

All rights reserved. No part of this publication may be reproduced, stored in a retrieval system, or transmitted, in any form or by any means, electronic, mechanical, photocopying, recording, or otherwise, without the prior written permission of the publisher.

Published by the University of Minnesota Press
111 Third Avenue South, Suite 290
Minneapolis, MN 55401-2520
http://www.upress.umn.edu

Library of Congress Cataloging-in-Publication Data

Abdi, Cawo M.
Elusive Jannah : the Somali diaspora and a borderless Muslim identity / Cawo M. Abdi.
   Includes bibliographical references and index.
   ISBN 978-0-8166-9738-0 (hc)
   ISBN 978-0-8166-9739-7 (pb)
1. Somali diaspora. 2. Somalis—United Arab Emirates—Social conditions. 3. Somalis—South Africa—Social conditions. 4. Somalis—United States—Social conditions. 5. Muslims—Cultural assimilation. 6. Immigrants—Cultural assimilation. I. Title.
   DT402.45.A23   2015
   305.893540088297—dc23   2014043030

Printed in the United States of America on acid-free paper

The University of Minnesota is an equal-opportunity educator and employer.

21 20 19 18 17 16 15   10 9 8 7 6 5 4 3 2 1

CONTENTS

Acknowledgments / vii

Introduction: Muslim African Refugees and Border Politics / 1

1 The Genesis of Contemporary Somali Migrations / 31

2 United Arab Emirates: Partial Belonging and Temporary Visas / 59

3 South Africa: Insecurity in Racialized Spaces / 111

4 United States: Slippery Jannah? / 169

Conclusion: Muslim African Refugees in Perpetual Passage / 231

Notes / 243

Index / 273

ACKNOWLEDGMENTS

Countless Somali men and women gave me their precious time and trusted me with their life histories at the five sites where I conducted research over the years (Somalia, Kenya, the United Arab Emirates, South Africa, and the United States). Their kindness often humbled me, and this book is dedicated to Somalis everywhere whose unbounded hospitality (*martigalis*) survived the political crises still plaguing that nation.

Like all books, this one was long in the making and owes a lot to colleagues, friends, and family. Donna Gabaccia, Teresa Gowan, Lisa Park, Jennifer Pierce, and Rachel Schurman commented on parts or all of the manuscript. Their friendship and incessant confidence in this book kept me going when the going got tough, and I cannot express enough gratitude. Many thanks also to Abdi Samatar for wonderful feedback on chapter 1 and to Janis Grobbelaar for a thorough reading of chapter 3. Working with freelance editor David Lobenstine was a delight. His superb eye and detailed feedback greatly improved this work. Thanks to Pete Kennedy and Mark Lindberg for the fantastic maps in this book.

Comments received at various platforms where I presented parts of this project were useful as well. These included the University of Minnesota; invited talks at the University of California at San Diego, the College of St. Catherine, Central Connecticut State University, Macalester College, St. Louis University, Denison University, Ohio Wesleyan University, St. Cloud

State University, and the University of Pretoria; and conferences of the American Sociological Association, the Canadian Sociological Association Congress, the South African Sociological Congress, and the African Studies Association.

I am fortunate to be in a great department. Our former and current chairs, Chris Uggen and Elizabeth Boyle, have supported this work. Thanks to my colleagues Ron Aminzade, Gabrielle Ferrales, Michael Goldman, Kathy Hall, Doug Hartman, Phyllis Moen, Josh Page, David Pellow, and Teresa Swartz. Thanks to Richard Black for great mentorship over the years. I am surrounded and inspired by wonderful colleagues and friends—Erika Busse, Njeri Githire, James Hendricks, Allen Isaacman, Meg Karraker, Trica Keaton, Diyah Larasati, Helga Leitner, M. J. Maynes, Eric Sheppard, and Anita Waters. Janis Grobbelaar, Maxi Schoeman, Charles Puttergill, Vangile Bingma, and Angela Ochse went beyond the call of duty to facilitate our stay in Pretoria. Thanks to Mary Drew, Ann Miller, and Hilda Mork in Minnesota and Martie Hanekom and Rita du Toit in Pretoria for essential administrative needs over the years.

I am most obliged to Nazli Kibria and Steven Gold for their constructive feedback as reviewers of this manuscript for the University of Minnesota Press. Steven Gold also provided indispensable follow-up feedback. It was fantastic to work with Jason Weidemann and other editorial staff at the University of Minnesota Press.

Too many to mention, but I would like to name a few individuals whose guidance in various settings facilitated the research process: in South Africa, Abdirashid Ibrahim, Amina M. Ali, Bashir Abdullahi, Sultan Ali, Ahmed Dowlo, Sheikh Ahmed Abdi, Mohamed Hassan, Osman Mohamed, Abdi Borama, Alas Jama, Mohamed Abdullahi, Ruqiya Mire Jama, and Fadumo Gaa'ir; in Minneapolis and St. Paul, Said Fahie, Maryan Dheel, Sheikh Abdirahman Sharif, Saharla Jama, Zuhur Ahmed, and Ahmed Yusuf; in Columbus, Jibril Mohamed, Mohamud Dirios, Doug Rutledge, Abdi Roble, Abdi Farah, Anita Waters, Ismail Ahmed, Roda Hassan, Nafisa Daud, and Sahrakiin Siad; in the UAE, Abdullahi Ali (Haybe), Alibadal Ahmed, Issa Hagi Farah, Fawsia Nur, Ahmed Naji Warfa, Ibrahim Sheikh, Sahra Saleh, and Fadumo and Muse Garow. My humble apologies to others whose names do not appear in this recognition but should have.

A grant from the University of Minnesota's Office of International Programs, a Multicultural Research Award, and a semester residence at the

Institute for Advanced Studies as well as a yearlong Fulbright Fellowship gave me the time and resources to complete this project. I would also like to acknowledge a Canadian Social Science and Humanities Research Council Fellowship as well as a British Commonwealth Fellowship for funding my doctoral work, from which the U.S. case draws. This book could not have been without the great commitment and professionalism of many research assistants. Thanks to Abdulkadir Ali, Abdifatah Mohamed, Saida Abdi, Ahmed Ali, Yasin Garad, June Msechu, and Guled Ibrahim. Adam Casey was an integral part of this book for the past four years and provided essential research assistance that aided its timely completion.

The unconditional love of family and friends makes everything we accomplish possible. Thanks to my siblings, Maryam, Safia, Saida, Habib, and Wa'an. My older sisters sacrificed their own pursuits to provide for dozens of family members while I pursued my education. I would not have accomplished half of what I have without them. Much love to my nephew and nieces, Mohamed Nur-Sed and Yasmin and Khadija Mohamed; my brothers-in-law, Jon Thorleifson, Rage Mohamed, and Ahmed Samatar; and cousins Ida, Edil, Hibak, and Deka and Bilan Hersi. My friend and sister Asha Issa fed me, housed me, and put up with my mess in my writing escapade to Ottawa. Thanks to Natasha Avakova, Geoffrey Dean, and Hodan Mohamed for decades of friendship. Thanks to my Minnesota family Amina Farah, Saida, Idil, Sagal, Nasra, and Ifrah Makarios for child care and absolute love. Special thanks to Abdi Samatar, who has been part of this book from its inception to its completion. It is impossible to quantify his contributions to my life and work. Our children, Sama and Tusmo, have learned the word *tenure* too soon. They accepted that Mom's project deserved weekend excursions to cafés and public libraries, and they, more than anyone, are most relieved it is now complete.

Most important, I thank my mother, Asha Qaalli. She raised eight children in the direst economic circumstances and encouraged us all to pursue education, though she has never had any schooling. She is a fearless poet and a pillar of courage, and we owe everything to her. This book is dedicated to her and to other mothers whose valiant efforts to create a semblance of normalcy for their children everywhere keep Somalia's hope alive.

INTRODUCTION

Muslim African Refugees and Border Politics

Osman, Sharjah, United Arab Emirates

"I am very aware that people [Somalis] are complaining in Europe, but then the only thing one really needs is that passport. I hear when you first go there [Europe] you will have to go to a camp in order to adapt to the country. And then you will have to wait for the passport for about five or six years and you lose all this time. Whereas I am now progressing and moving forward, it is clear that I would have to start life all over again if I went there. At least that is how I think about it. I mean, if it was possible to go there and get papers easily, then I think I would have gone. We know Somalis are people without proper legal status and that is what drives us to go to all these places."

Osman[1] and I are eating in a small Yemeni restaurant just outside of Dubai City, sitting on a mat on the floor with cushions at our backs, in a private cubicle with curtains used by families, couples, or women requiring privacy.

Osman is in his twenties, and he drove to the restaurant in an almost brand-new Toyota SUV that belongs to his much older brother, who brought him up in the United Arab Emirates (UAE) from his early teens. Since finishing high school, Osman has worked in the Somali ethnic economy, providing his language skills and cultural know-how of the UAE for Somali exporters to navigate the state bureaucracy in and around the ports. Export to and import from Somalia are the key industries employing almost all Somalis, with the UAE (and Kenya) now effectively the off-port economic center of Somalia.

Osman's brother is a successful entrepreneur in the import–export of goods and services to Somalia. Like all labor migrants in the UAE, Somalis endure a perpetual, costly, and at times uncertain visa renewal process—one of the many reasons that people like Osman desire another home to which to migrate. This is less of an issue for him, with his brother's enterprise providing a guaranteed work visa. But even Osman wonders if further migration would help him improve his future prospects. Return to Somalia is not an option, as the country remains in political turmoil, with millions still internally displaced and hundreds of thousands in limbo in refugee camps in Kenya, Djibouti, and Yemen.

For now, Osman feels very much at home in the UAE: "I mean, I do not want to leave here. This place is blessed. I am a man who understands the culture and the language here. I can also speak English and Urdu. So thank God I am living comfortably and I am not missing anything."

Osman portrays his situation in the UAE in religious terms, with "blessed" connoting the absence of financial, emotional, or spiritual need to seek further migration. But more important, "this place is blessed," and "it is a Muslim country," and "the locals respect you" are expressions I've heard from nearly all Somalis with whom I spoke in the UAE. These expressions tell us that migrants' evaluations of their welfare in their new land require a more holistic sense of well-being, a sense of comfort and peace, a sense of belonging akin to being at home. But the degree of this belonging can either be enhanced or diminished by the more rigid, bureaucratic realities of one's citizenship status and economic position.

The Somali designation for men who migrated to the Arabian Peninsula in the oil boom era of the 1970s was *Jannaalayaal* (*Jannaalle* in the singular). The root of this Arabic–Somali word, *jannah*, means "paradise." Migration to the Arabian Peninsula, with its oil-driven prosperity but also its particular spiritual significance for Muslim laborers as the birthplace of the revered prophet Muhammad, was imagined by Somalis as the closest one can get to earthy paradise. But this depiction of migration was imaginary, reinforced by the remittances these mostly male migrants sent back. The reality of their lives was mysterious to those they left behind. Families at home assumed that migrating relatives led lavish lives, with the remittances they sent back symbolizing their new socioeconomic standing in the countries to which they migrated. Osman's portrayal of making progress and living a blessed, jannah-like migrant life in the UAE is an instance where the Somali imaginary and the lived experience are aligned.

But behind this depiction of the UAE lies the closed-off option of return to and life at home, Somalia. Osman's narrative is one of many to emerge in this new era of Somali mass migration, triggered by the political instability plaguing Somalia since 1988. The UAE and other oil-rich Muslim countries, which defined the labor migration of the 1970s and early 1980s, have been superseded in the Somali imaginary by more far-flung destinations. These new destinations appear to offer refugee status, prospects for citizenship, and economic opportunities. Osman's acknowledgment of how content he is with life in the UAE still makes space for the necessity of more secure citizenship for Somalis, whose country has been in turmoil for more than two decades. We see Osman weighing the sense of belonging he feels in the UAE against the desire to seek the Western citizenship about which many Somalis dream.

Communication among Somalis who already made it to the United States, Canada, and Europe transmits information about the potential gains that migration to these regions entails, and this is often articulated in comparative terms with the locations in which Somalis are currently residing. This circulation of information and resources among Somalis located in different regions is one fruit of globalization, yet the ease of information flowing through diverse communication technologies does not necessarily mean that migrants are no less disappointed by the realities of their new lives. Such networks, together with Somalia's political crisis, inform Somalis' imaginary about destinations beyond the traditional oil-rich Muslim countries such as the UAE and Saudi Arabia.

Ardo, Bellville, South Africa

"I hate it here. At the beginning, it was very good and this was especially so when I was new because I came from Somalia. But now, with all my family still back home, I understand that I cannot just continue to ask my husband to send them money. These reasons, combined with the lack of proper legal papers here, are why I want to migrate further."

Ardo and I sat in her living room in the central business district of Bellville. The apartment was dark, with the heavy burgundy curtains still drawn, though it was midday. Ardo is in her mid-twenties, a short and heavy-set stay-at-home wife with an oval, expressive face. She came to South Africa through a flight from northern Somalia, to Addis Ababa, Ethiopia, to Maputo, Mozambique, where smugglers helped her cross the South African border to join her new husband, who lived in Bellville, on the outskirts of Cape Town. Her husband's clothing store business occupied the first floor of the three-story building at the heart of the town; the new couple lived in a one-bedroom apartment on the top floor of this building. Ardo was married to one of the most successful Somali entrepreneurs in the area, with half a dozen Somali and non-Somali employees working for him in the clothing store as well as a fast-food restaurant he runs.

Ardo explained that she has tried twice to leave South Africa using smuggled Western European passports. Such passports cost between $10,000 and $15,000, mostly payable only after successful entry to the hoped-for destination. She was caught both times at the airport but was negotiating with a third smuggler during the week I interviewed her. Though her husband is one of the most successful Somalis in South Africa, she still desires a life elsewhere.

Both Ardo and her husband, Shakur, held residency papers in South Africa, but these are not seen as "proper" documents. South Africa grants Somalis asylum as refugees from a war-torn nation (which is far more official recognition than they are granted in the UAE). But such a status does not help in Ardo's ultimate goal; American and European visas are beyond the reach of Somali refugees carrying African travel documents, unless these are accompanied by proof of major financial assets. We see, then, that for Somalis throughout Africa (and the Middle East), what are "proper" legal documents are only citizenship and travel documents granted by the European Union, the United States, Canada, or, to a lesser extent, Australia. Ardo's desired destinations were the Netherlands or England, where she had many friends. But Ardo insisted that this migration aspiration was not for her per se, but rather was necessitated by her family still in Somalia, and especially her widowed sister, who had ten children. Asked how much Shakur sends to her family, Ardo replied,

> Three hundred [dollars per month]. But when the need arises, he sends more money. But I do not want to burden him with them as business is

getting slow in South Africa. . . . It is hard for him to continue to support me and my family. So I want to go there [Europe] and get proper documents and then work and help my family.

Ardo's discontent with South Africa is intensified by what she imagines she can do for her family if she gets to Europe, compared to what she can do for them by staying on in South Africa as a stay-at-home wife dependent on her husband. Although she knows that she has no transferable human capital to help her easily integrate into the European labor force, she cites friends there who collect welfare to survive, insisting that they are doing well, able both to send enough money home and also to facilitate the migration of family members to join them. For her, as for Osman, citizenship status is of primary consideration, but equally important for Ardo is government support. Through her networks, she has come to believe that her best options are countries that offer state welfare services as well as the possibility of naturalization, family reunification, and ongoing mobility across borders—privileges denied to most Somalis who migrate to the Middle East or elsewhere in Africa. Ardo prioritizes the citizenship she can get by receiving refugee status from somewhere in Europe and imagines the eventual sponsorship and migration opportunities she can bestow on her sister, her nephews, and her nieces.

There is another powerful force behind the desire of many Somalis in South Africa to further migrate to Europe and North America: high levels of property and physical violence. Many of my interviewees in South Africa underscored the precariousness of their lives as township traders, the sector in which most Somali men are concentrated. The daily risk of violence makes South Africa less attractive as a final destination, overshadowing Somali migrants' considerable economic gains and the benefits of legal refugee status. South Africa's unenviable position as one of the world's most violent societies means that large segments of its own population experience multiple forms of violence, ranging from homicide to rape and robbery. This violence can disproportionately affect newcomers, such as Somalis, who are seen to benefit from postapartheid opportunities that remain out of the reach of the majority of poor, black South Africans. Thus, although Shakur sends more than $300 to Ardo's family and even more money to his own family, and although almost any young Somali refugee can afford *some* remittances, extreme levels of poverty plague South African townships. Migration to South Africa hence is often built on contradiction. Despite their alliances with and integration into the Indian–Muslim community and neighborhoods, Somalis' cultural distance from the majority South African black population in townships thwarts their sense of belonging. As a result, most articulate an urgent desire to continue on to a new destination, most often one that will bestow Western citizenship.

Adam, Minneapolis, United States

"They [other Somali men] say that it is paradise there. They mean one can relax there. They say the money you take with you can keep you for a while. It is peaceful; the people over there respect you. You are respected! Someone said as a joke that the woman's family will even prepare your ablution water: 'Oh, bring the ablution to the *Ugaas*' [*war Ugaaska u geeya ha waysiistee*]. I think that is why many people are going there, because they feel their manhood over there."

Adam had a big grin on his face, enjoying sharing with me how many of his Somali male friends imagine what a return to Somalia (or to neighboring countries with large Somali populations, or to the Middle East) would entail. What he doesn't say is this: these men only envision return with an American citizenship and some savings after years of laboring in the diaspora.

Notice that Adam uses the word "respect" twice in this short narrative, connoting that this respect is lacking in the lives of Somali men in the United States. Moreover, his discussion of how Somali male returnees will be welcomed and treated like royals by potential wives' families reflects a clear search for respect, prestige, and what one could call a "recouping of masculinity" missing from Somali men's sense of self in America.[2] The term *Ugaas* is a title of dignity given to a Somali clan chief. Adam uses this figuratively, to connote the deference that men returning with Western citizenship will get back in Africa and the Middle East, something they view as denied to them in a Western, non-Muslim country.

Still comparing "here" with "there," Adam continued,

> When it comes to here [the United States], he does not save anything of the money he makes. The man struggles in menial jobs, and the woman also has

to work. Both have to work. They are both suffering; America is like that. He wants to be pampered by her and she wants the same thing. There is a problem here; there is conflict that is leading many couples to fight and divorce. And this is due to the life we are leading being very difficult, and we are trying to fit into this environment. Let us be honest! We want to adapt to an environment that overwhelms us.

Though Adam was still an unmarried university student, he detailed what he perceived as the Somali Muslim refugee experience in the United States. Not only is the United States geographically distant from Somalia but it is also "an environment that overwhelms" the religiously, culturally, and ethnically distinct Somali sense of self. In Adam's eyes, this is an environment far from the earthly jannah imagined by Somalis in the Horn. In other elaborations, the key to Somalis' sense of alienation is articulated through gender-norm disruptions brought about by the role of state welfare institutions and the relative poverty of Somalis in the United States. Adam dwells on this socioeconomic stress as dismantling the family, creating gender conflicts and leading to disorientation.

Another source of stress when living in the United States, according to my interviewees, centered on the remittance demands from those left behind. Idman, a woman in her thirties, complained about how her mother in Galkaio, Somalia, hangs up the phone on her if she fails to send less than $300. With the United States as the pinnacle of migration destinations, Somalis in the United States say that those left behind never grasp the idea that those who have made it to the United States may not be able to send large sums. The impossible optimistic vision of the United States that Somalis in the Horn hold remains hard to alter by those family members who have successfully migrated, who themselves have to confront many difficult and unexpected challenges.

The majority of Somalis who live in the United States (including Adam) have residential papers, and many obtain their citizenship through naturalization once they fulfill the residency requirements. Thus a search for citizenship, which motivates further migration from the UAE, South Africa, and most other non-Western Somali settlements, is absent here. But although that longed-for dream has been fulfilled, other concerns about new challenges around gender and identity come to the fore.

From the tangle of aspirations and disappointments captured by the three preceding vignettes, we can appreciate the reality of borders and the hegemony of the nation-state in this age of globalization. Even before venturing to leave the place of birth or places of transit, globalization feeds refugees' and migrants' imaginations about the destination countries. We see how an idealized West beckons many Somalis still in Africa and the Middle East. But we also see how those in the United States may be beckoned back to Africa and the Middle East. How desired destinations are imagined is crucial in how migration is experienced.

These three vignettes also illustrate how transnational information exchanges include not only glamour but also details highlighting the challenges intrinsic in migration in this age of (in)security. Potential detention in camps, many years of waiting for naturalization, and economic and social marginalization as a welfare recipient are all cited as part of life in Europe and North America. And yet refugees continue to cross borders, continue to dream about a better life elsewhere. So we must ask, how do refugees and migrants utilize this information? Does it contribute to a reluctance to pursue this option, as it did for Osman? Why was this not the case for Ardo, who is still pursuing a route to Europe despite her previous failed attempts? What explains this steely determination to join those perceived to have made it to an earthly jannah, that reachable paradise? Clearly the treacherous trips and the extraordinary financial and emotional costs that refugees and migrants incur are all anchored by certain expectations about the destination. These ventures are often viewed as being worth the risks intrinsic in sea and border crossings—which can culminate (in extreme cases) in death, in detention lasting for years, or, if one is lucky, in legal citizenship that seals symbolic membership and basic rights.

But once entry happens, a given migrant's or refugee's "success" in fulfilling her dreams is contingent on a combination of the individual's human and social capital as well as the structural conditions in the context of reception.[3] Indeed, I argue in this book that migrants' evaluations of their own migration experiences—running the gamut from an earthly jannah to deep disappointment and alienation—depend less on achieving their initial goal of prized citizenship status than on how the receiving country's economic, political, and social dynamics align with the migrants' racial, gender, and religious senses of self. It is thus the feeling of belonging in the broadest possible sense that most profoundly colors the migration experience.

People on the Move: Complex Motivations, Simple Categories

As we know, human beings rarely fit into ideal, neat categories. In our case, as we strive to understand Somalis dispersed around the globe, our tendency is to see them either as "immigrants" or as "refugees"—the terms that states and scholars use to distinguish among them. In the literature, migration is viewed as involving people moving across administrative or political borders for a period of time to improve their economic situations.[4] In other words, they are seen as *agents*. Refugees, by contrast, are often viewed to be the victims of circumstances—civil war, political persecution, environmental catastrophe, and so on. As Yen Esperitu puts it, refugees become "objects of rescue" and eternally "incapacitated by grief and therefore in need of care."[5] But as we'll see, the distinction between migrant and refugee is not as clear as we assume. My study shows that for the majority of people on the move, these categories frequently overlap: people can meet every aspect of the United Nations definition of refugee and yet still be an agent, pursuing multiple strategies to improve their socioeconomic situations in highly constrained circumstances.

This book makes a number of key interventions into migration studies. First, it blurs the refugee–migrant binary. I argue that this blurring is most visible for groups that engage in step-migration, such as Somalis. By this I refer to those who cross multiple borders and stay months or even years at some of these stops, while still hoping to move on to further destinations. Thus while Somalis crossing to Kenya are easily categorized as refugees and put into refugee camps, we see throughout this book that this initial movement is often one of many stops for those ending up in the UAE, South Africa, and the United States. Ardo is a perfect example of blurring the refugee–migrant binary. She came to South Africa for marriage purposes and not in search of asylum, though she nevertheless sought such status. She dreams of pursuing better opportunities in Western Europe while already holding refugee status in South Africa. There is no doubt that Ardo is a "real" refugee: her homeland is in a state of profound political and economic collapse. Yet she is not a helpless victim in search of asylum in South Africa or at her desired European destination. Rather she is an agent, with clear understanding of how political refuge, economic opportunities, and travel documentation permitting her to cross borders more easily are intertwined for those like her.

The fact that the UAE does not admit refugees and all Somalis in this country are categorized as labor migrants further shows the situational nature of these terms; a person defined as a migrant in one country may be defined as a refugee in another. Through their transnational connections, people on the move are very aware of these categories and which it makes sense to embrace in a given destination.

In addition to blurring the migrant–refugee distinction, this book challenges the common disciplinary boundaries in migration studies. Although these disciplinary wedges will probably continue to persist for the foreseeable future,[6] this comparative study makes great progress in bringing together two dominant strands within migration and transnationalism discussions. The strand dominated by anthropologists focuses on issues of identity and belonging, while another, mostly led by sociologists, draws attention to questions of settlement and integration. As Brettell and Hollifield's commendable yet challenging effort to encourage scholars of migration to talk across disciplinary boundaries highlighted, these two approaches converge on some concerns but diverge on others. For example, anthropologists seek to home in on the "experience of being an immigrant and the meaning, to the migrants themselves, of the social and cultural changes that result from leaving one context and entering another."[7] Here great importance is placed on the cultural outlook of migrants and refugees themselves, which is shaped not only by the receiving country conditions but also by those of the sending country, as demonstrated by the burgeoning literature on transnational migration.[8] Conversely, sociologists mostly privilege the receiving societies, thus highlighting incorporation and examining access to resources facilitating or hindering settlement and integration.[9] A group's entrepreneurial pursuits, their human and social capital, and their mobilization of those resources for political incorporation become the center of analysis in understanding migration outcomes for different groups.[10]

In light of the limited work that successfully combines these two approaches, a second contribution of this book is to demonstrate the validity of both approaches.[11] I argue that the identity–imaginary approach and the resource mobilization approach are in fact interdependent facets in migrant lives and experiences and thus are necessary for a holistic grasp of the complexity intrinsic in migration and transnationalism. With this premise, the analyses provided throughout the book ambitiously pay close attention to individual and household articulations and representations of individual, ethnic, religious, and gender identities as well as barriers and opportunities in economic pursuits, including enclave economies, labor force participation, remittances, and public assistance. As the three vignettes that open this book clearly illustrate, migrant and refugee lives are affected, shaped, and informed by all these forces, at different times, at different places, and in overt and covert ways.

On the identify front, imagination is an important resource for refugees and migrants alike, as both negotiate global walls of restriction and exclusion. The first hurdle that migrants and refugees confront are the rules and regulations of entry to their destination, the reality of national borders, and the hegemony of the state. But even before they venture to leave places of birth or places of transit, transnational relations with those who have settled elsewhere in part feed their imaginations about the destination countries. Although much of the debate on transnationalism focuses on the social, economic, and political linkages across borders, little attention is paid to cognitive imaginings of the other place(s) where one is not at any given time. Aneesh Aneesh's work on Indian IT workers in the United States and their straddling of feelings of fantasy and despair of the place that they are not (India when they are in the United States, or the United States when they return to India) is a wonderful illustration of the value of paying attention to the role of the imagination in migration.[12] This is what Aneesh calls the "transnational condition," a complex subjectivity that "loses a single cultural or national mode of being."[13]

Attention to the role of imagination in migration does not discount the crucial role of material resources, family and community networks, and immigration regulations in translating dreams, desires, and imagination into reality. The fact that only about 3 percent of the world's population moves from their place of birth testifies to the myriad contingencies required to cross international borders.[14] Nor do I want to overplay the role of agency in this discussion of imagination. Rather, I suggest that with migration, imagination is essential, but not sufficient, to realize dreams, desires, and movements. As Andrew Smith puts it, "our imaginations are not placeless: even the most utopian dream is dreamed contextually."[15] Though global cultural circulation is real, then, its role in permitting people to access what they imagine remains limited. For instance, research in Somali refugee camps in Kenya shows that although many of these refugees dream of resettling in the West, only a small percentage actually get into refugee resettlement programs and manage to realize their migration dreams.[16]

How the desired destination is imagined in transnational lives is nevertheless crucial to how migration is experienced by those who successfully manage to migrate. The exchange of information, how earlier refugees articulate the alignment or discord between how they imagined their destination and what they encountered, and also how they reconcile any discrepancy between these are important for understanding the settlement process. The Somali formulation of migration as access to an earthly jannah discussed earlier speaks to the emotional and cognitive dimensions of pursuing migration dreams, with implications for social, cultural, and economic outcomes.

Transnationalism in this study connotes everyday real and imagined connections with the homeland as well as with other places where family, friends, and coethnics are dispersed. Refugees' and migrants' desire for social, economic, and political connections with those left behind is significant for their well-being; but as important as affective connections are repercussions from these linkages that dramatically affect settlement experiences. As Peter Kivisto suggests, we should view transnationalism as concurrent with settlement.[17] Transnational social ties are not disconnected from how a new group defines itself vis-à-vis the larger community that it joins.

This book conceptualizes transnationalism as both bounded and unbounded, as both freeing and constraining, permitting individuals to transcend some limitations while remaining subject to multiple national and international obstacles that carry real consequences in their everyday lives. As such, the analysis presented in this book encourages scholars to pay more attention to the complexity of transnational lives, which can call for celebration of new forms of identities and resource circulations but also for the burden that it represents for migrants and refugees struggling with basic survival. This is in line with a central question that Levitt and Jaworsky ask: "in what contexts [does] transnational migration [have] positive and/or negative consequences, in what combinations, and for whom?"[18]

This study also conceptualizes transnationalism and diaspora as closely linked. As Levitt puts it, "diasporas form out of the transnational communities" and entail networks across borders and a dispersed group that maintains real and imagined loyalties to a place identified as the homeland.[19] Also, I concur with Robin Cohen's recognition of the expansion of the meaning of this word, which is appropriated by all communities with members dispersed around the globe.[20] However, the fact that the word can no longer maintain its original association with victim diasporas, such as the Jewish and Armenian experiences, does not diminish its analytical utility. My Somali study participants define themselves as part of a Somali diaspora and even use the English word, suggesting that they appropriate the concept without regard for its historical origins.

What emerges from its Somali iteration, then, is a shared understanding that their initial migration was not planned but rather a "calamity" in the form of intense, protracted political conflict that has forced them out of their homeland. Because of their forced displacement from the homeland and the barriers to their return, Somali refugees around the globe strive to re-create the meaning of *home* in their new countries of settlement. Imagination, again, plays a crucial role in articulations of home, especially when return is not an option and when people's mobility is highly constrained because of their socioeconomic location and national origin in light of increasing border regulations.

These state border regulations in both developing and developed countries have become stricter following the September 11, 2001, terrorist attacks against the United States and now include the use of drones, enhanced technologies, detention, and deportation.[21] But the long reach of these security measures goes beyond the American or Western European nations, which are at the forefront of the War on Terror. For example, thousands of Somali refugees escaping war-ravaged southern Somali regions have been barred from entering Kenya over the last few years. Kenya justified this policy on security grounds that terrorists may hide within the refugee population. Moreover, as a partner in the War on Terror, Kenya receives major logistical and financial support from the United States to fight Somali and Kenyan groups viewed to be a global security threat.[22] These policies have dramatic impact and constrain the options open to many refugees and would-be migrants, especially Muslims, feeding a search for alternative routes. This is viscerally demonstrated by the thousands of migrants and refugees who continue to perish in the Red Sea and the Mediterranean while seeking to break into the Middle East and Europe.

Another phenomenon that the Somali diasporic condition underscores is the importance of the networks that grease the wheels of migration. Not only do the earlier arrivals assist with the search for employment but they also reduce the emotional costs and risks of migration to an unknown destination.[23] Networks hence are resources that heavily rely on relations between migrants and potential migrants across multiple regions of the world. For the Somalis in this study, such networks circulate ideas, strategies, routes, and financial capital to facilitate people's physical and emotional journeys as well as their settlement in a new country if they succeed in realizing their migration.[24] The implications of migration for identify formation (e.g., religious, gender, racial) hence remain concurrent with migrants' ability to translate their skills and networks into resources in their new settlements.

Thus attention to economic and political incorporation is significant as opportunities for entrepreneurship and access to state and federal resources and the human capital with which migrants and refugees arrive all shape how they fare in their new society. These, combined with how migrants and refugees interpret new cultural milieux (religious accommodation, gender norms, racial and ethnic structures), provide a multifarious lens through which to understand migration outcomes for groups differentiated on the grounds of nationality, class, race, and religion, as the analysis in the following chapters demonstrates.

Comparing Migrations

Migration research is intrinsically comparative, with most fitting into what Nancy Green calls the *linear model*—the study of one migrant group from its home origin to its destination. In most cases, the comparative element of the research is implicit.[25] Green also identifies a second approach, the *convergent model*, which examines different migrants within the same locale and compares how these diverse communities experience migration. What is held constant is place, while different migrants' socioeconomic positions, educational attainment, and other factors are compared.

This study, by contrast, builds on a nascent body of literature that focuses on the experiences of *the same group of people* as they migrate to different places, to a variety of hoped-for homes. The advantage of this sort of comparative approach—or what Green calls the *divergent model*—is that we can see how the interaction between the context of reception and the migrants' own characteristics shapes their integration and adjustment in each society.[26] Such studies of one population migrating to different locales are rare, despite their significance in revealing the multiplicity of factors that give rise to migrants' own—and others'—perceptions of the "success" of migration. Nancy Foner's comparison of West Indians in London to those in New York is one example of a study that takes this approach.[27] Foner shows how West Indians' success in New York is not replicated in the British context. Her findings challenge the notion that some universalized understanding of "culture" is the explanation for West Indians' position in New York, because the culture shared by this same group of migrants in London does not lead to the same economic experiences. Foner's study makes explicit how the *conditions of reception* in each location—in her case, London and New York—inform migrants' situations and can lead to very different social, economic, and political outcomes for migrants, both vis-à-vis their compatriots in other receiving countries and relative to mainstream and other minority populations in their new place of settlement. Immigration policies; the country of settlement's structural, ideological, and political practices; and the migrants' backgrounds and personal histories emerge as critical factors shaping migrants' experiences for this West Indian case study as well as for the few other migration studies that take this approach.[28]

As the narratives that opened this chapter suggest, the comparative approach anchors this book. I compare the experiences of one group of refugees and migrants—Somalis—who migrate to three different countries: the UAE, South Africa, and the United States. These countries are in three very different regions of the world and vary dramatically in their geographical, political, cultural, and religious characteristics. Although Somalis as a group share a common history that propelled them to migrate to different parts of the world, their experiences in their places of settlement have not been the same. Through these migrations, they come into contact with new social, cultural, and institutional arrangements in each destination. The divergent model, comparing the same group in three highly varied settings, thus permits us to identify the key factors that inform the migration process and outcomes in each location and to explain why the migrant experience in one location can be so different from that in another. In sum, this approach allows us to identify what is common about the migration experience for a particular migrant group.

To examine the options available (or not) to refugees and migrants navigating not only different state borders but labor markets, religious practices, gender relations, and racial tensions and alliances, Ann Swidler's discussion on the link between culture and action is a powerful tool for understanding the strategies that refugees and migrants utilize throughout their movements and transnational lives. Her formulation of "culture as a 'tool kit' of symbols, stories, rituals, and world-views, which people may use in varying configurations to solve different kinds of problems," is useful in analyzing migrant and refugee lives. The idea of a tool kit of resources of course speaks to the agency and strategies that individuals utilize in different circumstances. Strategies are defined as "the larger ways of trying to organize life (trying for example, to secure position by allying with prestigious families through marriage) within which particular choices make sense and for which particular culturally shaped skills and habits . . . are useful."[29] Though appreciating the use of the metaphor of a "tool kit" that Swidler formulates, I do not mean to overplay the role of agency in how individual actors use culture. Nor do I want us to think of culture as static, as it is constantly created and re-created by actors confronted with new structural dynamics and experiences, as we see throughout this book. Also, Swidler does not really address migration per se, but her discussion of how models of culture and action differ for "unsettled lives" and "settled lives" is applicable to migrants and refugees. In the latter case, the link between culture and action is much more difficult to articulate, as culture is practically invisible, taken for granted, and thus "people naturally 'know' how to act," whereas the former represents periods of "social transformation."[30]

Migration by definition involves actions taken by actors (migrants, refugees) in arenas where new models of relations and practices prevail, thus making actions and their consequences more explicit. As Swidler put it, in periods of transformation, "ideologies—explicit, articulated, highly organized meaning systems (both political and religious)—establish new styles or strategies of action."[31] I take this to be comparable to what Hess and Ferree in their gender analysis call the "points of change," when more spaces open up for negotiation, evaluation, and shifts in power dynamics.[32] Thus movement across multiple state borders by migrants and refugees renders explicit identity issues as well as barriers or opportunities in accessing the resources required to reestablish normalcy in new settlements.

The strategies migrants and refugees choose, or those that are at times imposed on them, are context specific. The situational nature of the strategies pursued, depending on what is defined as useful, what is permissible, what is possible and necessary even when defined as "illegal" in that context, for example, speaks to how strategies pursued are themselves constrained or enabled by structural forces in a particular settlement. As such, a third contribution of this book is to bring to the fore the tensions and outcomes between structure and strategies in various settlements. We will see that the cultural tool kit that migrants and refugees use, discard, and create is not only of their making but also shaped by how dominant groups perceive and treat them in their new homes. Culture is hence not used or created in a vacuum but rather in conjunction with power dynamics within each settlement. Is the cultural tool kit that Somalis brought with them useful or relevant for their needs in their new settlements? Do exigencies encountered in the new settlement call for modification or even the creation of new cultural practices? And how do these old and new cultural strategies contribute to changes or continuities in gender, family, religious, and ethnic–racial formations?

This study conceptualizes Somali migration as essentially involving strategies pursued within the exigencies of statelessness. Throughout the analysis that follows, we see the shifting situational cultural and economic skills and strategies that men, women, and families pursue to navigate various immigration policies. Immigration policies encompass both the regulation of immigration into a country and the conditions of reception.[33] As such, the focus of this book is the myriad intersecting factors—local and global, factual and fictional, political and historical—that shape Somali migration experiences in consequential ways. Comparing Somali settlement in the UAE, a relatively closed Muslim nation where citizens are a minority within a large South Asian population of labor migrants, with South Africa, a nation where apartheid's racial hierarchies determined immigration policies until very recently, with the United States, a traditional nation of immigrants with its own racial, socioeconomic, and political distinctions, sheds light on the significance of immigration policies in shaping migrant experiences.

Multisited Ethnographic Research

I chose my three sites because they represent significant destinations for Somali refugees in the Horn. South Africa has the largest Somali population in Africa outside of countries sharing a border with Somalia, with an estimated twenty thousand to thirty thousand now living in the country. The UAE represents one of the key oil-rich countries to which Somalis have migrated since the early 1970s and is now estimated to have about twenty thousand Somalis. The United States, long a beacon for refugee dreams, resettles the largest number of refugees in the world and is currently home to roughly one hundred thousand Somalis. These three sites are therefore significant "migration magnets" for Somalis and can help us better understand the process of migration and transnational connection within the Somali diaspora.

This study is built on 162 recorded interviews, about 50 informal interviews, and 10 focus groups with an additional 40 people. Of the recorded interviews, men outnumber women (ninety-nine versus sixty-three). This was intentional, as my informal interactions and time spent with women far surpassed my interactions with men. The interviews in this study were mostly semistructured.

I chose ethnography, a technique of immersion in the study setting that goes beyond interviewing and observing but pursues a comprehensive involvement and intense engagement in the setting.[34] Such immersion requires bodily and emotional presence and inevitably requires involvement in social situations in the lives of the research participants. To accomplish this full immersion in three settings is understandably difficult and was more fully attained in two of the settings. Though the active data collection for this book commenced with thirteen months of fieldwork in Minnesota across 2004 and 2005, the book has its genesis in my earliest work with Somali refugees in 2001, when I spent three months in the Dadaab camps in the Northeastern Province of Kenya. Subsequently, I conducted fieldwork in Ohio (July–August 2010) and in South Africa (in the areas of Johannesburg, Port Elizabeth, and Cape Town, between May and August of 2007, 2009, and 2011). I also lived in South Africa as a Fulbright Fellow between August 2012 and July 2013 and had many opportunities to speak again to my research participants. In the UAE, I collected data from Dubai, Sharjah, and Abu Dubai over December 2007 to January 2008 and then again from December 2011 to January 2012. Compared to my time in the United States and South Africa, my data collection efforts and time spent in the UAE were most modest, with a smaller number of interviews collected, though the results were no less rich.

This discrepancy is due to the serious barriers to researching migration issues in the UAE. Given the highly publicized and blatant human rights abuses of the millions of South Asian labor migrants in the Arabian Gulf region, academic research and any expressions of the rights of migrants and even citizens are highly sensitive and can lead to an expulsion from the country.[35] Knowing about this state of affairs, I opted to conduct my research in the most inconspicuous way possible. For the first visit, I spent close to twelve to fourteen hours a day with research participants, interacting, eating, talking, and observing without conducting a single formal recorded interview. Once I established trust within the Somali community, I fostered key contacts with community members and was able to conduct formal interviews during my second trip to this country. Again I strove to remain as inconspicuous as humanly possible, as I feared being incarcerated and deported if I was viewed to be conducting research that portrayed the UAE in a negative light. Fortunately, I completed my research without any contact with law enforcement officials and left at the end of January 2012.

The events of community organizations, political gatherings, religious ceremonies, and wedding celebrations all provided me with additional opportunities to interact with and informally observe the daily happenings of Somali communities in each of my three settings. The Cedar–Riverside area of Minneapolis and Global Mall in Columbus were crucial starting points for making connections in the United States and for immersing myself within these communities. In the UAE, the main Somali business establishment in Deira Gold Souk in Dubai served as my base for recruiting Somalis in other settlements. This gold market is where Somalis in the UAE and Somali returnees and visitors from around the globe congregate. In South Africa, Mayfair in the Johannesburg region was my point of entry into this ethnic enclave. I established contacts there with Somalis who were able to connect me to other major Somali settlements in Korsten in Port Elizabeth and Bellville in Cape Town.

As Somalia continues to produce an unceasing stream of refugees and migrants, these three case studies can help us better comprehend intersectionality. Somalis—as refugees, as Africans, and as Muslims—are a group in which key axes of migrant life chances and experiences coalesce. Moreover, a Somali case study can permit us to test many of the claims of globalization. As we will see, the lives of my interviewees manifest a key contradiction of globalization: that capital and ideas are boundless, while people, and especially those from poorer regions of the world, from failed and weak states, are increasingly bounded by stringent border regulations in this era of security. The comparative aspect of this case is therefore vital for a Muslim refugee group dispersed around the globe. Such comparison provides an opportunity to pose common migration questions but on a comparatively broader scale. Moreover, focus on a Western settlement as well as non-Western settlements expands and complicates our comprehension of the continuing hegemony of the nation-state, immigration policies, and resulting outcomes for people's everyday lives, within the web of geopolitical, socioeconomic, racial, and gender dynamics in communities they join.

Reflection on Self

I landed at Montréal–Dorval International Airport on December 9, 1988, having flown from Mogadishu, Somalia, transiting in Egypt and then in the Netherlands. I was still in my teens and was traveling with my brother to join our three older sisters, who came to Canada in 1986. This was our first trip outside of Somalia. There is nothing impressive about this story, as thousands of others cross international borders every day. But my brother and I proceeded to the Canadian immigration services to request political asylum.

Saying that we were terrified does not capture how we felt that night, but my name as it appears in this book and in the identification documents that I now carry is a daily reminder of that particular juncture of my life. Cawo Maxamed Cabdi is the Somali spelling of my name. But confronting immigration interrogation for the first time and being very nervous, I filled out the forms I was handed with a mixture of Somali (Cawo) and an English transliteration of my middle and last names (Mohamed Abdi).

I tell the story of my own migration to illustrate how my personal journey is closely intertwined with the journeys of the Somalis whose lives are detailed in this book. In no way am I drawing these parallels to claim that our migration experiences are the same. As stressed throughout the chapters that follow, the timing of migration, the resources one can access, the country to which one is hoping to gain admittance, the prevailing geopolitical forces at a given historical moment, and many other factors lead to different migration outcomes. Rather, what I want to show is that I share not only the Somali ethnic identity with my informants but also the experience of crossing international borders as a refugee.

What does it mean to be a Somali-born researcher studying Somali migration experiences in different parts of the globe? I briefly reflect on this topic, though not getting deeply into the insider–outsider binary, with ample literature already available on this topic. But touching on my role as an academic Somali–Canadian/American woman conducting ethnographic study with Somali communities further illustrates the need to avoid simplistic binaries.

It is not only others (outsiders) who expect those studying their own "group" to have an insider lens. It is in fact the "insider" researcher himself or herself who often starts with such an assumption. Without malice, and often for heuristic purposes, we like to think that there is one group, sharing common characteristics, a relatively homogenous collective. Age, education, gender, and cultural practices that differentiate members of the same group emerge as secondary when we assume that there is an "insider" position.

To provide a concrete example of how I was guilty of this assumption, I first traveled to Dadaab refugee camps in Kenya in 2001 for research for my master of arts degree, after having lived in Canada for more than a decade. Before my trip to Kenya, I consulted with my mother and borrowed a few dresses that I thought would be the only appropriate dress for a Somali woman hoping to interact with, build rapport with, and study Somali families in these camps. My premise in choosing these dresses was that Somali women's dress practices would be exactly as I remembered it, as it was in 1988 when I left Somalia, as I have lived and observed around me when I was growing up in Mogadishu. But that I needed to borrow these dresses, which were light, beautifully printed, flowing and transparent, long dresses, shows that these were not my normal wear in Canada, where I dressed like many mainstream women—trousers, skirts, and light summer dresses with no head covers. Thus, at the same time as I was aware of my own transformation with migration to Canada, I froze Somali women's dress practices in Somalia and other Horn African settlements to which they fled following the conflict that culminated in a state collapse by 1991.

My recognition of my own transformation and not that of Somalis living in Kenyan camps, or in Somalia, hit me once I arrived in Dadaab. From the first day in the camps, changing to what I considered to be Somali traditional dress, I observed that this dress was completely different from what the majority of the women in the camps were wearing. Instead of the flowing, see-through *dira'* and the shoulder-baring *guntiino* that women wore in the Somalia of my youth, almost all women wore what looked like uniform, full-covering heavy fabric in an array of different colors from black to blue to green to red and in between. Needless to say that I ended up going to the market to buy new attire, not similar to what other women were wearing but nevertheless more conservative than what I brought with me.

Differences in dress practices was also a salient issue for me in my interactions with Somalis in South Africa. I often joked that almost everyone offered me a gift of a head scarf during my multiple trips to South Africa. These offers were from people who have become friends over the course of the years of research in this setting, and though no one ever said that I should cover my hair, which I did during all my interactions with the study participants, I always got a clear message that they all knew that I was doing this out of respect for them. Internet images and TV interviews that some in this community have seen made it clear that I did not wear a head scarf outside of this research setting.

The preceding examples are illustrative of the initial challenges that my sense of authenticity, as a Somali woman who is an "insider" and who belongs to this community, that I brought with me faced. But the community recognized me as a partial insider, as the preceding sense of "othering" was often concurrent with expressions that I was also an ally who could best disseminate the many challenges that Somalis were experiencing in their settlements. I often reiterated my long absence from Somalia to make sure that people did not assume that I knew what they had experienced. But my being viewed to understand the plight of Somalis and the multiple migration barriers they confront made my study participants comfortable enough to openly discuss their migration strategies and share narratives that were different from those they often had to write for the immigration boards to claim asylum. Moreover, men and women openly discussed plans and activities that they would probably not reveal to non-Somali researchers. For example, a few successful businessmen in South Africa asked me to assist them in finding Somali women in Canada or the United States who would marry them, either genuinely or for a fee, so that they could gain entry into these countries. Moreover, Somali men who own small stores in South Africa and who confronted extreme levels of violence sometimes divulged information that they probably would never share with non-Somali researchers. Such information posed extra ethical weight on me, while the data collected also enriched the analysis.

This perception that I am an ally, bound to Somalia and Somalis by birth, gave the research participants certain comfort in expressing themselves more freely than may have been the case with non-Somali researchers. I spent hours and hours at the homes of families, watching them undertake their daily routines around me. I often only interviewed men in public places and at their homes only when there were other family members around. It was clear that despite some differences, research participants still viewed me as a member. For example, my being a Somali woman did not prevent some Somali men from discussing the importance of women being obedient to their husbands or at times to use language that I deemed sexist. Similarly, a few Somali interviewees spoke about South African blacks as "lazy" and used what amounted to racist language, as detailed in that particular case study. Thus interviewees expressed ideas that they often assumed that I would share, as a Somali myself. I made no attempts to intervene in these instances, as I did not see my role to be changing individual perceptions but rather to attempt to better understand the migration experiences of this group in different settlements.

My being an educated woman also gave me an honorary male status that placed me above other Somali women. As such, men often felt free to discuss topics that women were often not supposed to be privy to. For example, an elderly man in his mid-seventies whom I interviewed in Minneapolis went into detail about courting games and sex-related topics in the nomadic Somali society. He premised his discussion with, "You are an educated woman, thus there is nothing taboo with you." The discussion was humorous and in no way offensive. But I read his statement in two ways. First, I heard his intended compliment, with my education placing me above the censorship required when talking or interacting with Somali women who were not in my position. But conversely, there was an implied othering that women with "too much" education lack what is most desirable about women: modesty and ignorance about sexual matters, an innocence that I apparently lost with my higher education and my appearance.

A last but important topic for researching with Somalis relates to the place of clan identify in this community and how it may shape rapport during the research process. Unlike most books written by non-Somalis, and in some cases by Somalis, there is no section that outlines the Somali clan structure in this book. This is intentional and based on the nonrelevance of clan as a topic of discussion in my own interactions with Somalis in all the settings covered in this project. I grew up in an era when asking others their clan was frowned on. This remains so for many in my age group and especially for many in the Somali communities in the diaspora. But the place of clan and what it means in society has certainly become a major political topic since the collapse of the Somali nation in 1991. Nevertheless, the only Somalis who ever inquired about my clan affiliation were men and women in their sixties and seventies. In no interaction in Somalia, Kenya, South Africa, the UAE, or the United States did a research participant make an issue of what my clan membership was. This is not to say that interviewees did not inquire about what clan I belonged to with others, but it was never a point of discussion or contention with me.

It is probably that my being a researcher coming from North America and my education made some who would normally ask such a question censor themselves. But even the elders who asked this question often found a way to connect with me around shared kinship linkages. Thus, when I told one elder what my clan was, he automatically went on to discuss how his daughter is married to this clan, thus identifying a kinship affinity with me, even if it is through a level other than direct clan relations. My own position as someone whose clan is different from that of her children, and many of her own family members (cousins, uncles and aunts, grandmother, great aunts, etc.), puts me in position to be able to identify and have linkages with multiple Somali clans and regions. All Somalis in fact have such expansive kinship linkages that almost always crosscut clan lines. This way of conceptualizing the Somali clan system is different than that which is currently promoted by the Somali political leadership, which is partitioning the country into fiefdoms with clan borders, in territories that were historically inhabited by multiple clans. The international community, in its desperate attempt to create a stable Somali state, has accepted the warlord narrative of Somalia as a society that is steeped in an essentialized clan system that is rigid, primordial. My research experience contradicts this formulation of the clan system, which remains fluid and organic.

This brief discussion locates me within the lives of Somali research participants whose migration experiences are detailed in the following pages. While being a Somali and being able to communicate with Somalis sped up my entry into the settings where I conducted research, I heavily invested in building rapport with the communities where I did this research. My hybrid identity (citizenship, dress, languages) simultaneously positioned me as an insider and an outsider.

I thus present this work as a critical ethnography that reveals the strategies of survival used by men and women affected by political conflict and confronted with complex border regulations in a globally stratified nation-state system. I hope the portraits that emerge from this book show how fully human migrants and refugees are. I share their beauty and their flaws, their ingenuity and their failures to defy the exclusion of those deemed to have inflexible citizenship, those excluded from the fruits of globalization that many in the most prosperous regions of the world take for granted. I will feel that I have fulfilled my duty to the research participants if this book helps the reader better understand the challenges that migration entails in this age of security.

Organization

The narratives of individual Somali refugees and migrants are at the heart of this book. I privilege people's understanding of their particular lives alongside consideration of the larger sociopolitical and economic conditions of each country. These subjective articulations of lives as they are being lived serve as a thread for the chapters, providing a detailed lens that helps us to crystallize and comprehend the vast themes of migration and settlement, particularly as they are shaped by the equally vast themes of identity and resources (religion, nationality, race and gender, work, welfare, entrepreneurship, and remittances).

Chapter 1 provides background for understanding the scattering of Somalis as refugees and migrants. It examines the Somali civil war that erupted in the late 1980s and that led, by 1991, to a complete state collapse. This chapter provides an overview of the postcolonial Somali regimes and the regional and international political dynamics that continue to shape the country's ongoing crisis. I discuss how this crisis produced physical and material insecurity, forcing millions from their homes since the late 1980s, with hundreds of thousands crossing international borders in search of safe haven. Moreover, the emergence of the Somali diaspora around the world can only fully be understood when we first examine their former lives in refugee camps and urban areas in neighboring countries (primarily Kenya). Just like migration to the Arabian Peninsula during the 1970s was a means to finding an earthly jannah, in an era when peace still reigned in Somalia, the perpetual legal, physical, emotional, and financial insecurity in refugee camps and urban areas in neighboring countries produces new definitions of desirable destinations; again and again, the search for Western citizenship emerges as the most salient desire. Such an aspiration is unquestionably informed by the ongoing instability in Somalia, by the insecurities of refugees in neighboring states, by local and global border regulations, and by the imagined rewards of further migration.

Chapter 2 explores how two contradictory forces shape the lives and future plans of Somalis in the UAE. Somali migrants' religious affinity with the local Emirati population and institutions locates Somalis within a global *umma*, sharing a worldview and a belonging with a borderless brotherhood of fellow Muslims. They thus strategically enact their "Arab" and Muslim identities and do not experience any challenges to their norms and values in this context. But this religious and cultural belonging stands in sharp contrast to their temporary, and inherently insecure, legal status. Most Somalis, whose passports are tied to a hot spot in the War on Terror, are stuck with temporary work visas that must constantly be renewed, and they are mostly unable to travel outside of the UAE; as a result, they long for, and work for, a more flexible citizenship, found by a small number of Somalis who have managed to acquire a passport from other countries in Africa or in Europe, Canada, or the United States. Such documents facilitate transnational economic, political, and social pursuits and bestow a prestige denied to those carrying a Somali passport that is no longer recognized by most countries. Contact between these two groups, as well as the transnational circulation of information about the ease of citizenship in the West, fuels dreams of further migration.

Chapter 3 deals with Somalis in South Africa and their ambiguous position within this racially segregated society. I detail how Somalis exploit this ambiguity—strategically enacting their Muslim identity, and their brotherhood with the global umma, to cement ties with the small but economically established Indian Muslim community. This alliance emerges as crucial in Somalis' entry into entrepreneurial niches historically neglected by both white and Indian entrepreneurs. But the legacy of violence and communal crisis in postapartheid South Africa leaves these Somalis vulnerable to violence. This violence is gendered, as it is exclusively Somali men who enter poor black neighborhoods, whereas women work in more racially mixed urban centers. As in the UAE, Somali gender dynamics are rarely undermined here, where Somalis reside and socialize within the minority Indian Muslim community. In some aspects, then, Somalis' racial, religious, and gender identities remain stable and secure within the Indian enclaves where they settle, thus in line with the original sense of migration as leading to an earthly jannah. But the violence that Somalis confront, as well as a sense that South African travel documents do not permit Somalis' desired mobility in a world divided into sovereign nation-states, fuels the conviction that South Africa is ultimately not a home but a place of transition, with the final destination often imagined to be in Europe or North America.

Chapter 4 brings us to the United States, which remains the ultimate imagined earthly Eden for a majority of global migrants. But life for Somali refugees who actually succeed in reaching America is rife with challenges. The cultural and economic strategies that Somalis utilize in the UAE and South Africa have little currency in this setting. The chapter outlines how, from the first, state and federal refugee settlement policies unintentionally, but profoundly, disrupt Somalis' sense of identity. The eligibility requirements for refugee status, based on the structure of domestic welfare programs, means that women are usually granted the "head of household" title, a deep threat to the gender prerogatives most Somali men claim. The continuous involvement of social services in Somali refugee family life erodes the legitimacy of Somali male authority, while its material base is undermined by the availability of unmediated economic resources for women. In their turn, women perceive these same resources as essential for the survival of the family, given that the only employment opportunities open to low-skilled refugee men and women are in the lowest tier of the economy. Challenges to cultural norms become most visible in this context, and this calls for strategies other than those that have worked in Somalia, Kenya, the UAE, and South Africa.

Despite these profound struggles, family members left behind in Somalia and its neighboring countries still idealize the United States and expect much higher remittances than from relatives in other countries, further exacerbating the economic pressures on refugee households. For all these reasons, Somali experiences in the United States often fail to align with the image that they brought with them from the Horn. Paradoxically, despite access to permanent residence documents and even highly coveted American citizenship, first-generation Somalis do not develop a strong sense of belonging, as they become painfully aware that their lives and those of their children are now defined by their refugee status, their Muslim faith, and their newly acquired black identity, leaving them struggling at the bottom of a heavily racialized and profoundly unequal economy.

The last chapter compares and contrasts the findings in the three case studies. It underscores the convergence of the local and global that prods so many people to move across borders, a convergence that is rarely a simple matter of identify versus resources but instead of a complicated culmination of a search for physical, economic, cultural, and spiritual well-being. It also shows how refugees and migrants develop distinct adaptive strategies in each social context, depending on economic opportunities and the religious, social, and political milieux they encounter. Migrants' religious, social, and political locations within both their immediate environments and the broader society all remain key to the process of migrants' integration or exclusion, to whether they are able to realize their aspirations for an earthly jannah. Each of my case studies, in various permutations, shows how Somalis' search for citizenship, security, and a new home leads to unanticipated conditions that confound their expectations. Ultimately, we find the great complexity of migrant and refugee lives, and we see how our understanding of successful migration and integration must go beyond the achievement of legal, economic, and physical security to encompass a sense of religious, cultural, and social belonging.

1 The Genesis of Contemporary Somali Migrations

> When the war erupted. It all happened so fast, within a few days. There was an uprising one day, and within a few days, the community was divided into opposite sides. This clan, that clan! Most people fled from the disaster following the onset of the conflict. Bringing rural practices to urban centers is catastrophic![1] Some fled to Kismayo, and some fled to other regions. *Alhamdulillah* we reached Kismayo safely. My wife was accompanying me, and we had a young niece who got separated from her family by the confusion. . . . Everyone was thinking that this [war] will be over, that it will last for a couple of months, and then we will all return. This [hope] still continues. We do not even know what we fought over, and the problems are still ongoing and we are still searching for answers.
>
> —Guray, teacher assistant, Minneapolis

When a country is in crisis, its people are in crisis. For more than two decades, Somalia has been engulfed in political turmoil, which has created vast uncertainty for the country's citizens. The scale and the composition of the mass displacement that this uncertainty produced is unique in the history of the Somali people. Yet migration itself is nothing new to Somalis. Starting in the early twentieth century, a small number of Somali men migrated to East Africa and across the Middle East, and then to Europe (mainly England and Italy) and America, in search of adventure and economic opportunities. These men established small communities in Aden, Rome, London, and New York as well as in Cardiff, Kampala, and Dar-es-Salaam.[2] But these earlier migration trends involved a very small percentage of the population, who were mostly male.

Somalia's crisis—like all other national calamities—is rooted in a longer history. Here we briefly explore the political trajectory of Somalia within the history of the Horn of Africa.[3] The state-building projects that sprouted across postcolonial Africa were often brave efforts at self-determination, yet they resulted in the creation of many fragile states. Experiments in governance were undermined by the complexity of dictatorial rule, colonial legacies, and endless internal fissures. The tumult of recent migration, both to and from this region, emerges from the effort of states such as Somalia to accommodate competing internal and external interests. In this chapter, I briefly explore this history and subsequently turn my focus to the experiences of Somali refugees in Kenya, the country that, since 1991, has hosted the largest Somali refugee population in the world. I demonstrate how experiences in this initial "safe haven" inform subsequent migrations to other parts of the world, including the UAE, South Africa, and the United States, which are the focus of this book. I show that once their basic physical and material needs of survival are met, these refugees dream of more, imagining destinations where they can reach higher summits than has been possible in Kenya. As citizens of a failed state, a combination of other factors that they confront in their host nation—from limited socioeconomic opportunities to state corruption in an environment where a majority of citizens are themselves marginalized—hinders Somali refugees' sense of well-being in Kenya as well as their future prospects in the country. As a result, Somali refugees in Kenya often imagine, and pursue when possible, further migration. Indeed, Kenya is only the *first* point of a step-migration for Somalis who end up in South Africa or the United States. Hence it is important to understand their experiences in Kenya, and their sense of there being "no going back" to Somalia, before we turn to the dynamics of their secondary migrations.

Calamity and Collapse: A Brief History of the Somali Political Crisis

Somalia was outside the purview of global attention prior to 1991, when global news outlets brought its spectacular breakdown of violence, famine, and destruction to living rooms all over the world. It was in January 1991 that Mohamed Siad Barre was ousted from power, ending his twenty-year-long military dictatorship. This led to widespread killings, rape, and looting, producing a massive migratory movement both to other regions within

Somalia and then to nearby countries, especially Kenya. In addition to the death by violence and starvation of an estimated three hundred thousand people, this crisis led to the displacement of close to two million people in a population of less than eight million in the mid-1990s.[4]

Somalia is located on the tip of the northeastern part of Africa, with the Indian Ocean on its east, Ethiopia on its western border, Kenya to the southwest, and Djibouti in the northern tip. With a population now estimated at ten million, and about the size of Texas, Somalia's prominence in recent history far outweighs its population and geographic size. Unfortunately, much of this attention revolves around its exceptional condition as a failed state in a world divided into nations. The Somali people mostly share a common language (Somali) and religion (Islam), although Somalia is also home to many minority ethnic groups, some of which were historically excluded from political power.[5] The majority clans that make up the Somali people and that are in great part the key players in the Somali political crisis are the Darod, Hawiye, Isaq, Digil, and Mirifle clans. Although international nongovernmental organization (NGO)-created "clan maps" indicate a neat geographical separation of clans, in reality, Somali clans physically overlap in much of their territories (e.g., the Isaq and Darod in the north and the Darod and Hawiye in the central regions). Somali regions thus house multiple clan residents, the majority of whom are interlinked through marriage. This is to say that though clan identity is significant to Somalis' identity and group relations, clans are not isolated from one another but are mostly meshed through shared pastoral and water resources, family relations, and other forms of communal interests.

Similar to other regions of the world, the lands the Somali people inhabited became part of the loot divided up by Europe's imperial powers at the 1896 Berlin Conference, with Ethiopia the only non-European country to partake in this scramble for Africa.[6] The creation of borders that cut through areas inhabited by peoples of the same ethnic groups was an intrinsic part of the imperial land grab. In the process, Somali lands were sliced into five different administrations, controlled by four colonial powers: British Somaliland, Italian Somaliland, Ethiopian-controlled Western Somaliland (also known as the Ogaden region), French Somaliland (what is now Djibouti), and the Northern Frontier District (NFD), or what is now the Northeastern

Province of Kenya, which also came under British rule. These divisions, shaped by European imperial interests, would stoke all manner of African problems. In the Somali-inhabited regions of the Horn of Africa, the European division produced Somali regions in what eventually became Kenya, Ethiopia, and Djibouti (Figure 1).

Most African nations obtained independence starting in the late 1950s, usually after decades of either armed or nonviolent resistance to colonial domination. Subsequently, two of the Somali territories—British Somaliland and Italian Somaliland—came together to form the Somali Democratic Republic following their independence in 1960 (Figure 2). Djibouti got its independence much later than most African nations (in 1977), whereas the

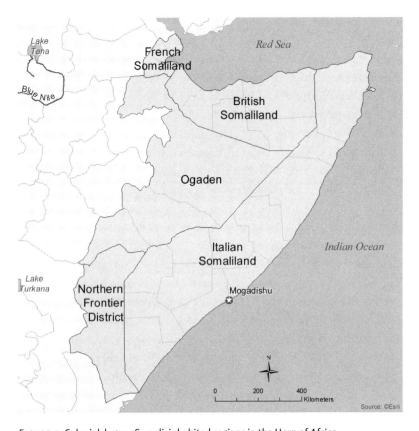

FIGURE 1. Colonial-legacy Somali-inhabited regions in the Horn of Africa.

British allowed Kenya to keep the NFD, following its independence in 1963. Western Somaliland (the Ogaden) remains part of Ethiopia.

The trajectory across Africa, from colonies to independent nations, has been marked by conflict. These conflicts have in some places brought about complete state collapse, whereas in many other places, fragile governments stay in power by brute force and the subjugation of their citizens.[7] The devastation of Somalia in the early 1990s is an extreme case of complete collapse. As mentioned earlier, Somalia inherited colonial borders that were drawn without regard to the identities of its inhabitants, with the very notion of national borders, without regard for the pursuits of nomadic peoples whose ways of life are dependent on movements over large territories in search of pasture and water for their livestock. Even in the second half of the twentieth century, amid African independence, Somalis were still predominantly nomadic and moved seasonally through territories that are now in Djibouti, Ethiopia, Kenya, and Somalia.[8] Somalis disregarded these borders during the colonial era, and the colonial administrations themselves did not always enforce them, recognizing people's need to continually move. However, with the ferocious blooms of independence, and the adamant effort at state building, borders left by colonial powers became more permanent yet contentious divisions that emphasized the existence of independent nation-states. Conflict over the legitimacy of these imperial-drawn borders was, perhaps, inevitable in shaping the political evolution of the countries in this region.[9]

The Era of Democracy

The first Somali government, led by President Aden Abdullah Osman (who served from 1961 to 1967), with prime ministers Abdirashid Ali Sharmarke (1961–64) and then Abdirisak Hagi Hussein (1964–67), prioritized the inalienable right of Somalis to be under one administration and passionately pursued this project, albeit in a peaceful manner.[10] In the heady atmosphere of nationalism, particularly in the first few years following independence, the proper fate of these "missing" regions was seen as intrinsically linked to the larger movement for reunification of Somalis in the Horn. Somali political leaders thus insisted that Somalis outside of the Somali nation were still under colonial rule. This is to say that the Somali-inhabited regions that remained under Kenyan and Ethiopian rule were considered still

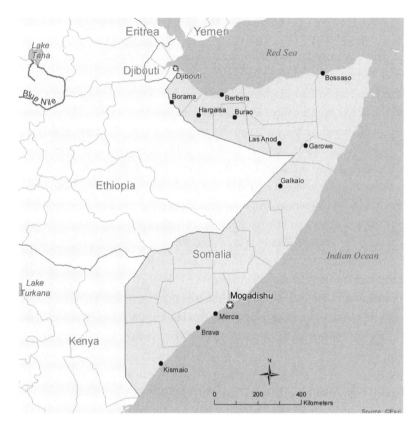

FIGURE 2. Postcolonial Somalia represents only two out of the five territories of the Somalilands.

colonized (Figure 1). Somalia's goal of uniting its peoples living under different African states contradicted the charter of the recently created Organization of African Unity (OAU), which stipulated that each African state would respect the borders inherited from the colonial powers and the integrity of all other African states.[11] OAU leaders feared that a secession of Somali territories from Kenya and Ethiopia would set a devastating precedent for the continent's many multiethnic states and were determined not to open the door to the possible fragmentation of other African states.[12] Somalia consequently attracted very little support from OAU members, who instead sympathized with Kenya and Ethiopia.

Somalia got military support from the Soviet Union following independence, which came not out of sympathy for the Somali nationalist project but rather in exchange for military bases in the country. Soviet backing, albeit limited and temporary, was consequential, as it began the earliest Somali militarization. The first military confrontations between Somalia and Ethiopia occurred in 1964, when Ethiopia bombed northern Somali towns.[13] The bombings were precipitated by Somalia's military support for the Western Somali Liberation Front (WSLF), a Somali guerrilla movement, as well as other rebel movements within Ethiopia.[14]

Abdirashid Ali Sharmarke and Mohamed Ibrahim Egal's government, which came to power in the 1967 election, followed a different approach than the two previous Somali regimes (1961–64, 1964–67). Perceiving the political tactic of previous governments as unsuccessful, because they led to Somalia's isolation from the international community, the new administration pursued a policy of détente.[15] Instead of hostility toward its neighbors, this regime negotiated with Kenya and Ethiopia, agreeing to terminate conflict and accept the colonial borders. It also reestablished relations with Britain, which had been severed by the earlier government. Finally, the administration agreed to stop all support for guerrilla fighters operating in Somali territories in Kenya and Ethiopia.[16]

This regime's 1967 election and its first years of power were plagued by allegations of corruption and nepotism.[17] Many felt that President Abdirashid Ali Sharmarke had abandoned those Somalis still under colonial rule and gave up on Somali nationalism enshrined in the constitution. On a trip outside of the capital on October 15, 1969, the president was assassinated; within a week, a military junta led by Mohamed Siad Barre overthrew the government in a bloodless coup. People celebrated all over the country, with the hope that the new regime would combat corruption within the government and also pursue the liberation of missing Somali territories.[18]

The Era of the Dictator, 1969–1991

The new regime embraced a socialist path from the beginning, creating a twenty-five-member Supreme Revolutionary Council that consisted of army and police officers led by Siad Barre. This abruptly ended the democratic electoral system that had been in place in Somalia from independence. As the cold war heightened, the military leadership deepened the country's alliances with the eastern bloc and received increased military support from the Soviet Union and other communist countries.[19] The implications of this alliance were complex. As the historian, Abdi Sheik-Abdi aptly noted, a Muslim nation choosing "'scientific socialism' as its guiding ideology in its bid to modernize, Somalia had to deftly straddle several dichotomies, including Africa versus the Middle East and Islam versus Soviet-style socialism."[20] Despite these contradictory ideological strands and the renewed tension with its neighbors, the Siad Barre government enjoyed great support from the population in the early 1970s, cemented by its large investments in education and public infrastructure.[21]

As the military government pursued a modern state apparatus, its policies continued also to be informed by political decisions reached in Berlin almost a century earlier and by subsequent European colonial policies in this region. Siad Barre rekindled the nationalist project to liberate the "missing" Somali territories and reestablished military support for WSLF. The regime also provided bases for other rebel groups, including the Eritrean, Oromo, and Tigray liberation movements fighting against the Ethiopian military regime of Mengistu Haile Maryam.[22] Ethiopia itself was experiencing political crisis in the 1970s, which provided Somalia with what seemed like the perfect opportunity to attack.[23] In 1977, Somalia's army enacted the country's long-simmering nationalist aspirations and went to war with Ethiopia. Though Somalis had major successes in capturing much of the Somali-inhabited territory at the onset of the war, the Ethiopians soon gained the upper hand, after the Soviet Union switched sides and provided military and personnel support.[24] The Somali army had to retreat. Ethiopia, bolstered by Soviet military and intelligence support as well as Cuban and South Yemeni army and air force equipment, offered this smaller nation a humiliating defeat. Obviously, then, cold war politics meant that, not just Soviets, but also Americans played an instrumental role in the regional conflicts in the Horn. The Horn region was and still is considered a strategic area because of its proximity to the Red Sea and the Middle East, essential to the cold war chess game played by world powers in the region. A contest for regional domination by these world powers therefore meant Somalia and Ethiopia were not alone in manipulating cold war politics to build military might.[25]

The Somali defeat by Ethiopia in 1978 was a national humiliation, accompanied by economic devastation. The war exposed Somalia's weaknesses and turned the nation's focus inward.[26] What came in the wake of war exacerbated the country's problems: a startling increase in Somali–Ethiopian refugees fleeing Ethiopia in fear of ethnic persecution. By 1980, the border between Somalia and Ethiopia was home to the worst refugee crisis in the world: an estimated six hundred thousand Somalis had fled Ethiopia, a vast burden on a nation of only about four million people at that time.[27] Though this number is contested, and the Somali government was known to have inflated refugee numbers to obtain international aid, the refugee crisis was still unprecedented for the Horn of Africa.[28] If nothing else, it further weakened a regime staggering from the latest round of isolation and from a costly military defeat.

For Somalia as well as many other African countries, the 1970s and the 1980s were a "period of disillusionment," a brutal follow-up to the "romantic period" that characterized the euphoric years following independence.[29] Despite the Somali government's socialist rhetoric, the ruling class became increasingly sectarian. Siad Barre's dictatorial rule, as well as the nepotism that had grown throughout the Somali leadership, alienated the majority of the population and led to the first overt challenge to the administration's rule. A few months after the Somali defeat, a group of army officers attempted to overthrow Siad Barre. The coup was crushed, with seventeen of its leaders publicly executed in April 1978.

This mutiny further exposed the chasm between the rulers and the population and marked the beginning of the end of any pretence of progressive legislation and socialist ideals that Siad Barre's government claimed to espouse in its first decade. Attitudes toward the regime became hostile, and distrust toward it soon manifested in unprecedented ways. The Somali Salvation Democratic Front (SSDF), formed in 1978, was the first armed Somali rebel movement organized against the Somali government, supported by and operating in Ethiopia. Members of the military who were involved in the failed coup founded the SSDF. Siad Barre reacted to this opposition by indiscriminately punishing people living in central regions (Mudug), dominated by clans deemed hostile to the government.[30]

Other rebel movements subsequently sprang up in other regions of the country. The Somali National Movement emerged in the northwest and, by the late 1980s, was contesting the regime's power in Somalia's main northern towns. In response, the state's military apparatus turned on its own citizens in 1988, with brutal military attacks in major cities, such as Hargaisa and Burao, killing tens of thousands of people and creating hundreds of thousands of refugees.[31] The year 1988 represented the beginning of the end of Siad Barre's rule and the beginning of Somalia's fragmentation into the small fiefdoms responsible for the continuing political turmoil of the nation.

The Era of Warlordism and Fiefdoms, 1991 to Present

The group that finally succeeded in toppling Siad Barre's rule was the United Somali Congress (USC), led by General Farah Aideed. This rebel group, mostly comprising the Hawiye clan, ousted Siad Barre and his clansmen from Mogadishu in January 1991. But instead of laying the groundwork for a new government to replace the old, the country descended into mayhem, with killing, looting, and famine. Within days of Siad Barre's fall, it became clear that there would be neither stability nor transition to a new regime. Young armed men started a witch hunt that targeted anyone belonging to the clans that they thought had benefited from the old regime's largesse with public funds. The resulting violence pitted clans against each other, with many who were outside the government apparatus feeling forced also to partake in the internecine conflict to protect their kin and property.

It did not take long for members of the USC to turn their guns on each other, however. The USC leadership's lack of any concrete plans for the post–Siad Barre era, and its growing internal divisions, became apparent shortly after the collapse of the old administration.[32] The leader of the group's civilian wing, businessman Ali Mahdi, was proclaimed president of Somalia; General Aideed, flush from his successful command of the USC's military branch, contested this nomination and waged a new war, this time against those loyal to Mahdi.[33] This conflict exposed the fragile basis and complex alignments of what had been depicted as a clan movement: these two men belonged to the same clan, but different subclans, and turned on each other a few months after ousting their common foe. In fact, fragmentation of clan-based rebel movements and cross-clan alliances became a recurring phenomenon throughout the conflict following Siad Barre's demise. The militias initially mobilized by warlords on the basis of clan interests to oust

Siad Barre turned into lawless, revenge-seeking thugs. They killed and raped while also looting both the public and private property of all those displaced by the conflict, regardless of clan affiliation.[34]

Though some scholars have argued that the state collapse in Somalia was due to "tribal" cleavages, there is ample evidence that the current clan rhetoric used by warlords and leaders such as Siad Barre drastically differs from the use of the term in Somali rural and nomadic history and is thus anything but ancient or primordial.[35] Moreover, clan identities are themselves malleable through migration and marriage relations.[36] It is fair to argue that manifestations of the recent clan constructions have their roots in elite manipulations of clan relations for political purposes, as practiced by Siad Barre and his government as well as some members in the postindependence governments. Catherine Besteman's research on minority and marginalized groups, such as the Somali Bantus (Jareer), a group excluded from the Somali imagined community, also adds racial and class dimensions that challenge the reductive, clan-based analysis of Somalia's crisis.[37] These more nuanced arguments bring to the fore the point that "clan" is a social construct, shaped by historical and social processes, including particular forms of stratification, such as race and class. Such multifaceted arguments expose the complexity of interactions between different segments of the population and the state apparatus, both colonial and postcolonial.

Unfortunately for Somalia and for Somalis, however, a clan-based political dispensation has now been instituted. This has led to the manipulation of power politics associated with financial returns for leaders bolstered by economic resources from national and international interest groups. In the post–Siad Barre era, holding office in Somalia has become characterized by usurpation of public funds and nepotism, a pattern that further fuels sectarian politics and protracted instability. Similar to the many previous transitional federal governments (TFGs) that the international community facilitated to reinvigorate a Somali central government since 1991, the current Somali government is plagued by corruption and ineffectiveness. Somalia has topped the corruption index list from 2009 to 2013, for example, with Transparency International reporting that "Somalia faces many of the major corruption challenges that affect conflict-torn countries, with rampant corruption and a deeply entrenched patronage system undermining the legitimacy of the internationally recognized Transition Federal Government.... Corruption is, of course, partly linked to the absence of a strong and accountable functional central government, a lack of resources and administrative capacity, weak leadership structures, and a limited ability to pay public officials."[38] Similar to other previously concocted administrations, the current government is also paralyzed by infighting, with President Hassan Sheikh Mohamud recently sacking his prime ministers, Abdi Farah Shirdon, in December 2013, after only thirteen months in office, and Abdiweli Sheikh Ahmed, on December 6, 2014, after eleven months in office. Such perpetual quibbling has crippled any attempt to craft political stability in Somalia over the last twenty-odd years. The current leadership, guarded by African Union forces, has little power beyond the government compounds to which it is confined in Mogadishu. Worse yet are the sectarian warlords all over the central and southern regions of the country waging a continuing struggle for territorial power. This fragile state of the Somali nation is largely responsible for the continuing plight of millions of internally displaced Somali refugees who are seeking to migrate around the globe.

Mass Displacement and the Emergence of Somali Diasporas

Conflict of the scale Somalia experienced after 1991 led to the complete destruction of all public and private institutions in Mogadishu, the capital and the seat of government. Yet before discussing the refugee flow to Kenya, it is important to highlight that this lawlessness went beyond Mogadishu to affect most regions of the country. Following the air bombardment and destruction of northwestern cities in 1988 by the Somali military, the collapse of the center and the ousting of Siad Barre led this region to take another path. Following a period of interclan conflict, the northwest claimed independence in 1991, reinstating the old colonial boundary demarcations left by the British when it was known as British Somaliland. The northeastern region, Puntland, also established an autonomous regional authority in 1998 and was generally spared the destruction that devastated most of the country, though many of its main centers continue to experience intermittent sectarian conflict.

This is to say that Somalia has become divided into small fiefdoms, with a weak central government that the international community has attempted to resuscitate over the last twenty-three years yet that barely controls any part of what represented the "Somali nation" prior to 1991 (Figure 2). The violence and destruction around the country since 1988, when Siad Barre bombarded and massacred his own citizens in the north, and since 1991, when he was toppled from his seat in Mogadishu, produced political, social, and economic instability that continues to fuel migrations to all parts of the world. In the cases of the northwest (Somaliland) and northeast (Puntland) of the country, hundreds of thousands flee these regions in search of better opportunities via the Red Sea. These people come to the northeastern ports (Puntland) from all parts of the country as well as from Ethiopia, moving on to Yemen, where they live in refugee camps.

Illustrating the scale of this crisis, the United Nations High Commissioner for Refugees (UNHCR) reports that "by September 2012, Yemen was hosting some 230,000 registered refugees, with Somalis making up 95 per cent of the caseload."[39] As Yemen is one of the poorest countries in the world, it is never the desired destination but rather is imagined as a stepping-stone on the way to more prosperous destinations. Many of these Somali refugees want to move on to Saudi Arabia, the UAE, and other countries in the Arabian Gulf to become Jannaalayaal. Others dream of entering Europe and North America. Hence it is clear that these latter migrations involve not only a search for place that will provide a safe haven from the Somali political crisis but also a migration toward imagined opportunities in more prosperous regions such as the Middle East and Western nations.

More often than not, these refugees have gained negative international attention as the Somali "boat people," particularly with thousands perishing in their quest to enter Yemen on overcrowded boats. Brutal smugglers operate these boats illegally, some dumping their human cargo in the middle of the seas to avoid Yemeni port security.[40] Some of those who survive this ordeal do make it all the way to the UAE, Saudi Arabia, and other Gulf countries, whereas others trek to Libya or other North African countries, where they continue their risky ventures through the Mediterranean on their way to Europe. Some perish in the seas or, if they are lucky, end up incarcerated in Malta and on other European shores, awaiting an uncertain future.[41]

Heading South

The Somali state collapse ravaged the livelihoods and the physical security of its inhabitants, especially in the south. This region was the breadbasket of

Somalia, and its people include some of the most politically and socially marginalized minority groups in the country (the Gosha people, for example, also known as Jareer and Somali Bantus). Thus the displacement of all the residents of the southern regions, with warlords vying for control over the land between Mogadishu and the Kenyan border, destroyed people's properties and livelihoods with massive death and displacement.[42] As a result, more than three hundred thousand Somali refugees had sought to cross the Kenyan–Somali border by mid-1992.[43] As men, women, and children fled the physical and material insecurity that had become Somalia, they were directed by the Kenyan government and international aid workers to a series of hastily planned refugee camps in northeastern Kenya. Hagadera, Ifo, and Dhagahley are the three refugee camps (collectively known as Dadaab) in this region. These camps sit about sixty-two miles from the Somali border. In a semi-arid land and sparsely populated remote region of the Northeastern Province of Kenya, this is home to the Somali Kenyans, who live in the disputed territory that we referred to as the NFD (Figure 1). Massive logistical and financial resources were required to accommodate such a large influx of people in such a short time. As this was a gargantuan task, the majority of the refugees self-settled, utilizing the limited natural resources found in the area. Consequently, these refugees depleted the twigs and acacia trees in the region to build their homesteads, also using plastic sheets, metal tins, or any other cover they could access to shelter their huts from the elements (Figure 3). Although the number of refugees Dadaab was originally intended to house was 90,000, more than 463,000 refugees had come to live in the camp by 2012.[44]

It was with great reluctance that Kenya permitted these refugees to live in its territory following the 1991 Somali crisis.[45] Although these refugees were allowed in, the expectation was that they would remain in their allotted spaces and would not have freedom of movement outside the camps. The UNHCR, with the cooperation of a revolving list of international NGOs, including CARE and Médecins Sans Frontières, manages these camps. The refugees collect rations that are distributed bimonthly and that have been dwindling over the years because of the limited resources UNHCR can garner for this protracted crisis. To supplement these rations, some refugees depend on remittances from families around the world, whereas others

FIGURE 3. Somali refugee girls in search of firewood in Dadaab camps, Kenya.

undertake petty trade within the camps to survive.[46] But despite these economic pursuits, the problem of malnutrition plagues many camp residents. Though this has been a problem for more than two decades, it has recently reached acute levels, with 40 percent cuts to the international funding for these camps leading Médecins Sans Frontières to report increasing fears of disease outbreaks owing to a lack of funding for basic needs.[47] The crisis has been exacerbated by new refugee flows to the camps, simultaneous with donor fatigue for a protracted situation that is now in its third decade.

We can rightly ask what the forecast is for Somali refugees in general and for those in Kenya in particular. In its refugee management policies, UNHCR identifies three "durable solutions" to protect the dignity of refugees: integration into the host nation, return to the home country, and resettlement to a third country.[48] These lofty goals, as we can infer from the protracted existence of Dadaab, are extremely difficult to implement. This explains why refugee camps that are often created as short-term solutions to political crises unfortunately metamorphose into semipermanent towns or villages.[49] To briefly see what the barriers to these solutions are, let us examine why none of these solutions has materialized for Somalis in Kenya.

To start with *integration,* some refugees self-settle in urban centers where they establish their families, seek livelihood opportunities, and, if they are lucky, secure residency papers, through legal or illegal schemes.[50] But integration as a government policy is elusive for the majority of the half million Somalis living in Kenya. Kenya, similar to other host nations (such as Yemen), has its own intractable social and economic problems to address. Half of Nairobi's population lives in slums and informal settlements, and the Kenyan population faces extremely high rates of unemployment, with only 27 percent of the employed holding formal-sector jobs.[51] The severe challenges Kenya faces render the refugees' plight more acute, with some claiming that refugees in camps may in fact be better off than millions of Kenyan citizens.[52] The government's inability and lack of political will to deal with the overwhelming refugee flood to Kenya leave most refugees with limited options, including remaining in closed refugee camps, where international aid organizations provide basic necessities but not much else. This lack of alternatives often leads to a life in limbo, at times in an inhumane living situation and with a level of physical and material insecurity that is barely an improvement from the Somalia that they fled in the first place.[53]

The experience of those who try to evade this lack of freedom of movement in the camps and the lack of opportunities outside exemplifies the lived experiences that fuel desire for further migration by Somali refugees. Thousands of Somali refugees live in Nairobi, Garisa, and other large urban areas in Kenya. But their refugee status puts them in constant fear of extortion from law enforcement personnel. Refugees become vulnerable to multiple types of power abuses, whether from the police force, border security, or even state bureaucracies.[54] Transparency International–Kenya found that the nation's police force was "the most bribery prone institution in Kenya," occupying the top position on the East African Bribery Index for the tenth year in a row.[55] This report notes that "there was a 67 percent chance that you would be expected to pay a bribe every time you interact with the police"[56]—and those polled for this index are born in Kenya. The situation for refugees and migrants is much worse.

An elderly Somali refugee woman in her sixties who came to Nairobi to care for a sick family member informed me that she recently paid $200 to leave Hagadera, one of the three camps in the northeast, to come to Nairobi (see Figure 4). She gave this money, sent by relatives in Canada and the United States, to a smuggler, who procured a forged medical permit for the woman. Some of this money was also used as bribe, which the bus driver distributed among the dozen or so traffic agents working at the checkpoints through which they passed during the three-hundred-mile journey from Dadaab to Nairobi. That the "pass" from Dadaab refugee camps for the Kenyan capital now costs a hefty $200 was very surprising. In Kenya, $200 is about what a public servant with a university diploma earns in a month.[57] The surprise was not the bribe itself, because such bribes are commonplace for refugees and even citizens in many parts of the globe, but rather the inflation in the price of the bribe since my earlier visits to Dadaab in 2001 and 2003. In fact, the cost of movement for refugees within Kenya in 2011 was *about twenty times* what I recorded in 2001, when I traveled by road from Dadaab to Nairobi to observe the constraints on movement that so many of my interviewees had described.[58]

FIGURE 4. Eastleigh, the Somali enclave in Nairobi.

As I subsequently learned, bribes for travel were not the only costs that had risen exponentially over the last decade. There is pervasive corruption among all ranks of Kenyan law enforcement officials, who target refugees in urban areas as a vulnerable source of income. Corruption within the police is so entrenched that it involves those at the top as well as low-level traffic and police personnel. Somali refugee women in Kenya report having their gold earrings and chains taken from them to escape imprisonment, whereas cell phones, watches, and any cash a refugee is carrying can also act as ransom currency. Many Somalis in Kenya told me that the police refer to them as "an ATM," guaranteed either to have money on them or to have family members who are willing to bail them out if they are taken to local police stations. This constant fear of being "shaken down" (often in the name of law enforcement) shapes how Somalis view life in Kenya. Although they did find basic physical and economic security, their lives are still filled with vulnerabilities and insecurities linked to their immigration status that impact their sense of well-being and belonging.

The second "durable solution"—to return home—is also extremely difficult, although for very different reasons. Returning to Somalia remains an option that a small number of refugees choose, especially after living in camps in neighboring countries. Recent political developments in Somalia and Kenya, including the September 21, 2013, terrorist attacks by the al-Qaeda-affiliated Somali terrorist group at Westgate Mall in Nairobi, where sixty-eight people were killed, have now accelerated calls to return Somali refugees. As such, Kenya, Somalia, and UNHCR signed a Tripartite Agreement on November 10, 2013.[59] This agreement stresses that "any refugee has the right to choose whether to go home, after they have been given information about conditions on the ground in Somalia so they can make an informed decision.... It also means returns should be conducted in safety and dignity."[60] The "voluntary" nature of the agreement may prove key to how many of the close to half a million Somali refugees in Kenyan camps return. The idea that Somali refugees, most of whom have lived in the camps for two decades, can just pack up and go restart a life in Somalia without concerted international financial and logistical support is unrealistic. The Kenyan government's rhetoric of ordering all Somali refugees to return to Somali may also be a mere political tactic designed to appease its population's fear of further terrorist attacks, with refugees scapegoated to deal with the state's failure to prevent these attacks. Nevertheless, these recent developments add further to the uncertainties that refugees in Dadaab have endured for the last twenty-three years and may push many to seek alternative migration destinations to avoid having to return from camps in Kenya to uncertainty in Somalia.

Finally, resettlement to a third country is the last solution for protracted refugee situations. Such a solution is realized for a small number through resettlement to Western refugee status–granting nations willing and able to absorb refugees. UNHCR data for 2011 show that globally, sixty-two thousand refugees were accepted for resettlement in twenty-one countries. The United States resettled the largest number of these refugees (43,215), followed by Canada (6,827) and Australia (5,597) and, to a lesser extent, the Nordic countries.[61] Of these refugees, 21,300 were from Myanmar, 20,000 from Iraq, 15,700 from Somalia, and 13,000 from Bhutan.[62] These four countries have remained among the top refugee-producing countries in the world over the last two decades. But most important for this study, the United States is the country that accepts the highest number of Somalis for resettlement and thus occupies a prominent role as a desired destination for migration. This fact creates a domino effect, as those Somalis resettled to the United States are able to initiate family reunification opportunities for other family members, creating a chain migration to this destination. As such, the U.S.–Somali refugee flow is particularly prominent in the Kenyan setting, given that the United States (and, to a lesser extent, Canada, Australia, and Scandinavia) provides the most opportunities for legal routes to those with families in the United States. As we see later, this flow is not as straightforward as it may seem, although it is quite distinct from the smuggling routes that migration to South Africa involves.

Journeys to South Africa and the United States

The preceding discussion outlining the protracted refugee crisis in Somalia and the refugee experiences in Kenya anchor the multidirectional Somali dispersal around the globe (Figure 5). As this project compares Somali communities in the UAE, South Africa, and the United States, the rest of this chapter provides a window into how these Somalis get to their particular

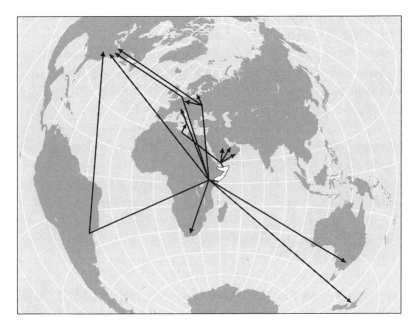

FIGURE 5. The creation of a Somali diaspora: migrants move anywhere they can rather than where they want to go. Map created by Dr. Mark Lindberg, senior cartographer in the Department of Geography, Environment, and Society at the University of Minnesota.

destinations. But because Kenya is more of a springboard for Somali migrations to South Africa and the United States, I focus exclusively on these two destinations here. The next chapter will incorporate the UAE migration journeys, which mostly involve direct flights from Somalia and are thus less informed by the refugee experiences in Kenya.

Somali migration from Kenya to the United States mostly involves three main routes: resettlement schemes in which developed nations allow a certain number of refugees to resettle to their countries, as detailed earlier; family reunification, where Somalis already in America sponsor their immediate family members to join them; and through smuggling, where Somalis request asylum on arrival at American ports. Given the distance between the departure point (Kenya) and the destination (the United States), the first two paths account for the bulk of this migration.

The most common route for Somali migration to the United States is through the UNHCR-facilitated resettlement program mentioned earlier. The United States by far remains the country that resettles the most refugees around the world through this scheme. Some refugee categories are selected for resettlement on humanitarian grounds. As such, women who have suffered from rape and other types of sexual-based gender violence as well as families with parents or children with physical or mental disabilities receive priority status by countries such as the United States, Australia, and Canada. A young Somali interviewee in her early twenties now living in Columbus, Ohio, for example, reported how her own mother's health situation expedited the sponsorship her grandmother in America filed for them:

> We came to America in 1997. Before leaving for the U.S., we lived in Dhagahley refugee camp (one of the Dadaab camps), having fled the Somali conflict of 1991. My grandparents who were in America sponsored us and the sponsorship process was sent to my mother, who then appealed for my dad and all her children. As far as I know, the process did not take that long mainly because my mother is disabled.

The most distinctive humanitarian resettlement program granted to any group in the Horn of Africa involves a Somali Bantu minority group, who continue to be resettled to the United States. This group historically occupied a lower socioeconomic and racial status relative to the majority clans, which have dominated Somali politics since independence. As a group that traces its origins to other African nations, such as Tanzania and Mozambique, a culmination of material and physical insecurities in the camps in Kenya and the continuing political turmoil in Somalia makes the possibility of repatriation dim. With the limited capacity of other African nations willing and able to integrate this population, the U.S. government granted more than ten thousand Somali Bantus resettlement in the United States. This group met one of the U.S. refugee resettlement priority categories: priority 2 (P2), or a group that is of special humanitarian concern to the United States based on its persecution (in this case, because of race) within the home country.

Reductions in resettlement opportunities as well as increased scrutiny and DNA testing requirements for those coming through the priority 3 (P3), or family reunification, scheme nowadays render the third option more attractive, despite the hardship and high cost of transiting through multiple regions to make it across the Atlantic Ocean.[63] Heightened security measures following the 9/11 terrorist attacks have prolonged the legal means of entry to the United States by many years, sometimes as long as a decade. With such a stringent system, more and more young people resort to crossing oceans with smugglers, with some reaching the Mexican–U.S. border after literally dozens of border crossings and many months, even years, in detention centers, as well as thousands of dollars in costs.

The case of a young Somali man who came across the Mexican–U.S. border exemplifies the risk-filled routes that some Somalis take to migrate to the United States.[64] Dalmar arrived at the border after having traveled through a dozen African, Asian, European, and South American nations. While still in his twenties, Dalmar left Somalia for Kenya, from which he traveled by air to the UAE, then to Russia, and subsequently to Cuba. Once in the Americas, he traveled through Colombia, Nicaragua, Honduras, Guatemala, and Mexico using multiple smugglers who transported him on buses, by foot, and on mules. Another young man also came to the United States, where he requested asylum, across the Mexico border via Angola, Brazil, and eight different Latin American countries. Only a small number of Somalis currently take this treacherous route, though it is likely to attract more migrants desperate to leave the uncertainties of refugee life in Kenya and the political paralysis in Somalia.

These cases underscore the sensitive and serious nature of "legality" and modes of entry into the United States as well as other destinations such as the UAE and South Africa. Some of these interviewees must often rewrite their migration histories to fit the asylum-granting countries' immigration policies. This is to say that though a Somali may have transited in Kenya and even South Africa for many years, her narrative for requesting asylum in the United States may need to focus only on escaping the Somali conflict. The sensitive nature of asylum requests and the narrow legal frameworks that countries implement to categorize refugees and migrants shape the types of questions that the researcher can ask study participants. As a result, this study took cues from participants and intentionally avoided discussing this sensitive topic in detail. The recent coverage of fraud in one of the key legal routes for migrants and refugees to the United States, and the stringent new regulations for family sponsorship for many groups, including Somalis, who are now required to undergo DNA testing to prove biological relationships, informed my decision.[65] The post-2008 DNA testing requirements for family reunification aim to eliminate the possibility that unrelated individuals will fraudulently claim to be family members in exchange for payments of thousands of dollars to their U.S.-based sponsors.[66] Though the majority of study participants came through legitimate family reunification schemes, or through the U.S. resettlement process, and openly discussed their migrations, others remained silent as to their modes of entry.

Leaving aside details about who sponsored them, some interviewees use the vague "family" to explain how they came to the United States. One such woman in her early thirties stated, "I came to America in 1994 with my family; we were sponsored by a family member." Others explicitly state their relationship with the sponsor. For example, a woman in Minneapolis in her early sixties who came in 1996 reported, "We were sponsored by my sister. My mother and I, accompanied by fourteen other family members, came through my sister's sponsorship." She offered no details as to who the other fourteen were and whether they were all blood related, and I chose not to query further. Clearly migration research is fraught with ethical questions for researchers as the data collected can entail serious legal repercussions for migrants and refugees.

It is nevertheless important to highlight that although some of these cases may be seen to involve fraud by American immigration officials who define the term *family* narrowly (to mean nuclear family), many Somalis use the term to refer to extended family and thus would sponsor nieces and nephews, for example, as their biological children. Comparing those who would "sell" sponsorship to unrelated strangers willing to pay them thousands of dollars with those who seek to use sponsorship to bring their close kin, such as uncles, aunts, cousins, nieces, and nephews, is really comparing apples and oranges. Nonetheless, the closing of this sponsorship loophole by requiring DNA testing has greatly slowed the number of Somalis entering the United States through legal means. Here, then, we see how the U.S. immigration system, which defines family as nuclear family, imposes a cultural construct that applies in the dominant narrative within the United States but is foreign to Somalis, whose definition of family is much broader, similar to some minorities within the United States itself.[67] Aynte, a man in Minneapolis, described how these new regulations impacted his family:

> My sister came to America in 1992, just after my mom died. She was in Minneapolis. I stayed behind for a while with the kids and [our] father, and my sister then helped me get into the U.S. And after I left, I continued to want to help them [siblings] and worried about them. Our dad stayed with them, but he passed away in 1997. He died in Nairobi after being ill for a while.

I asked what happened to his younger siblings.

> We tried to sponsor them. One girl went to Australia, but now moved here. Four of the kids are still in Nairobi; we sent them sponsorship, and they were asked to take blood tests to prove that they are my sister's kids. So the kids did not do that as they are in fact brothers and sisters and not my sister's kids.... That is how the situation is now and we provide for them. The oldest is twenty-two years, and the youngest is fourteen.[68]

Biological children are given priority in the family reunification process. Knowing this, Aynte and his sister decided to present their siblings as the sister's children, as she is the oldest child of her father and mother and is now their main guardian, because both biological parents have passed away. Aynte reported that he and his sister in the United States are now planning to sponsor their qualifying siblings, those still eighteen years or younger, and will still be required to prove their relationship through DNA testing. These tests are very costly and can climb to thousands of dollars per family. This is a cost they said they could not afford at the moment but were on track to saving for.

Though the most common source country of Somali migration to the United States is Kenya, it is by no means the only route to the "land of the free," as illustrated by the smuggling networks in Latin America referred to earlier. A small number of Somalis were also already in North America. When the Somali state collapsed, some of my study participants were in the United States for educational purposes, for example. One such man, Bashir, stated that he was "at an airport traveling from Pittsburgh to Richmond, Virginia, when I stumbled on CNN reporting the collapse of the Somali state." His student visa subsequently expired and he requested political asylum in Virginia, where he brought his wife and five children. Class and connections with high government officials were instrumental in how the earliest Somali cohort secured bursaries to the United States and other Western nations. Thus, though class divisions in Somalia were not widespread, connections with those controlling major ministries, such as the educational institutions, produced opportunities for some people. Consequently, those already in the United States could sponsor their kin, opening up more opportunities for migration. Nevertheless, Somalis from all walks of life are represented among the migrants to the United States, including large numbers of people who have lived in Kenyan refugee camps and who have few resources to their names. Networks of kin made it possible to undertake migration, with the majority of people whom I interviewed referring a sister, or a brother, or an uncle and at times distant family members or even neighbors to the United States, England, Sweden, Italy, Germany, the UAE, and other places instrumental to their migration.

Those unable to make it to the most desired migration destination—the United States—pursue other options to escape what they perceive as a restrictive and marginal life in Kenyan camps and urban areas.[69] Some choose to seek their fortunes in postapartheid South Africa, a migration that almost always involves travel by land. As Somali migration to South Africa mostly commenced in the mid-1990s, border agents in the countries separating Kenya and South Africa were not familiar with this refugee group. Their trips were also facilitated by their strategy of traveling in very small numbers, and they often arrived at the South African borders without much hassle or exploitation. The most common route to South Africa involved a voyage from Kenya through Tanzania to Malawi, Zambia, or Mozambique, entering South Africa either through the latter or through Zimbabwe. For those starting their trip in Somalia, border crossings into as many as five or six countries may be necessary to arrive in South Africa. At times, migrants go back and forth across the same borders if border control agents catch them and they are unable to pay the bribes that are now required to proceed to their final destination.

Somali refugees' decision to venture into South Africa often emerges from family calculations that encourage this migration as a venue for individual and family well-being. Such migration is considered a brighter alternative to staying on in Somalia or Kenya. But the chain migration that started with small numbers of refugees going to South Africa has now evolved into increasing numbers of people flocking to South Africa and entering through its vast and porous borders. These road trips have become harder and more expensive because of both the emergence of abusive smuggling networks and the border agents who control entry and exit privileges in these nations. Those with family in the West often call for economic assistance during these journeys, and Somali remittance companies in fact now operate at all of these stops. Others may plead with families in Somalia, who at times sell their property or bond them to finance these trips. Those with no other options may seek employment within the small industry catering to the refugees and migrants. For example, there are Somali "stop stations" in Tanzania, Malawi, Zambia, Zimbabwe, and Mozambique, and one woman and two men in this study recounted having to halt their trips to gain enough money to pay the smugglers to get them to South Africa. Another man who left Nairobi for South Africa detailed the creativity necessary to afford these expensive trips for those who don't have family members in the West to pay for the trips or to bail them out when their money runs dry. The latter negotiated with the smugglers, offering to gather enough potential migrants willing to pay the hefty fees in exchange for a reduced fee for himself.

Many Somalis and other African migrants, then, imagine South Africa as a second-best destination for migration to the Western world. This view was expressed not only by those who didn't already have family in the West but also by many who had sisters, brothers, and extended families in the United States, Canada, Europe, and Australia. Some whose families attempted to get them to the West through family reunification chose to move on after years of waiting for their immigration cases to be processed. This was illustrated by Aragsan, a woman in her fifties who ventured to South Africa:

> I left Somalia on October 12, 1995. I went to Addis Ababa. My sister who was living in the U.S. said she will sponsor me. When I was there for a year and the sponsorship still did not come through, I phoned my sister and told

her that South Africa gained its independence and many people are going there. I asked her to send me money to go there too. So she sent me eight hundred dollars. There were no smugglers [*mukhallas*] at that time and there were no soldiers hunting you down. I left Addis Ababa and I came to Kenya.

The recent discovery of the dumped corpses of dozens of Somali and Ethiopian men who suffocated on the truck in which they were traveling on their way to South Africa—along with other horrific incidents—does not seem to dampen people's burning will to undertake these journeys.[70] The adventure and hardship continue because of the hope migrants associate with their imagined lives in South Africa and the potential to find the physical, material, and psychological security they did not have in Somalia and Kenya, where they spent years or even decades.

A Somali proverb one of my South African interviewees used says, "Dad dad buu dugsadaa dugaagna geed"—humans seek shelter with other humans, whereas animals seek forests or trees for protection. The context of this proverb relates to Somali refugees' reliance on kin and community for protection and nurturing to survive the long trips necessary to reach their destinations. Having family, friends, or even coethnics in a new place softens the initial culture shock, alienation, and lack of resources many newcomers experience in a new land. Any analysis of Somali migration and the emergence of the Somali diaspora around the world needs to be anchored in people's lived experiences: their former lives in Somalia and in the camps and urban areas of Somalia's neighboring countries. In addition to the material, physical, and emotional turmoil of war and conflict and the dispersal of family that continues to be generated by the ongoing instability in Somalia, widespread abuse by law enforcement officers in Kenya curtails refugees' sense of well-being. The context where they sought protection threatens their material and psychological security. Their status as stateless refugees locates them in a distinct and separate, vulnerable position vis-à-vis the mostly Kenyan workers who dominate all the employment opportunities in these camps as well as the smaller but dominant expatriate supracitizens (read European/American/Canadian) who enjoy stringent protection and compensation.[71] Their experiences shape their expectations of a destination and the hope of family members left behind. Thus the journeys discussed here convey an understanding that the investment in migration ultimately improves not only the lives and prospects of individual refugees but those of whole families and communities.

This chapter also alludes to the many possibilities as to what might happen to each individual, or family, who flees Somalia. Each decision that a refugee makes closes off other possibilities (e.g., when a Somali decides to flee south to Kenya, she doesn't travel to the northeast and potentially on to Yemen). Each decision also opens up possibilities for additional decisions (does she stay in Dadaab or try to continue farther south, or to return to Somalia, or . . .). We all make countless decisions, each and every day, yet the choices many of us make are often far more banal and do not have the same future-altering consequences as those of the refugee and migrant: where to flee, where to seek shelter, whom to ask for help. Though the majority of the civilians displaced from Somalia have escaped to neighboring countries, many also undertake further journeys elsewhere within the continent as well as to other regions of the world.[72] Focusing on three of the most popular destinations to which Somalis head can provide us with a sense of how the expectations they hold of these places align with the realities they, their families, and their communities confront when they get there. The next three chapters outline the experiences of Somali migrants in each of these "receiving countries," seeking to identify how particular immigration policies, economic opportunities, race and ethnic relations, and more interact with the agency of these migrants and the cultural tool kits that they bring with them. How are the pain and hope of the voyages articulated, imagined, and reimagined through the migration experience? Is the initial optimism about migrating realized, or are people's hopes dashed as the context of reception trashes their expectations?

2 United Arab Emirates

Partial Belonging and Temporary Visas

> This is a Muslim country. For example, if the natives are working with you, they always express supplications for you from Allah, which is something very interesting. I have to say that what we encounter in this country is mainly good. There are Somali guys who are here without proper documentation but continue to work and live without ever confronting any harassment. So, this is a Muslim country, and as soon as the locals discover that you are a Somali, they really respect you.
>
> —Fuad, shipping broker, Dubai

We know that the state—with its ability to grant, deny, or regulate immigration status—shapes migrants' and refugees' sense of economic, political, and emotional well-being.[1] But state policies are only one of the forces that shape migration experiences. One's religion, citizenship, gender, and other axes of power can ameliorate or deepen constraints or privileges that migrant groups experience. This chapter reveals how Somalia's position in today's geopolitics shapes the migration options of Somalis as they cross multiple borders.

I outline how Somalis in the UAE are subject to two overlapping but contradictory forces that shape their everyday lives and inform their future plans. The first is Somali migrants' religious affinity with the local Muslim population and its institutions. A common religious heritage locates Somalis within the umma, a global community of believers, an ancient and still-potent concept that dictates that all Muslims belong to a borderless brotherhood. The umma can be equated to Anderson's "imagined community," but with a shared global religion rather than the limited nation binding countless strangers.[2] This affinity gives Somali migrants in the UAE a strong sense of physical and emotional security, with their cultural tool kit mostly in harmony with that of the citizens of the UAE. As such, Somalis express a sense of well-being in distinction from many other migrants, who suffer multiple types of abuse.[3]

The religious belonging of Somali migrants in the UAE, however, stands in sharp contrast to the second dominant force on their lives: their temporary and insecure legal status. Here the blurred refugee–migrant categories are most noticeable. Under UAE law, migrants are ineligible for the kind of residential and citizenship rights that some countries, including the United States and South Africa, bestow on select newcomers, as discussed in the following chapters. Neither the UAE nor any other Gulf state has signed the United Nations's 1951 Refugee Convention.[4] All migration to the UAE is therefore considered to occur for labor purposes and to be temporary and contractual. Most Somalis, whose passports indelibly link them to a hot spot in the War on Terror, thus experience permanent insecurity and immobility in the UAE. The result is a jarring clash, as the comfort of religious belonging must coexist with the lingering reminder that you are temporary. I argue that, except in a few unusual circumstances, being citizens of a failed state diminishes the legitimacy of Somalis' travel documentation and renders their citizenship inflexible. Most Somalis, as a result, either actively pursue or passively dream about a more flexible citizenship.

Yet only a few Somalis—mostly primarily entrepreneur returnees from the Western world and other established entrepreneurs who hold non-Somali passports—enjoy this flexibility. Their American or European passports and bank accounts facilitate transnational economic, political, and social pursuits. This privilege is denied to the majority who carry Somali passports, which are not recognized by most countries. Contact between these two groups, as well as transnational social ties that circulate information about the ease and legal security of refugee life in the West, fuels dreams of further migration. Amid the religious and psychological well-being of Somali life in the UAE exist perpetual rumblings and reminders that this is not really their home and that a better life beckons elsewhere.

Meeting Place and Melting Pot

In the Dubai gold market in Deira, you can find shop after shop selling the distinctive printed fabrics that Somali women use for dresses (Figure 6).

The storeowners, usually Arab or South Asian men, stand in the doorway enticing customers to come into their stores. "Kaalay waryaa, dhar raqiis, soo gal soo gal soo dhowow soo dhowow" (Come here, good prices, come in, come in, welcome, welcome), they say to anyone who looks like they might be Somali. Although I have conducted research on three continents where Somalis have settled since their country fell apart, the UAE is the only place where I have seen non-Somali store owners and employees who are fluent in Somali. These men are Indian, Pakistani, Afghani, Bangladeshi, and Yemeni. This unique fluency is evidence of the large number of Somalis who live in the UAE, who continue to visit after settling in the West, or who come to the UAE to buy wholesale goods for their enterprises in Somalia, Kenya, Ethiopia, and Djibouti. As a Somaili transit and trade center, Somalis who visit this country add to the estimated twenty thousand who live in the UAE.

This familiarity with Somali, a language spoken by only about ten million people around the world, is also illustrative of the UAE's status as a hub, not just for international trade, but also for international labor. Over 80 percent

FIGURE 6. Deira Market in Dubai, a place of gathering for multiple nations.

of the country's labor force is expatriate, predominantly from the Indian subcontinent.[5] A visitor to this region rarely interacts with Emirati men and women, except in mega-luxury malls such as those in Dubai and Abu Dhabi. Urdu and Hindi, not Arabic, are heard in the streets, and many non-Asian port workers, including Somalis, become fluent in Urdu. The UAE's historical sea trade with the Middle East, northeastern Africa, and the Indian subcontinent continues, intensified by new technologies in transportation and communication.[6] From early pearl trading to textiles, gold, and electronics, to its current reputation as a destination for tourism and real estate investment, it continues to serve as an intermediary between regional and global powers—economic, social, and political alike. Such powers include everyone from the American military to small traders from eastern, western, and southern Africa.

As host to one of the most diverse populations on the globe, the UAE may be called a melting pot as far as contact with and interaction among different peoples are concerned.[7] But beneath the surface, there is very little melting; this diversity coexists with segregation and entrenched socioeconomic and political hierarchies. Some residents imagine themselves or others as privileged natives, whereas others are seen as cheap, temporary skilled and unskilled labor, potential consumers, and importers and exporters. Thus there emerges a hierarchy of privileges and rights, with citizens at the top, foreign investors and successful entrepreneurs in the middle, and low-skilled labor migrants, mostly from South Asia, at the bottom. Despite these severe divisions, all these people share a common pursuit: making money, or at a minimum, guaranteeing the survival of self and families left behind.

Everything changed, and seemingly all at once, for the previously tribal peoples in the vast Arabian Desert with the recent discovery of oil. The cosmopolitan, global cities of Dubai and Abu Dhabi, with their eclectic societies, stand in complete contrast with the backwater status of this region only half a century ago. What are now the Gulf States were "parochial and inward-looking; until the discovery of oil, they appeared to be places where time had stood still."[8] Like other Gulf countries then, contact with the British in the late eighteenth and early nineteenth centuries greatly shaped the UAE's current system of governance. Its connection with other Arab nations was limited, while its trade with the Indian subcontinent flourished, as a result of both its location and the common British connection; until formal independence from the Crown in 1971, the rupee was the most widely used currency in the region.[9]

It was Britain's conquest of India, a century prior, that immediately rendered the Gulf strategically important as the primary path between Britain and India. Arab sheikhs, who had long held informal rule over small populations of camel herders and traders of pearls and dates, came into contact with British imperialism. All the sheikhdoms were forced to sign treaties in which they guaranteed that they would never attack British interests in the region and in which Britain promised not to interfere in local affairs or seek territorial or political control.[10] The treaties also committed the sheikhdoms never to establish bilateral relations with another state without Britain's consent.[11]

Though they were not colonized in the traditional sense, after India's independence in 1947, Britain deemed the states of the region as its protectorates. That arrangement guaranteed the British full control over the waters of the Gulf and prevented interference by other European imperial powers, such as France and Germany, or regional powers, such as Iran and Oman. Each of the seven small states within what is now the UAE (Figure 7)— known then as the Trucial States—formed a one-on-one relationship with Britain, minimizing conflict not only with this superpower but also with each other. Britain also often acted as a mediator for conflicts between the states. A series of treaties between Britain and these states followed by the concessions required for oil exploration in each of the states further consolidated the power of the sheikhs and ruling families, transforming an informal power structure that worked through shifting tribal alliances and porous borders into one in which a small number of families took permanent hold over state resources and thus dictated state largesse.[12]

Britain ended its treaties with countries in the Gulf in 1971, and seven of the former Trucial States—Abu Dhabi, Ajman, Dubai, Fujairah, Ras al-Khaimah, Sharjah, and Um Al-Qaiwain—came together to form the UAE. (Qatar and Bahrain opted out of inclusion in the UAE.) This union among unequal states was dominated by Abu Dhabi and Dubai—particularly Abu Dhabi, which occupies 87 percent of the UAE's land and has 95 percent of its proven oil reserves and 92 percent of its gas reserves.[13] As Heard-Bey notes, "At the time when the UAE was created in 1971, Abu Dhabi's revenues from

FIGURE 7. The United Arab Emirates in the Arabian Peninsula.

oil that year were some $450 million, while Dubai's were about $40 million—and the other emirates had none."[14] The sheikhdoms all had the status of states on paper, but population, economic strength, and territorial size all favored Abu Dhabi, followed by Dubai, leaving their sister states dependent on their largesse.

Oil wealth has permitted the creation of a state infrastructure, but that infrastructure in turn is dependent on the large expatriate labor force imported to work on development projects. The borders of the UAE are open to all citizens of the Gulf Cooperation Council (GCC), a regional body consisting of the UAE, Saudi Arabia, Qatar, Bahrain, Kuwait, and Oman created in 1981, which models itself after the European Union. GCC member states permit free movement of their citizens, do not impose customs duties on domestically produced goods, and impose only low tariffs on imported goods. Goods in transit within the GCC are also exempt from taxes. GCC members can travel to and work in member states without any complications. Citizens of non-GCC countries, however, confront stringent visa requirements to live in the UAE, implemented to protect the small population of the native born and their oil wealth.[15]

With the large migrant population imported to carry out unskilled and even skilled jobs, Emiratis can all be classified as "middle class or above."[16] The UAE, like some of the other Gulf States, enjoys one of the highest per capita incomes in the world; in 2012, it ranked sixth at $47,500, trailing only Qatar, Luxembourg, Singapore, Norway, and Brunei.[17] Only the small number of residents who are citizens, however, shares this wealth. The privileged position of UAE citizens is made possible by a very generous welfare state that distributes oil revenues to them, protects their employment in the public sector, and offers them preferential treatment in the private sector.[18] However, over the last decade, public-sector saturation and reluctance by private-sector firms to hire nationals are leading to increasing unemployment among Emiratis. Employers often see Emiratis as unwilling to work in certain sectors that they believe debase their social status and as preferring the public sector over the private, with its longer hours, lower wages, and more competitive environment.[19] As Kapiszewski puts it, "unlike in Western countries where foreign workers have generally complemented the national workforce by filling lower-status jobs, in the Gulf monarchies foreigners now dominate the labor force in most sectors of the economy and in the government bureaucracy."[20] About one million Emirati nationals, in a population of more than seven million foreign workers in 2011, confront balancing their national developmental needs, which require these temporary foreign workers, and the fear of being a minority in their own land.[21]

When oil was discovered, none of the GCC countries had the skilled workforce needed to harness it. Bahrain, Kuwait, Oman, Qatar, Saudi Arabia, and the UAE thus have had to import massive numbers of workers while protecting their small populations and their wealth. They established immigration policies that created the highest migrant–native ratio in the world.[22]

UAE policies were designed to attract both skilled and unskilled workers to transform the country into a global economic power while guaranteeing that the migrants would only stay as long as they were needed.

The rapid, oil-infused economic development of the Gulf countries places them at the center of debates on globalization. Dubai in the UAE exemplified this debate with its aggressive pursuit of international investments in its real estate boom prior to the recent economic crash. Dubai is now home both to the world's tallest building and to its largest mall. The current strategy of places like Dubai and even this whole region—replacing dependence on finite oil reserves with a robust service industry catering to national and international markets—remains reliant on the availability of a labor force with no basic rights who are paid very low wages.[23] In this strategy, migration exists only to meet the state's economic needs and priorities. However, as the German and French guest worker programs after World War II demonstrated, the import of millions of migrant laborers often produces new dynamics; such populations—and their offspring—are never as easy to manage as the government hopes. Though pressure from the International Labor Organization as well as scathing international human rights reports have recently drawn more attention to the treatment of migrant laborers, the region's competing needs—for cheap labor, developmental growth, international competitiveness, and protection of the privileged citizen minority—have thus far limited any concrete steps to minimize these contradictions.

Thus study of migration to the UAE, as well as to other GCC states, requires a different approach from the standard focus on settlement, integration, and assimilation—usually the core concepts in the analysis of migration to Europe and North America. The seemingly insatiable labor needs of the Gulf region as well as the overwhelming numerical dominance of migrants in the population produce anxieties, stringent immigration policies, and contentious power dynamics between citizens and migrants (Figure 8). The push to ensure that migration remains temporary creates a pervasive sense of insecurity among migrant workers.[24] Yet, as we shall see, the needs of the employers tasked with national development create further complications and tensions. Certain UAE policies limit the number of consecutive years a migrant worker can stay to discourage demands for rights and naturalization. Yet these policies are undermined by employers' preference for

FIGURE 8. Migrant workers in the UAE are a silenced majority.

keeping workers for long periods to avoid loss of their investment in worker training.

The foundation of the strict immigration policies throughout the GCC is the *kafeel* system. *Kafeel* literally means "sponsor" and represents employer-sponsored visas. A work visa, which is required for anyone to work in the country, can only be obtained through a contract with regional employers in construction, oil drilling, domestic work, and other service domains. An important segment of the labor force was initially drawn from Arab neighbors outside of the GCC, such as Egypt, Iraq, Jordan, and the Palestinian territories. These migrants were preferred because of their linguistic, cultural, and religious affinities, but over time, they have become a minority within the larger labor population. Political, economic, and cultural rationales abound for what Kapiszewski has termed the Asianization of the Gulf, with Arabs representing 72 percent of the foreign population in 1975 but only 32 percent by the early 2000s.[25] One factor influencing this trend is that many Arab migrants brought their families with them, thus creating anxiety that they might settle permanently and eventually demand naturalization rights. As workers, Asians are also perceived as being easier to manage, because they often migrate alone, without their families, and have less of a basis (linguistic, cultural, religious) for claiming rights.[26] But reliance on this large Asian migration is also viewed as problematic. An example of the existential cultural threat that Emiratis perceive is the fact that only 1 percent of nannies in the UAE are Arabs.[27] At the GCC labor ministers' meeting of 2004, the Bahraini minister of labor and social affairs stated that "non-Arab foreign workers constitute a strategic threat to the region's future."[28]

However, political anxieties are directed not only toward the non-Arab labor force but also toward Arabs. The growth of those fears corresponded with a concurrent reduction in the number of Arab migrant workers and in the reliance on labor from the more geographically and ethnically distant Bangladesh, India, Indonesia, Pakistan, and Philippines.[29] Many South Asian and Southeast Asian migrants are Muslims, but their language, their ethnicity, and their citizenship in poor and overpopulated Third World countries render them weaker in the global power hierarchy. These migrants, not surprisingly, have emerged as the preferred workers in the Gulf.

Political and cultural developments in the postcolonial Middle East have reinforced this trend. For more than a half-century, the region's sheikhs and monarchs have felt threatened by increased Arab nationalism, pan-Arabism, and secularism. Recent revolutions in the Middle East, the emergence of Muslim militancy around the globe, and the subsequent dominance of America's War on Terror all reinforce the preference for migrants from South Asia over those from the Middle East. UAE's labor laws state that when UAE citizens are not available to fill a position, "the priority in employment will be given to Arab nationals and then workers of other nationalities."[30] But in reality, preference over the last two decades has been for cheap South and Southeast Asian labor, along with a much smaller number of highly skilled technicians and other knowledge workers from the West.[31]

Somali Migration to Arabia

Somali migration to the UAE and other GCC countries is distinct from that to other regions. Though the insecurity triggered by the Somali civil war prompted most of this migration, that reason is—at least officially—

irrelevant, because refugee status doesn't exist in the UAE. The word *refugee* rarely came up in my interviews in the UAE, except as a term in reference to Somalis seeking asylum in the West or to those people living in Kenyan, Ethiopian, and Yemeni refugee camps. Somali identity in the Gulf seems to exclude the common identification conferred on Somalis who have settled in refugee-accepting nations. Somali migration to GCC countries (none of which, as mentioned, are signatories to the 1951 Refugee Convention) thus conforms to the larger labor migration flows across the region. Categorizing Somalis as labor migrants, when they are refugees almost everywhere in the diaspora, speaks to the UAE's immigration policies as well as to the malleability of these categories in different contexts.

Though migration to this region started prior to the late 1980s, the UAE has become an even more desired destination since the collapse of the Somali state and the subsequent political turmoil that sent Somalis to all corners of the globe. The UAE emerged as the cheapest, though not necessarily the easiest to migrate to, of the three destinations covered in this study. Except for new flights by Turkish airlines to Mogadishu, the UAE has remained the only nonadjacent country with direct weekly flights to and from Somalia over the last two decades.

The geographical proximity of Somalia and the Gulf underpins the historical relationship between these two regions. Somali adventurers have traveled to the Gulf for centuries, for trade and exploration alike. Abdinur Ali Yusuf, the first Somali ambassador to the UAE (1973–81), recounted his meeting with a Somali man who traveled in his teens with his father in the early part of the twentieth century to what is now Abu Dhabi but who stayed behind after his father returned. The young man settled in this region and became part of the local community. There are also communities of Somali descent in Oman and Bahrain. The few Somali traders who traveled to this region by sea in the early twentieth century were followed by a larger number of men attracted by the oil economy that transformed the UAE and the larger Gulf region in the 1970s. Though there are few records of these early migrant men and women, my interviewees described a wave mostly made up of young, unskilled Somali men working in the oil industry, construction, and other development activities. These early Somali migrants, however, did not consider smaller Gulf countries like the UAE and Bahrain to be ideal destinations. One interviewee who spent the last thirty years in the UAE reported that he and many others chose the Emirates in the mid-1970s because they were unable to get into Saudi Arabia, their preferred destination. Saudi Arabia was by then already economically flourishing with a fully established oil industry, whereas the UAE, having severed its treaties with Britain in 1971, was just starting to develop its infrastructure.

These early Somali migrants were a tiny fraction of the region's rapidly increasing labor force. Their numbers, however, inevitably grew, both as these migrants had their own children and with the increased migration that came on the heels of Somalia's political crisis. Members of the "1.5 generation"—children of the earliest migrants, who arrived in the region as small children as well as those who were born there—occupy an ambiguous position within the Somali community and within Emirati society. The only home they know is the UAE. Though often multilingual, most speak Arabic as their first language and Somali, English, and often Urdu or Hindi as additional languages. However, the fact that the UAE's only option for nonnative residents is labor migration means that visa renewal requirements for longtime residents are no different than those for the latest arrivals.

Following the Somali state collapse, these earlier migrants and their children were joined by two new groups—an elite business class from Somalia and the diaspora and a mostly unskilled laborer group working in export–import businesses owned and managed by the former group. On the margins are another category of migrants who are smuggled into the country. The elite Somalis, to whom I refer as transnational entrepreneurs, mostly hold passports from Western countries or non-Somali passports (Djiboutian, Ethiopian, Kenyan, and Ugandan) and fly in and out of Dubai or Abu Dhabi engaged in trade with different parts of Africa and Asia. The majority of Somalis in the UAE are unskilled migrants who arrive from Somalia, Kenya and even Yemen. Somalis often fly into the UAE from Mogadishu and Berbera (which is close to the major Somali urban cities, such as Bossaso and Hargaisa). Others fly directly from Nairobi, having spent time in the refugee camps or having lived in Kenyan urban areas. Some are smuggled in, thus ending up undocumented in the UAE. As we will see throughout the chapter, we can best understand the place of Somalis in the UAE by distinguishing these groups: old migrants, transnational migrants, new migrants, and undocumented migrants. These groupings will be presented in terms of visa acquisition and employment experiences.

Perpetual Search for Visas

Since Somalia's political crisis in the late 1980s, the UAE has taken on a prominent role in Somali economic and social life. Somalia's collapse, not surprisingly, also resulted in a breakdown of bilateral relations between Somalia and all other states. Alas, a prominent Somali shipping entrepreneur in Dubai, described the vacuum that followed this state collapse:

> Back when Somalia was a functioning state, goods used to come from Europe. A lot of these goods came from Italy. For example, cars used to come from all over Europe. Some of the Somali imports were even from China.... There were functioning bilateral agreements between governments. When the country collapsed, all of that went with it.... Most of the Somali businesses back then had some ties to the government. When the government went out of the picture, the people who came to Dubai had to build something from scratch. Somali businesses slowly spread to other countries, as far away as Pakistan, India, or China.

By 1991, the country's infrastructure had been destroyed and law and order were absent, making the largest Somali city, Mogadishu, a lawless and dangerous place, as was detailed in the last chapter. Somalis had to formulate a new type of economy. The new Somali reality transformed Dubai into a de facto offshore Somali port. It is thus not far-fetched to argue that Somali businessmen (and a few businesswomen) based in Dubai replaced the state in managing trade within and to Somalia. Peter Little's aptly titled book *Somalia: Economy without State* shows how a thriving informal economic sector emerged to fulfill many state roles.[32] Through the Dubai port, sugar from Brazil, secondhand cars from Japan, rice and fabrics from India, and building materials from China find their way to Somalia. These small transnational corporations are exclusively owned by Somalis based in Somalia or the UAE or, to a lesser extent, by Somali returnees from the West. Many of these Somalis migrated to Western Europe and North America either prior to the Somali political crisis or in the late 1980s to early 1990s. Either way, they often return with Western citizenship and at times some capital to pursue business ventures in the region. More often than not, some of these create enterprises with many investors, some of whom may return, while others stay behind in the United States, Canada, and the United Kingdom, for example. These entrepreneurs have established offices in the port cities of Mogadishu, Bosasso, and Berbera in Somalia and in Djibouti and Mombasa in Kenya. They and their associates procure the bulk of the visas that enable Somali migration to the UAE.

Class is key for how the preceding group emerges as the bedrock of the visas that Somalis use to enter the UAE. We know that people with enough money to invest can quite literally "buy" residence visas in many countries. To qualify in Canada, for example, "investors, entrepreneurs, and self-employed persons" must "show that they have business experience; have a minimum net worth of C$1,600,000 that was obtained legally and make a C$800,000 investment." Investors are reassured that their "investment is managed by Citizenship and Immigration Canada and is guaranteed by the Canadian provinces that use it to create jobs and help their economies grow."[33] The U.S. Citizenship and Immigration Services (USCIS), similarly, has a "Green Card through Investment" path: "You must invest $1,000,000, or at least $500,000 in a targeted employment area (high unemployment or rural area). In return, USCIS may grant conditional permanent residence to the individual."[34] This is the type of opportunity only accessible to migrants that Ong called "astronauts," an elite group who strategize in pursuit of economic opportunities while also securing their children and family's social capital, including coveted western citizenship and education.[35]

In the UAE and other Gulf nations, visa policies also privilege those with money to invest—without the potential for naturalization or citizenship but with extensive social and economic benefits.[36] This system shares some features with Western nations but also has Gulf-specific characteristics. Every citizen has the right to become a sponsor, or kafeel, for foreign migrants. Any enterprise a foreigner aims to establish must be co-owned by a citizen and must contribute to the economic well-being of citizens and the nation.[37] Clearly this system further empowers Gulf citizens and companies, as the migrants they sponsor are dependent on them, with some calling the system a golden dirham.[38] This represents the fees for the visa that the citizen charges the migrant, further enriching Gulf citizens, especially in light of the weak institutional support for migrants.[39] The law requires that all foreigners starting a business go into partnership with a UAE citizen, who must control 51 percent of the enterprise. Often the UAE citizen involved in such a contract is a "sleeping partner"; the contract documents 51 percent citizen ownership, whereas in reality, the small company is migrant owned. A better term for this arrangement may be "free rider," because the citizen–partner's status grants her a guaranteed income for the visa and business licensing without contributing to the capital financing of these projects. Though costly for the migrant, such contracts open up opportunities for chain migration, permitting the sponsored migrant himself also to start bringing in relatives and friends using the connections established with the sponsor.

Of the more economically established Somali migrants in the UAE whom I interviewed, none came to the UAE with millions of dollars, but most brought a willingness to pay a yearly stipend to entice an Emirati to enter into a contract with them, abiding at least on paper the 51 percent local ownership clause. Though simple in formula, this process requires a strong network and a relationship based on trust built over time. Musa, a Somali returnee from the United States with two successful businesses in the UAE, described the significance of strong ties between Somalis and Emiratis for his own visa application. Hassan, another prominent Somali entrepreneur whose company exports goods to Somalia, Djibouti, Kenya, and Ethiopia, also emphasized the importance of trust and networks. For him and his business partners, the kafeel is a genuine partner, even if the 51/49 percent formula does not represent their real shares, as the local sponsor only controls a small portion of the company. He described how he and his Somali business partners found this sponsor:

> Someone who already established a respectable business with this citizen recommends you to him. For us, we found our business kafeel through a former Somali sports official working with FIFA[40] and thus connected to the sports ministry here in the Emirates. Our sponsor works for the UAE FIFA office and we have had him as our sponsor for close to two decades. But since he works for the government, he assigned another Emirati to run his businesses for him and we deal with this man now.

I asked Hassan if he could make major decisions in his business, such as hiring and other transactions, without the consent of this sponsor. He replied, "If you respect the rules and run your business well, then you may not even see this guy for years. I mean there are those who pay fees, but not us. This guy is actually a co-owner of our business and thus we do not pay any fees." Somali entrepreneurs have found success in a variety of sectors. Livestock importing from Somalia to the UAE is a key activity for Somali entrepreneurs and an important supply of meat to Gulf countries, despite the absence of a functioning Somali state apparatus. Another important enterprise is the transfer of remittances to Somalia, an offshore financial industry that has replaced the collapsed Somali banking system. All Somali money transfer companies have their central offices in Dubai and are licensed by the state. A third activity is the extensive, and nonregulated, export of charcoal from Somalia to the Middle East. But the most dominant Somali economic activity in the UAE is the export to Somalia of goods that pass through the UAE, primarily from China, India, Taiwan, and Brazil (Figure 9). The majority of Somali industries thus have their headquarters in the UAE, leading to an increasing Somali presence there. Commenting on the situation of Somalis in the UAE in the late 1980s and early 1990s, Alas, who trades in cargo boats and livestock, and who first came to Abu Dhabi in the early 1980s to go to university, stated,

> There were not a whole a lot of Somalis here back then. There were few of us, mostly business traders but also some workers.... The businesspeople were always in Dubai and the workers were at Abu Dhabi. The locals welcomed us because Somalis were well known businesspeople. They had and still [have] businesses that were very dynamic. Back then, ... if you were coming by sea, you didn't need a passport, but if you were coming by air, then all you needed was a visiting visa. All you needed back then was an ID, and that is what I used to use to get in. When the collapse happened, I was here. Thank God we survived, and our business actually boomed when that happened. Somalis fled from the country in all directions, and the country and people turned to us for help.

The businesspeople and laborers who were already in the region when Somalia imploded became sources of visas for Somalis seeking everything from education to business opportunities to health care. For example, Alas refers to the visitor visas that Somalis would obtain to come to the UAE prior to the conflict. This is a temporary visa for which one has to apply before coming to the UAE, consistent with what many other countries require for visitors. But because there is no Emirati embassy in Somalia, these are now harder to get, with those already in the UAE applying for visas for their relatives, who may want to come to work or even to visit for a variety of reasons.

Unlike Somali migrations elsewhere, here there is no reference to refugees, safe havens, or asylum, no discussions of trauma, of violence, of forced displacement. The topic of refugee status for Somali migrants is anathema in the UAE. Labor and business investment, and, in rare cases, education or health care, are the only permissible criteria for migration to the UAE.

Over the last two decades, those Somalis who have gone into business with Emirati partners have become the source of visas for the vast majority of Somali migrants. Sometimes a company's Somali and Emirati partners

FIGURE 9. Exports heading to Somali ports at the UAE transit port in Dubai.

reach an agreement that authorizes the Somali partner to procure visas for workers. As was mentioned earlier, these contracts open up new chain migration opportunities, which are undertaken legally but exploit loopholes in the kafeel system. Hundreds of migrants may enter the country in a chain that began with one original sponsor.

The dozen Somali entrepreneurs I interviewed, like all migrants in the UAE, were dependent on a kafeel. With the exception of Hassan and another woman, all the other entrepreneurs depicted their partnerships with their local sponsors as mere facade and as fee based. However, all these Somalis had brokered visas for other newcomers. This second-tier visa procurement industry has been key to migration for those coming from Somalia, who do not have access to recruitment firms such as those that exist for Indians, Pakistanis, and Filipinos, for example. The Somali entrepreneurs I interviewed who ran either import–export firms or small retail stores each had at least two and as many as a dozen workers listed on her business license, including both Somalis and non-Somalis. For example, Musa had Somalis, Bangladeshis, and Ugandans on his payroll. Discussing the hiring of employees, Musa clarified the flexibility of the sponsorship arrangement:

> This guy gave me authorization. We went to the court and he gave me the authorization to hire people if I want to. If I need anything from the immigration [office], this document permits me to do it all on my own.

Such authorization frees the sponsored partner from much of his legal dependency on the sponsor. Loopholes in the UAE visa process allow a certain level of migrant independence as long as the migrant obeys the law and pays the agreed fees to the sponsor. Sponsorship contracts also provide opportunities to support the labor migration of others in both legitimate and fraudulent ways. With his sponsor's authorization, Musa metamorphosed from a dependent to a job creator in his own right; he became a visa source for other migrants, some of whom came to the UAE and worked for him and others of whom sought employment elsewhere:

> For example, in my garage business, I have twelve people working for me. So I brought these people from Bangladesh, India, and Pakistan and even

from Uganda in Africa. I also have two Somali workers.... I put down three thousand dirhams [about $850] for every worker.... The potential employees send me their documents, including passports, and I take them to the Labor Department. The Labor office checks to see if this person has been here before and if his credibility is in question. So, if they do not find anything on this person, they will approve. After that I apply for the visa, which he would use to come to this country. When they come here, they then have to go through fingerprinting and eye scans 'til they complete the process to become legal residents.... This adds up to eight thousand dirhams per employee, including costs for Labor office fees, health checkups, etc. If you add the three thousand dirham visa deposit, each employee costs me about eleven thousand dirhams [$3,000].

Sponsored employees are typically paid reduced wages until their debt is paid off. But some of the migrants who receive visas through Musa may never work for him, though he still provides them with a visa through his business, with the expectation that they will subsequently transfer their employment visa elsewhere. This arrangement provides most migrants a legal means of remaining in the UAE while maintaining a visa market that profits both Emiratis and their foreign business partners.

A Somali American businesswoman, Ebyan, provided a very different, and far less common, example of how business partnership can work:

> The kafeel sponsors your business. You will pay money to a [citizen] and they will take responsibility for your enterprise. For my clothing store, I pay about seven thousand dirhams [about $2,000] per year, but if your business is an LLC, for example, my cargo company, then you would pay about fifteen thousand dirhams. But in my case, I actually do not pay anything because my kafeel for this company is my best friend. She is a Somali who has Emirate citizenship through marriage. She is cosigner of my business. Also it is interesting that you cannot sell your business without the kafeel. She is my business partner, legally speaking. All the actions that I undertake, my kafeel must know about them. Unless your kafeel gives you permission, you cannot even open another business. This was a shock to me when I tried to open another store. They asked me, "Is your kafeel on board with this?"

For Ebyan, the kafeel system did not involve economic transaction. Her narrative was also the only time I had heard of a Somali woman who obtained Emirati citizenship through marriage. This type of cross-ethnic marriage with the local population is extremely rare. For the majority of migrants, thousands of dollars per sponsorship go to an Emirati, who benefits from the privileges that come with his citizenship.

The UAE government recognizes that there are loopholes and is very aware that companies that migrants and citizens register may be in fact not even exist in physical terms. *Gulf News,* the main newspaper in the UAE, discussed this same topic: "Unofficial estimates now put the number of workers sponsored by these fictitious companies as high as 600,000, or around 27 per cent of the total work force in the UAE.... Out of 400,000 companies registered in the country, no fewer than 180,000 are bogus."[41] Such numbers testify to the widespread practice of visa-for-a-fee utilized, not only by Somalis, but also by almost all the groups who have large enough numbers in this country. A visa to enter the UAE does not therefore guarantee legitimate work or a visa renewal while in the UAE. Though the UAE government instituted these migrant–Emirati citizen partnerships to guarantee a mutually beneficial cooperation—providing the labor migrants work while the local sponsor also benefits from the investment the migrant is supposed to bring into the country—implementing such a partnership is often much more complex than its original purposes suggest.

Although entrepreneurs may be able to pay Dhs 15,000 ($4,000) per year to license a business in the UAE, unskilled migrants—from Asia and the Horn of Africa alike—have to find affordable and safe ways to pursue their migration dreams. For Somalis, these challenges are complicated by the lack of a recognized government to legitimate their travel and identity documents. Many Somalis nevertheless continue to navigate borders as if reciprocal laws governing human movement still existed. The Somali passport continued to be accepted for visas to the UAE beyond the collapse of the Somali state. However, the lack of a legitimate central government to issue valid passports has created a market for forged passports that can easily be bought in Somalia and Kenya, among other places. A drastic consequence is that many countries have stopped recognizing the Somali passport because of its widespread abuse, with allegations that drug dealers from other African countries are using falsified Somali passports to gain entry to the UAE, for example. The UAE stopped issuing new visas on the Somali passport starting in 2005. But many Somali migrants continue to use the Somali passport because they have no other choice. Those who obtained a visa with a Somali passport before the ban continue to renew their visas and can also sponsor immediate family members. However, those without such networks are forced to resort to using smugglers to get into the UAE, as discussed later in this section. Others who can afford it also seek other passports to disassociate themselves from the stigma of statelessness associated with Somali travel documents.

Hassan, for example, carried a Djiboutian passport, one of the hardest to get for non-Djiboutian Somalis without a birth certificate. He and his business partners had an import–export office in the UAE, which gave them economic status, and he had connections with powerful businessmen and politicians in Djibouti. With this passport, he regularly traveled to India, Malaysia, and China for business. The Djibouti passport, combined with banking details testifying to his profitable enterprise in Dubai, even made it possible for him to get a visa to Germany for health reasons, something that would be impossible for the average individual carrying a Somali passport. For those lacking Hassan's status and resources, an Ethiopian passport is both possible and affordable, given that country's large Somali population and pervasive corruption. It is certainly easier for wealthier people to cross a border, especially from underdeveloped to developed countries. But regardless of class, citizens of Somalia arguably now confront considerable mobility constraints, and they must continuously devise ways to subvert these barriers to pursue their regional and international migration goals.

For example, Nasra, a woman in her late thirties, gained a UAE visa when she married a Somali man already settled in the UAE but remained in Mogadishu for four years while her husband traveled throughout the Gulf region for work. He eventually brought her to the UAE but died unexpectedly two years later. Nasra's visa was renewed a few weeks before her husband's death, and she continued to use it for its full three-year term.[42] A few days after I interviewed Nasra, she left the UAE for neighboring Qatar, where she did a turn-about at the airport to reenter on a new employment visa procured for her by an unrelated Somali woman with a Swedish passport who owns two clothing stores in Dubai; that move gave Nasra an additional two-year UAE visa.

Others have entered the UAE through family visas as dependent children—in some cases claimed by relatives as their own children, whether or not they were actually underage, and in other cases smuggled in by Somalis matching visa buyers and visa sellers. As far as I could ascertain, those coming through this method were rarely children but mostly young adults who were presented to be younger than their actual ages. Once their first visa expires, these migrants have to find new sponsors through employment or through a family member's business license. Some end up in the visa market. Faysal, a man in his early twenties, said that the initial entry visa is the only one that matters and that every migrant, legal or undocumented, eventually finds a way of managing his situation:

> If you do not have any business that will renew your papers whether you have legal documentation or not, when your time ends, then you are done. For example, some have *baja,* the legal visa documentation for sponsored children—that is, if your parents sponsor you.[43] It is like you bring someone because you claim they are your children.... So the person who brought you will get you a two- or three-year visa. And when that visa expires, you will need someone or someplace to sponsor you or else you have no place to stay. The person who sponsored you cannot continue to be your parent any longer after the two or three years.[44] You will need a store or business that will take you on and give you a visa to stay. And the cost can be huge.... For me, for example, my aunt, who is like my mother, is going to transfer my visa to her shop where I now work.

Somalis take advantage of the legal loopholes and the black market visa industry to pursue their migration dreams, often facilitated by smugglers (*mukhalas*) with networks in the UAE and other countries. Sometimes some Somali visa holders "rent" their passports to other Somalis coming from Somalia or other countries in the Horn to get into the UAE. If the smuggling is successful, the new migrant then returns the passport that she used to the smuggler, who then may use it for further transactions. This method is mostly used by women seeking domestic work in the UAE. The majority of the undocumented Somalis whom I met in the UAE were women, some leaving their children and husbands in Somalia and becoming the main breadwinners for their families. One such woman, Suhur, working as a maid in Sharjah, described her experiences:

> I told my mother that I was thinking of leaving for the Emirates. She advised me to seek information as to how and what was required for me to make this move. I went to my cousin and told him that I wanted to migrate and asked him if he could assist me. He outlined what the possibilities were. One, if I wanted to get a visa, pretending to be a wife or a daughter of a legal resident, then the cost would be nine hundred dollars; but if I was willing to travel on a bogus passport with a UAE visa that belongs to another woman, the cost would be seven hundred dollars, with three hundred of that going to the ticket and the rest to the man who rents out the passport. So, they brought me a passport that belonged to another Somali woman. They removed her picture and pasted mine in its place. That is how I left Somalia and came to this country.

Waris, another woman who worked as a maid in Ras al-Khaimah, came to the UAE to join her husband, who had himself entered on a fake visa and thus could not legally sponsor her. Instead, he paid another man with a valid visa to bring her in. Within a year of her arrival, however, Waris had to stop using this visa, as the man who smuggled her wanted to use the passport he used to bring her in for further transactions. Waris's marriage also fell apart, as her husband could not afford to rent a room for them, and she became one more tenant in a two-bedroom apartment already housing a dozen Somali maids.

Waris's and Suhur's stories illustrate the flexibility and constraints of the UAE's visa industry. UAE citizens can, at their discretion, bestow certain limited legal rights on the people they sponsor. As long as the facade of legitimacy remains, neither migrants nor citizens encounter any problems.

Relative accessibility of UAE visas partially explains why so many of my interviewees perceived the visa renewal process as easy and the UAE as a safe and welcoming place for law-abiding people. Fuad, a young man who works in the shipping industry, said, "They really welcome you. It is like you are the same as natives here"—assuming you go through the immigration bureaucratic requirements of finding an employer able to sponsor you as an employee and seek proper legal documents. Among everyone with whom I talked, the UAE was commonly hailed as a safe haven for Somali Muslims, where visa acquisition and renewal are almost always guaranteed unless a person commits a crime. One perception expressed several times was that Somalis, as citizens of an Arab League state, occupied a privileged position within the UAE. One interviewee, recounting his experience renewing his visa, said that although there were long lines, mostly of Asian labor migrants, he walked straight to the front of the line—being an Arab exempted him from waiting. I have not found any documentation attesting to such privileged status for citizens of Arab League countries, making it hard to ascertain whether this man was exaggerating or was just helped by a government bureaucrat who gave him preferential treatment over South Asian migrant workers. Such claims also represented Somalis wanting to distinguish themselves from the groups that occupy the lowest echelons of the economic and racial hierarchy in this country. We thus witness Somalis strategically self-positioning themselves as citizens of an Arab League nation, thus enacting a particular cultural framing that is relevant and instrumental in the UAE. Despite the exclusive privileges accessible to UAE citizens when compared to labor migrants who have temporary labor status visas and who are barred from accessing any public services, such as health care and education, all the Somalis I interviewed said they derived comfort from their sense of belonging within the Muslim community and still felt privileged when compared to other non–Arab League migrants.

Visa acquisition can be a long, risky, and stressful process. But these difficulties were viewed as worthwhile, as they gave migrants a chance at economic independence and the ability to support families left behind. Differences in class are clear, with those with the capital to invest in the UAE having a much easier time with their visa renewals, while many others find themselves stressed about what will come next. Not surprisingly, some end up staying on without a visa, working in the margins of the economy.[45]

Economic Opportunities: Diverse and Constrained

In addition to their diverse modes of entry into the UAE, migrants find a variety of ways to make a life and a living once they arrive. Family and community networks not only influence who gets into the UAE but are also crucial in determining who survives there. Vital for Somali chain migration is the ethnic economic enclave. Somali businesses in the UAE are centralized in Dubai and easily conform to Portes and Jensen's definition of the enclave as a "firm of any size which is owned and managed by members of an identifiable cultural or national minority."[46] Moreover, this enclave employs a significant proportion of Somalis, though these remain differentiated by legal status, citizenship, socioeconomic position, age, and gender. As the new Jannaalayaal, these Somalis bring with them aspirations that at times make everything seem possible but at other times lead to a life too insecure.

Transnational Entrepreneurs and Returnees from the West

Ebyan, a fifty-one-year-old woman who spent more than a decade in the United States before settling in the UAE, embodied the dream driving the migration of millions around the globe. Ebyan now owns a home in one of the most popular residential areas of Dubai and runs two businesses that employ and sponsor seven people. Though Ebyan's level of success is not common, it is a general truism that many Somali men and women with Western passports hold higher socioeconomic positions than Somalis who have never gone farther than Africa and the Middle East. The social capital that Western naturalization is perceived to provide further fuels the desire to migrate there.

Ebyan's transformation—from a part-time helper in a family business in the United States to a divorced, highly successful businesswoman raising three children alone—deserves attention. Enabling her to carry out her work successfully are a full-time Ugandan nanny and tutor and a full-time live-in Somali maid, both of whom have been with her for close to ten years. I asked Ebyan to compare her life and work in the United States to her current position in the UAE:

> The economic potential is just not the same. You cannot make the same amount of money there [in the United States] compared to what you can make in Dubai. But you know every place has its advantages. In America if you are really stuck and are experiencing financial problems, there are places where you can get help, but here if you don't have anything then you are in for a tough life. But it is much better to live here if you are financially stable.

Many people with whom I spoke expressed the notion that life in America, and by extension most of the Western world, is more attractive for migrants and refugees who are poor and thus more in need of public assistance. Though appreciative of those resources and supports, Ebyan insisted that her quality of life in Dubai would have been next to impossible to attain in the United States. Here we see a clear class distinction of how different groups of Somalis view themselves but also how different destinations are categorized as being appropriate for economically differentiated people. Thus it is clear that Ebyan is implying that the UAE is not for people without resources, whose lives are constrained. But as a successful businesswoman, she states that the UAE provides her with more than was possible for her in the United States, including servants, but also a sense of belonging in a Muslim nation that is a stone's throw from home—Somalia. She said that she was more relaxed and that the pace of life was healthier and more consistent with her philosophy, values, and identity. In addition to the maid and the nanny, Ebyan employs five workers in her two clothing businesses— three Bangladeshis, one Indian, and one Somali. Thus Ebyan created seven jobs, and these employees depend on her for their visas.

Ebyan's comment about the lack of a safety net for less fortunate migrants to the UAE is well founded. For the lucky minority who are UAE citizens, the UAE provides generous employment opportunities in the public sector as well as government-funded education and health care coverage and both loans and grants for homeownership. Since 2002, Emiratis making less than Dhs 10,000 ($2,800) a month get grants to build their own homes.[47] But these benefits are available to UAE citizens only; everyone else faces high housing costs. Exacerbated by real estate speculation, housing in Dubai is unaffordable for most migrant workers, who commute to jobs in Dubai and Abu Dhabi from Sharhah, Ujman, and the other less developed and more affordable Emirates (Figure 10).

Some successful Somali entrepreneurs are able to pay Dubai's high rents, permitting them to live where they work. As we have seen earlier, one of them is Musa, the Somali American man who worked as an unskilled laborer in the United States but now employs fourteen individuals, mostly Pakistanis and Bangladeshis but also Somalis and Ugandans. Unlike Ebyan, Musa lives alone in the UAE, with his current wife and their three children living in the

United Kingdom and another four children from two previous marriages there and in the United States. Musa has not invested in any property in the UAE but has invested heavily in businesses and properties in Somalia and Kenya. He has partners in most of his businesses. Musa attributes his success partially to the openness of the UAE system, which he said enables entrepreneurs coming with tens of thousands of dollars—rather than hundreds of thousands of dollars—to thrive and expand. The other factors in his success that he cited were his American passport and his English language skills, which allowed him to become a trader to China and India on behalf of not only his own enterprises but also those of other Somalis unable to obtain visas to these destinations.

This fundamental difference—that Somalis carrying Western travel documents can cross international borders in a way that the majority of those carrying Somali passports cannot—opens more opportunities within the UAE, where Somalis with Western passports can act as mobile representatives in global trade for the larger community. The global power hierarchy

FIGURE 10. UAE migrant housing on the outskirts of Abu Dhabi.

thus is not only expressed through Western economic and political hegemony but also trickles down by constraining the mobility of the citizens of much of the Third World, who do not have the assets to override the limitations inherent in their nationalities. The majority of Somalis can be labeled as global wanderers with little capital and are, as Muslims, objects of suspicion in the post-9/11 world. A small number of upper- and upper-middle-class Somalis can translate their social and human capital, including Western travel documents, into hard currency, while citizenship in a failed Muslim nation and limited financial resources hinder border crossings for the majority.

A common theme among Somalis in the UAE who had returned from the West after many years of residence and eventual naturalization is that their lives in the countries that granted them citizenship were not satisfactory, primarily because they were unable to achieve the economic autonomy that they have found in the UAE. Beilleh, for example, lived in the UAE from 1988 to 2000 and worked a business exporting cement and other construction materials to Somalia. With the collapse of the state in 1991, he requested a tourist visa from Holland for himself and his family and then applied for asylum for his family once they landed there. He stayed with them for nine months and returned to the UAE to continue to work. Asked how he was able to secure a visa to Holland given the difficulties Somalis usually have getting visas to Western nations, he credited his export–import business and UAE residence, which differentiated him from typical asylum seekers. Another factor that could explain this exception is that the majority of Somalis believed that the conflict would be short-lived and were not rushing to these embassies in 1991. Thus the now common association of Somalis with asylum seeking was absent in the early 1990s. Though Beilleh returned to the UAE after settling his family in Holland, he eventually migrated to the United Kingdom, where his family joined him and where he earned a master's of business administration degree as well as British citizenship. But after losing a middle-management position in London, he decided to return to the UAE with his three youngest children and wife, while leaving his three oldest children, two in university and one finishing high school in London. He reported that his income is about $6,000 a month, a salary that is very high in the UAE, where the majority of unskilled laborers' monthly wages range from $250 to $300.[48] This income also compares well with what he made in his last job in London and is, in fact, higher. Beilleh works as a marketing manager for an oil company, though his salary barely covers private tuition for his three children, the rent of a three-bedroom house in Ajman, and remittances to his children in the United Kingdom.

Complicating the commitments of these migrants to their immediate family were the incessant demands of relatives still in Somalia. The more educated or successful the migrants were, the higher demands from their families became. More secure incomes permitted professionals and entrepreneurs to care for those left in Somalia as well as their own children, whether they lived in the UAE or the West. For example, Roble, a Somali Finnish marketing consultant for a telecommunications company, reported that though he had worked in the white-collar sector in the UAE for the last seven years and earned more than $5,000 per month, his savings were very limited. He sent money, not only to his wife and two children in London, but also to family members in Somalia: he bought two trailers for his brothers in northern Somalia, built a home for his parents and other siblings, and brought his mother to the UAE for medical care.

Some of these successful entrepreneurs and professionals keep their wives and children in the West while they take advantage of the trade and employment opportunities that exist in the UAE for Somalis with Western passports. This phenomenon is mostly explained by the high cost of living in the UAE. In North America or Europe, their children can get a free basic education, and their families, who almost always claim refugee status, are at times eligible for affordable and even subsidized housing. Somalis without Western papers also settle their families in the Middle East, but in countries seen as offering stability and affordable or free education. Until very recently, many Somali families settled in Syria or Egypt while the fathers stayed in the Horn, North America, and Europe or in other Middle Eastern countries.[49] This has created complex Somali transnational family networks where shifting legal, financial, political, and emotional decisions influence where each family member may reside, and when.

Old Migration and the Myth of the Jannaalle

Jannaalle, as mentioned in the Introduction, is a Somali term used to refer to those who migrated to the Gulf during the oil and construction boom of the 1970s and 1980s; its literal translation is "those who went to heaven." These early migrants, though often working in the Arabian Gulf's lowest-paying jobs as cooks, cleaners, and drivers, were highly regarded by people in Somalia who had little knowledge of the occupations they entered but were in awe of the money they sent back. Men from this group were also considered ideal marriage partners.

The migrants who came to the UAE prior to the collapse of the Somali state have experienced modest economic success. Thousands moved on to the West after the first few years of the Somali conflict, realizing that the precariousness of their UAE legal status could be exacerbated by Somalia's collapse. Others have remained in the UAE and now have adult children and even grandchildren, some of whom have professional careers. There are vast differences in education and class within the group and across generations. A Somali couple I interviewed came to the UAE in the 1980s after finishing their university education in Iraq, on bursaries given to the Somali government. As the political turmoil in Somali worsened in the mid-1980s, they saw no prospects of returning home. Because of their educational and linguistic capital, Abdiqani and Rodo were both able to join the Abu Dhabi police force, where they are still working, the husband for close to thirty years and the wife for twenty. As public-sector workers, they are relatively comfortable, though their combined salary of Dhs 19,000 (about $5,200) has long been stretched thin paying for private school for their five children, with the two oldest daughters now completing medical school in China. As government workers, they qualified for public education when their two oldest girls were younger, but Abdiqani and Rodo decided to send them to an Indian private school where English was the language of instruction. But this costly choice meant that they had to send their three youngest children to less expensive Arabic schools in the UAE. Medical school in China, though expensive, still costs much less than it would in the UAE. As long as the parents work for the government, their visa renewal is relatively routine, though this is expected to end when they retire. The police department determines the timing of that milestone. The hope is that when the two oldest daughters complete their education in China, they will return to the UAE and take over the family responsibilities, including UAE visa procurement for the whole family.

Another couple I interviewed shared some of these characteristics. Abdalla, a weathered, gregarious man with a limp, lives with his nine children in Mussafah, a small industrial town just outside of Abu Dhabi. He has worked as a tractor operator since the early 1980s. His case, like many of those of the earliest cohort, testifies to how much of a myth the attainment of an earthy jannah by early Somali migrants to this region was. Abdalla came to the UAE as a single laborer in the late 1970s but returned to northern Somalia to get married in the early 1980s. Abdalla had the opportunities afforded to Jannaalayaal, who were considered good marriage partners in Somalia as they often remitted money not only to their own families but to their in-laws. Abdalla only brought his wife and children to the UAE in the late 1980s, after the Somali government bombarded parts of the north; they lived with him in labor camps outside Abu Dhabi. His wife, Asha, described how devastated she was when she saw the shacks for labor migrants in the middle of the desert in which she ended up living. In this housing, the family confronted extreme weather and rudimentary living conditions. Telling of this shock after her arrival, Asha depicted images that are in complete contrast to the jannah she and others often associated with migration to Arabia. This was closer to hell than the paradise that the term *Jannaalle* carried. She said she often thought of giving up and returning to live with her family back in Somalia. But the attacks on the north from the Somali government in 1988 displaced her family to Ethiopia, and return was not an option for her.

Abdalla and Asha's family consisted of nine biological children as well as two of the wife's younger siblings, only a few years older than their oldest biological child. Asha's siblings were smuggled into the UAE as biological children. Asha is a homemaker, whereas Abdalla, now in his early sixties, has driven a tractor for the Abu Dhabi municipality for the last thirty years. As a large family with a low-skilled laborer as the primary breadwinner, they also relied on the wife's young sister, a nurse whose starting salary of Dhs 7,000 in 2009 (just under $2,000 per month) matched what Abdalla earned after three decades as a driver. The oldest biological daughter, age twenty-one, had just completed a nursing degree and was looking for employment when I interviewed her parents in 2011.

Owning a house was unimaginable for this family. As a government employee, Abdalla got two adjacent apartments of subsidized housing from the government in the 1980s. But the Abu Dhabi government has recently contracted out many municipal-sector jobs, and he now does the same work for a private company that does not provide housing subsidies for its employees.[50] He and his family continue to live in the same two units but have lost the government subsidy. To make ends meet, the family has rented out two of the three rooms in one of the apartments. After Abdalla retires, the employed daughters are expected to sponsor their parents and younger siblings.

Abdalla had in fact renewed his visa (which has his wife and all their dependents on it) during the week I interviewed him and his wife. Because of difficulty getting time off from work, Abdalla was a couple weeks' late filing the visa renewal documents and had to pay a fine of Dhs 900, or $250. Despite working for the public sector for three decades, his visa is no more guaranteed than the visa of the person who came to the country a year or two ago. Abdalla and his family are obligated to renew their visas every two years for as long as he works in the country.

Asha, Abdalla's wife, reported that she relied on different charities to clothe her children. Her husband's income, even when combined with the salaries of their nurse sister and daughter, cannot cover tuition for the six children still in school. Public schools, free for Emiratis, charge tuition to foreigners. The family pursued and received full tuition coverage from an educational charity funded by members of the ruling families in Abu Dhabi.

As for all migrants, then, intergenerational dependency, reciprocity, and resource pooling are common survival strategies among the earliest migrants and their families. For example, Ubah, a woman in her late twenties who had a university degree from Syria, worked in a major department store. She shared a home with her brother, an engineer; his wife, a nurse; their two children; and the sons and daughters of a brother who had returned to Somalia—a total of thirteen people. Ubah and her siblings also provided for several relatives in Somalia, Yemen, and Uganda. Asked how the family managed financially, she stated,

> We are all staying together now. . . . My father's youngest wife and the children were also here until about two years ago. But she wanted to go to Aden, Yemen, and not to Somalia. She was too afraid about the whole situation there. And you know what is happening in Yemen now.[51] Anyway, we are

providing for her and the kids over there. To be honest, it is much easier for us now.

I asked how much they send to their father every month, and she replied,

> Around one thousand dollars. It comes to about thirty-six hundred dirhams, and we can manage it because we used to spend more than that on them [when they were here]. For the moment we are sending her a fixed amount each month, and it is my sister and me who contribute. My sister also has her own mother back in Somalia, and I have my own mother to support. I send her 200 to 250 dollars a month.[52]

Ubah said that, despite all these financial commitments, she still considers her family very fortunate, as many of her siblings—including sisters in the United Kingdom, the United States, and Sweden—all chip in to support this large and dispersed family.

Somalis who are long-term residents of the UAE and who came to this region in the 1970s and early 1980s, and their children, are rarely entrepreneurs. For example, Asha and Abdalla have a son who works as a clerk for a major private hospital and another son who is a gas station clerk, while one daughter works as a nurse and another just completed a nursing degree and is looking for employment. Three more educated members of the "1.5 generation" interviewed for this study work for a major retail outlet, a global pharmaceutical company, and an Arabic TV station in Sharjah. Thus those who were born in the UAE, or came there as children, are able to seek employment in more mainstream sectors than recent Somali migrants whose Arabic skills are limited. Some of these young Somali men are able to enter the police force with a high school diploma, and young Somali women work as nurses and nurse assistants. Somalis report that jobs in the health sector are an attractive option, with many nursing programs offering full funding in exchange for a commitment to work in a specific hospital for a few years, though this has begun to change in recent years. Work in the public sector in health and law enforcement remains accessible to those fluent in Arabic who are also citizens of the Arab League, while the Somali enclave in which Somali is the lingua franca is dominated by more recent migrants with more immediate links with Somalia. Despite their shaky legal status, then, long-term Somali residents still articulated that they consider themselves better off than most Asian migrant laborers in terms of their salaries, their treatment by Emirati citizens, and their visa acquisition process.

New Migrations: Unskilled Migrants

Other than professionals and early migrants concentrated in the public and private sectors, the majority of Somali men and women currently in the UAE make a living using multiple strategies in an environment where financial security is uncertain. This group can be called "new migrants"—those who have arrived in the UAE since 1991, as a result of Somalia's collapse. Many young men and some women, when asked their occupation, said that they worked as a *dullaal,* or middleman. This generic term allowed them to avoid being too specific about their work, either because they were undocumented or because their work was intermittent and not easily definable. But they primarily used the word *dullaal* during the initial conversations; later, a more detailed and diverse picture emerged as they described working as independent small traders and working for more established Somali entrepreneurs, and even as occasional intermediaries on commission for Somali traders in the Horn, Europe, and North America.

I chatted informally about job opportunities with three young women in their early to mid-twenties who lived in Ujman but were shopping in the Dubai Somali enclave. They reported domestic work as an area in which some can get part-time work paying Dhs 600–700 per month ($160–$200). Two of the three were unmarried and worked for private elementary schools, accompanying children on the bus to and from school. This part-time job also paid about Dhs 700 per month. One of the women said she complements this income with another part-time job cleaning houses a few times a week. Between the two jobs, she could make as much as Dhs 1,500 per month ($420). The youngest woman, who only works for schools, said she lived with her aunt and did not pay rent, and thus her income covered basic remittances to her family as well as pocket money for her.

Emirati women's job opportunities are often limited because of cultural constraints; in GCC countries, female labor participation is less than 20 percent.[53] But recent UAE policies have encouraged Emirati women to enter the public sector, especially in education, which is dominated by foreign teachers. This is partly because of increasing anxieties about contact between non-Arab foreigners and Emirati children.[54] Women from Arab or Muslim nations, including Somalis, are considered attractive candidates to work as guardians and school helpers, given their ease with Arabic and their religious and cultural affinities with Muslim Arab children. Some of these women are also attractive as cheap labor. An undocumented Somali woman who works in a public school in Mussafah, just outside of Abu Dhabi, said that her supervisor asks her to disappear whenever documentation checks are planned for the school but that she returns to her position as soon as the inspectors depart.

Combining incomes from multiple sources, including part-time work in day care centers and elementary schools as well as domestic work, was a common and effective livelihood strategy for Somali women in the UAE. The combination offered a relatively reliable source of income even when one source dried up. Nasra, the widowed woman discussed earlier, started work at 5:00 A.M., boarding a school bus that picked up children beginning at 5:30 A.M. and got them to school by 7:00 A.M. She also worked at a women's clothing store in Deira Gold Souk from 3:00 P.M. until closing time at 10:00 P.M. This only paid Dhs 700. Thus her combined income of around $400 per month allowed her to send her mother $100 a month and still support siblings, cousins, and other extended family members who may call for help. Nasra does not pay rent and lives with her married sister; she is also saving money to start her own business. During our conversations in the clothing store where she works, she often called her family in Somalia to discuss the fate of a sister who was caught in the Libyan conflict at the end of 2011 and the beginning of 2012. Nasra sent $1,000 to her sister, who later traveled to Malta by boat to seek asylum in that country, with the hope of moving on to other European countries with large Somali communities.

Even women in better socioeconomic positions than Nasra often used similar financial strategies to minimize their cost of living in the UAE. Unlike most new migrants, small-scale traders who are in the entrepreneurial category avoided commuting to Sharjah and Ujman, where rent was cheaper, in favor of apartments in the areas around the Gold Souk, where most Somali businesses are based. But to afford these more expensive apartments, they sought tenants for each room and even for each bed in a room to minimize the cost of their own lodging. Ridwan, who runs a small Somali women's clothing store, rented a large apartment with four bedrooms. She turned the kitchen into a bedroom, which she shared with two other related women. The yearly rent for this second-floor apartment was Dhs 45,000 ($13,000) in 2009.[55] The four bedrooms were filled with beds—one room housed five men, two had four men each, and the smallest had three. With the three women who shared the kitchen, nineteen people shared this house with Ridwan. Each man paid around Dhs 350, or just under $100. This covered the rent and the utilities while the three women did not pay rent, with one of them providing cleaning and cooking services while the other worked with Ridwan at the store.

The primary renter bears all the risks, including the possibility of empty beds. For those female renters with apartments around the bustling market, that possibility rarely seemed a concern. Still, such ventures are not guaranteed to succeed and can entail high financial risks. One woman who tried to sublease an apartment in Sharjah could not rent out all the rooms, and her lease was terminated when the Emirati landlord found out that she rented rooms to men and women who were not blood relations or married. While this was problematic for the Emirati owners of the properties, Somali men and women never expressed concern about this practice; sex segregation is far less rigid in Somalia than it is in some other Muslim countries, though this has been changing somewhat over the last twenty years.[56] Somali women only rented to men with good referrals and good standing in the community. Although they lived with a dozen men, neither Ridwan nor her roommates expressed any fear of sexual abuse or stigma when I talked to them after they invited me to their house. Thus the socioeconomic strategies that these women use to meet the high cost of living are never interpreted to challenge the Somali gender order, with relative acceptance of these women's vital roles in the economic well-being of families in the UAE and elsewhere.

Young men are often in a very similar position as the young women described earlier. Sponsors paid to bring them as their own children may have smuggled them to the UAE. I found this to be less true for young women and have not encountered any woman in her teens who came alone to the UAE. The Somali gender norm of fearing that young women may confront sexual exploitation outside of their protective family surroundings accounts for this differential treatment between young women and young men. Young men, however, are often expected to fend for themselves once on UAE soil, with the expectation that they will also provide for their parents and siblings and, at times, their own children left behind in Somalia. Initial jobs open to such young men are at the bottom of the ladder—loaders and packers for the Somali shipping industry or for small stores that send packages to clients around the globe.

These men—along with undocumented Somali women whose only option is to work as maids or to rely on charity if they are single mothers—occupy the lowest rank in the community and are often said to struggle the most with life in the UAE. These young men, who may even lack work visas, can still achieve limited social mobility as they gain experience and build networks within and outside the UAE. For example, Baddal, a man in his mid-twenties, reported working as a packer for a shipping company for three years, until he saved enough to buy a car, which he uses as a taxi within the Somali community. Though this work is unlicensed, many of the men who work as taxi drivers said that the police were aware of it but rarely punish them. In addition to shuttling UAE-based Somalis, living for the most part in Sharjah and Ujman and commuting to Dubai for work, these taxis cater to the Somalis from the West passing through the UAE and in transit to Somalia, Kenya, Ethiopia, or Djibouti and also to those in the UAE for business or pleasure coming from around the globe.

Such men supplement this income in various ways. For example, Omar reported working as a private driver for a Somali family and getting paid under the table. His employers are an entrepreneur who exports goods to Somalia and his stay-at-home wife with both school-age children and toddlers. With a combined salary that exceeds $1,000 a month, and a rent of only $170 per month for a room he shares with two other men, Omar supports his parents as well as a wife and child in Mogadishu. His income would not have been sufficient if his wife and child were in the UAE, especially because he would still support his parents in Somalia. This way, he is able to visit his family once a year. His employment visa, procured for him by a relative with a store in which he does not work, is key to his ability to enter different sectors and own and insure a car, and thus not only survive but also cover his family's needs.

Maids: Struggling on the Margins

The employment opportunities for most low-skilled migrant women in the UAE revolve around domestic work, which remains loosely regulated and managed by networks of private agencies and unscrupulous middlemen.[57] Domestic work is one of the most racialized employment sectors, with Asians considered the most ideal workers.[58] Women from poorer regions in Asia, whose families depend on their income, endure financial, physical, and sexual abuse, leading some to call this work tantamount to "contract slavery."[59] These domestic workers are part of the women-dominated international circulation of domestic workers whom Rhacel Parrenas calls "servants of globalization."[60] Millions of these women are integrated into the global economy, and lead complex transnational lives, but remain dislocated from the home country as well as their host countries.[61]

Some highly publicized cases of domestic worker mistreatment by Arab employers have led to international furor and bilateral tension, with some nations, such as Sri Lanka, banning or threatening to ban travel of young women to the Gulf.[62] The UAE government claims to have made some progress on the treatment of domestic workers and human rights in general. But citizens remain the ones enjoying legal protections in this context, with very little recourse for domestic workers.[63] Cognizant of the abuses of domestic workers in this region, Somali women were more willing to talk about their dislike of working for native Emiratis. It is common for Somali women to see themselves as superior to the Asians who often predominate in this sector, seeing Asians as obedient and willing to endure mistreatment and themselves as high-spirited, independent, and, despite their legal status, equal Muslim brothers and sisters of the native population.

These Somali women often enter the UAE through the same smuggling networks as men, including by renting passports or paying someone to sponsor them as a wives or as biological children. Also, just like men, the women are expected to fend for themselves after they arrive. Women in this position seek out friends, relatives, or family acquaintances and even former neighbors willing to assist them until they find jobs. Nevertheless, interviewees unanimously said they were confident that no Somali will starve or be homeless as long as other Somalis live in the area. The nomadic culture of hospitality and Islam's emphasis on charity are often said to be the foundation of this profound commitment to sharing resources, no matter how meager.

Suleikha, a woman in her early thirties who has lived in the UAE since 2005, came to join her husband, though he could not sponsor her himself on his visa. She traveled from central Somalia to Mogadishu, which has strong smuggling networks with the Gulf. Once she arrived in the UAE, her husband could not afford to rent a room for the two of them. As a result, he took her to a woman who was a distant relative of hers, who was already sharing a house with many others:

> Men lived there. One room had six men and the other had seven.... The men sometimes asked me to make tea for them. So whatever was left over from the money they gave me to buy sugar, I used that to buy bread to use with the tea. A year later, I found a job, thank God.

Suleikha not only received shelter from this distant relative but was also able to eat thanks to male tenants of the apartment who asked her to cook for them. Some of the women worked as full-time maids and only came to the apartment on Thursday nights, as they had Fridays off. Others, however, worked as maids for a few hours a day for two or three days and thus always returned to sleep in the house. Before Suleikha got a job, she ended up getting a divorce from her husband. He failed to provide for her or to shelter her, responsibilities considered in Islam to be a husband's duty, and her family pressured him to let her go.

The process of finding work as a maid can be long and at times painful, involving both the mundane realities of culture shock and the horrible risk of sexual exploitation. Hiring an undocumented maid is a clear violation of UAE law, and though Emiratis sometimes do this, the Somali maids I interviewed all opted to work for non-Emirati Arabs such as Sudanese, Syrian, Omani, or Lebanese families. This is not to imply that these groups don't request papers but that they are less stringent in their documentation requirements. For example, Suleikha reported that the family for whom she worked asked for her work visa and that she told them that they were with her brother and that she would make copies for them. She has not done that, and the family has not insisted.

The most common shock among the Somali maids I interviewed concerned alcohol consumption. For many, it is the first time they have come into contact with alcohol, which is consumed in Somalia, but only in top hotels serving expatriates and Somali elites and never in public places. In the rich Gulf nations, alcohol is publicly prohibited but often consumed in private. A recent report found that "almost 81 per cent of all traffic offences in Dubai in 2011 were due to drunk driving."[64]

Two maids recounted quitting their jobs after encountering practices that they viewed as contrary to their cultural and religious beliefs. Rukia's first job was in a house where alcohol was stored in the refrigerator. It is common for Somali women to have never known anyone who drinks, and these women view alcohol as forbidden in Islam and those consuming it as untrustworthy and potential violators of everything sacred. Rukia said,

> The wife talked to me one night and she advised me not to sleep without locking my door. She told me keep it locked and to even leave the key inside the hole.... She advised me to be aware and watchful when I went to sleep.... Another time, their daughter and I also had a conversation. She told me that I should move away if her father ever came close to me. She said he has no memory as he drinks. I asked her if he drinks in the house or outside and she said that he does both.... The wife also told me to leave the kitchen once her husband comes in there. One day while I was in the kitchen, he came in and took his glass. He went to the pool, took out a black bag and poured something out of it.... [He] came with it into the kitchen and added cold water to it. He took it and drank it. That day, I thought to myself, "Allah, have mercy on me!" In my whole life, I have never seen anyone who ever drank alcohol, I only heard of it. It was surreal to me. I said to myself, this cannot be happening!... After this incident, I called the friend who got me the job and told her that the man was alcoholic and that I could not wash his glasses, but also that I could not live in his house. I told her that I could not continue to work in this house. She spoke with the man and told him that I am homesick and he should bring me down for one day at the end of the month.

Rukia never went back to that family and in fact quit two other jobs before finding an acceptable arrangement.

Another Somali maid had similar experiences; her employer was a Moroccan woman who was a second wife and only saw her husband in the daytime, when he visited her on his way back from work. The husband was an Emirati and had a local wife who did not know about the second wife and their son. The woman drank alcohol and also smoked tobacco in a *shisha*, a Middle Eastern pipe. This maid, too, expressed incredulity and shock, not only at the presence of alcohol, but also that a woman would consume it. She quit the job within a few days and told the woman that she did not expect to be paid for the three days of work she had put in. She just wanted out.

Another persistent theme in these interviews was fear of sexual violence, expressed not only by these women but also by their parents. One woman, Suada, described her mother's concerns and frequent statements that she should come back to Somalia if things did not work out in the UAE. This young woman, who was single, expressed her enthusiasm the first time she collected her wages and sent $200 to her mother, who nevertheless remained concerned about her being alone and unemployed for many months after arriving in the UAE. Suada found an older female acquaintance of her family to talk to her mother on the phone, to reassure her that Suada was fine despite her initial trouble finding steady work. Fear for her safety, but also for her reputation, created a lot of stress for her mother in Mogadishu:

> She told me that she was not going to tell me to come back, but that I should not hesitate to return home.... She told me that I should not do anything stupid if I become desperate, and that I should call her and she will try to help.

This motherly concern was in part informed by Somalis' understanding of what maids experience in the Middle East. Anecdotes told by Somali women who worked in Saudi Arabia in the 1970s and 1980s often mentioned the constant fear of sexual abuse and exploitation by the male heads of these households or their sons. One common anecdote refers to Somali maids being told by the women they work for never to clean the floors bending over, as that would emphasize their posteriors, which could tempt the men in the household to make sexual advances. These old stories continue to trigger parental concerns for Somalis' daughters in the UAE.

Language barriers exacerbated fear of sexual abuse. Somali women who sought work as maids often had very limited formal schooling and did not initially speak any Arabic. But many knew some Koranic teachings and thus started picking up the basics quickly. The five maids with whom I spoke said they all had to learn Arabic on the job, often lying to get employment but then adapting to the situation quickly. One of the maids was fired from a job on the second day as she could not follow basic orders or comprehend the tasks she was assigned. But after a few months, they all reported picking up enough Arabic to do their jobs cleaning, cooking, and caring for children.

These women overwhelmingly expressed a preference to work as maids but still live in their own apartments, no matter how crowded, rather than to work as live-in maids. Finding jobs in the schools as child care assistants or cleaners was cited as more preferable to working as maids. Many Somali women work in the latter sector, but for this, documentation is often required, though some private schools hire undocumented workers, who are cheaper and more vulnerable than those with work permits. After months or even years of changing jobs, some women find good jobs with families. One maid has now worked for more than two years for a Sudanese couple, both medical doctors, with two daughters and one son. Another one has been with a Palestinian family, two middle-class professionals with two daughters, for the last three and a half years. Both said they were content with these jobs, which they found after many trials and tribulations.

Somali maids' wages are the lowest of all those reported by Somalis and are closer to those of low-skilled laborers from Asia. Their income can range from Dhs 1,000 to Dhs 1,200, or just about $270 to $330 per month. These are also the salaries paid by the Somali entrepreneur families who can afford to hire a maid. Live-in maids and nannies usually do not incur rent and food costs.

Despite their low incomes, these women still provide for their families. Even a maid making $300 per month reported building a one-bedroom stone house in a small village in central Somalia, where her family lives, while she still saves up to $50 a month: "I save it for them [her parents], for future construction projects." Another maid without a banking account said she saves up a couple of hundred dollars every three months or so and buys small pieces of gold jewelry—earrings, rings, or chains—as these are easily storable, don't require her to have a bank account, and are safe investments. These migrants meet the needs of immediate families left behind in the Horn. They often find ways to support their families, even if this happens after months or years of living a precarious existence marked by unemployment or dependency on the charity of others.

Identity of Quasi-Belonging

With the possible exception of the Somalis who are better off and who often hold non-Somali regional or Western passports, migrants in the UAE face fundamental and ongoing obstacles. Yet there is a remarkable sense of contentment among these workers. Every one of the people with whom I talked said something along the lines of "this place is really good to Somalis—it is a Muslim nation and we feel good here." No matter the overarching insecurity of visa renewal, or the lack of access to any state services, they could still hear the call to prayer five times a day wherever they worked, and there were no major conflicts between their cultural tool kit (faith and gender norms, for example) and those of the host country. Such elements played a key role in this sense of well-being. Many Somalis also expressed appreciation for what seems like a hands-off approach by the government: as long as Somalis obeyed the law, the common view went, the government did not intrude because of its sympathetic view of the precarious position of Somalis as fellow Muslims whose country is in turmoil.

Interviewees were convinced that Somalis were treated differently than South Asians and that only Muslims originating from Arab League nations got special treatment from the government and fellow citizens. Despite the fact that a large segment of the labor migrants in the UAE originates from other countries with large Muslim populations, such as Pakistan, Bangladesh, and India, Somalis often brought to the fore their Muslim and Arab identities to differentiate themselves from these other migrants as more closely affiliated with the Middle East. The number of Somalis who use their private vehicles as unlicensed taxis throughout the UAE without penalty was seen as evidence of this special bond. Though video cameras are mounted on most UAE street corners, including areas where unlicensed Somali taxi drivers solicit their customers, the police almost never arrest or even give warnings to these taxi drivers.

Yasin, a man in his early twenties, elaborated a key reason why Somalis are tolerated:

> It is true that Somalis are very much respected in the UAE. If you and someone else were stopped by the police and the Somali guy had no documents, it is very likely that they will let go the Somali person.... The police in this country are mostly not Emiratis; the majority of them are non-natives like Yemenis, Iranians, Sudanese, and Somalis. The police are made up of mixed people. So if you are stopped by Somali, Sudanese, or Yemeni police officers, they really would not give you much trouble. Unless you stole or killed someone, they would just let you go.

The fact that many UAE law enforcement personnel are from groups with which Somalis have great affinity, such as Sudanese and Yemenis, was seen as important. The police force remains one of the key areas of public-sector employment open to young Somalis who have gone through the UAE school system. For example, one young woman whose mother was in the police force for more than twenty years was given a position in the same field after her mother passed away. This woman now provides the visas for all her siblings as well as her father, who retired after thirty years as a municipal clerk in Dubai. Another young man in his early twenties in the Sharjah police force reported that hundreds of young Somali men were trained and entered this sector in the last few decades. Yasin's statement underscores how Somalis rarely interact with Emirati citizens, as non-Emirati public servants often man public institutions that Somalis frequent. Somalis concentrate and work in their own ethnic enclave, which produces a different reality than what many South Asian migrants experience, who live in labor camps and work in construction under foremen and in harsh conditions. In such conditions, South Asian labors who are Muslims do not identify their faith as an asset that enhances their sense of belonging in the Gulf, as Nazli Kibria's work in this region has shown.[65]

Interviewees rarely mentioned experiencing overt racial discrimination. This does not mean that race does not matter. The absence of blatant discrimination and racism reported by Somalis may best be explained by the absence of direct contact between Emiratis and the majority of Somalis.

During my stay in the UAE and my fieldwork in places where Somalis work and congregate, it was exceptional to come into contact with UAE citizens. Except for Emiratis who produce visas for fees, occasionally visiting workplaces where they are listed as co-owners, the people with whom one comes in contact are almost always other migrants, who visibly dominate the landscape in the UAE. Thus the sense of well-being described earlier is experienced through the state's hands-off approach to law-abiding Somalis, as any dealings with native-born people are mostly limited to government agencies, such as the immigration office and various licensing offices.

Discrimination was more likely to be reported by Somali professionals, some of whom are returnees from the West and others who are first-generation and 1.5-generation Somalis who don't have UAE citizenship but whose whole lives have been spent in the UAE. There was no clear consensus on the impact of racism in the UAE from these Somali professionals, though they all acknowledge a clear—if usually implicit—racial hierarchy in their workplaces. One Somali returnee from the United Kingdom insisted that for middle-management positions, the United Kingdom was a nightmare, and he found it very difficult to find a job after losing a well-paying position with an international marketing firm in London. He said that the hierarchies based on nationality in Dubai had been less detrimental in his case than what he had experienced in the United Kingdom. In his current job, he finds that South Asian workers, no matter their level of skill, are treated the worst, with American and European whites occupying the pinnacle in terms of both pay and respect. This observation is in fact consistent with research on group dynamics in the UAE, with Emiratis at the top, followed by Western expatriates (American, Canadian, European), followed by Arabs, while the South Asians (Indian, Bangladesh, Pakistani) are the bottom of this hierarchy.[66] Beilleh, who lived in the UAE from the late 1980s to 2000, acknowledged that his British passport and his graduate education afford him a more privileged position, even if that privilege is restricted by his Somali identity. This experience, he argued, is shared with all other Africans, Asians, and Middle Easterners still tacitly treated as inferior to white westerners by native-born Emiratis.

Another challenge some interviewees mentioned was related to the global War on Terror and its impact on Somalis everywhere. The UAE is a major ally of the United States and the North Atlantic Treaty Organization (NATO), and some Somalis say that visa applications in the UAE by people with Muslim names now take much longer to process than they used to. The current political turmoil and uprisings in the Middle East, the fact that UAE citizens are so outnumbered by foreign guest workers, and the UAE's alliance with the United States and its War on Terror all create more stringent attitudes toward Muslim migrants. Ubah, who came to the UAE when she was two years old, was hesitant to switch jobs for fear of visa transfer problems:

> Changing visas is not easy.... I hear this is especially so for Somalis. They are making the visa process very difficult for them. You have to be hired, and then go through a visa application and approval process. You will have to be hired and then approved. One of my friends is going through this. She was working for a firm and her family left, her mother and her sister. So when she switched [visas], it required multiple levels of approvals.... We Somalis are always under suspicion. So, this is one of the reasons stopping me [from switching jobs]. What if I move and the company does not help me and I cannot find [another] company to get a visa?

This new scrutiny of Muslim migrants, combined with nonrecognition of the Somali passport, constrains Somalis' sense of security in the UAE and fuels further migration in search of a more secure legal status or even naturalization elsewhere. For those unable to obtain a passport from a country neighboring Somalia—Ethiopia, Djibouti, or Kenya—a contradiction emerges between a sense of well-being in the UAE and a need for recognized citizenship and travel documents.

In Search of a Western Passport and Its Privileges

The continuing political turmoil in Somalia increases the vulnerability of Somali citizens not only in the Horn but elsewhere in the diaspora. This protracted instability leaves those Somalis already in the UAE with two options. The immediate choice for most is to remain in the country and manage employment and visa processes with the help of the highly functioning community networks established there. A concurrent option for some of those not already holding a Western passport is to imagine, and if possible actively pursue, further migration to fulfill personal and professional aspirations not achievable in a place like the UAE, where most migrants live within the confines of low-level employment, constraints on mobility, and lack of access to further education and technical training.

The upper stratum of Somali migrants in the UAE includes successful entrepreneurs who profited from the collapse of Somali state institutions and who now monopolize Somalia's import–export sector. They have established major transnational offices in the UAE and trade with China, India, and Brazil. As discussed earlier, this stratum also includes returnee entrepreneurs from the West, who also partner with the preceding group. Most members of the former group carry passports from a regional country, such as Djibouti, Ethiopia, Kenya, or Uganda, whereas the latter carry American, Canadian, or European passports. Some, like Alas and Beilleh, have sent their wives and children to Europe or America and eventually obtained Western passports, though they never settled in these countries themselves but rather only visited to fulfill immigration requirements or see their families, who often come to the UAE for summer vacations.

The mobility available to those with Western or non-Somali African passports, especially those with the financial assets required for visa eligibility in many countries, was often cited as a rationale for pursuing further migration, especially by men and women who carry a Somali passport. As one young man put it,

> It is clear that we are all in search of a good life.... Because of uncertainty, most of the young adults prefer to go to Europe even when they know others are coming back from Europe complaining that there is really nothing there for them. People still want to get that passport. And we know that Africans and Arabs respect those European passports very much. If you and a second person pull out Somali and European passports, the one with the European passport will definitely get the proper treatment. And because of that you want to go to [Europe]. In my case, even though my aunt is very good to me and she is telling me to stay here and she tells me to settle down and get married and open my own business, this is still not something my heart wants or is content with.

Various others substantiated Faysal's analysis. For example, an elderly Somali woman I met in the Dubai airport was on her way to Somalia. Because she only had a Somali passport, even though it was accompanied by an American travel document issued to her as a U.S. permanent resident, she was barred from entering Dubai and had to spend her day-and-a-half layover at the airport. With an American passport, she would have had no problem getting out of the airport to spend that time in the city.[67] In the minds of those who have never migrated beyond Africa or the Middle East and whose experiences are shaped by the nonrecognition of their Somali passports, seeing Somalis returning from the West fuels their desire to acquire, not just Western travel documents, but naturalization and a passport. The elderly woman who migrated to the United States but still has not acquired American citizenship is confined to the airport as she carries a Somali passport, which is outside of the privileged group of countries whose citizens are exempt from visa requirements to the UAE (the United States, all of Western Europe, and a few other countries, including Singapore, Malaysia, Japan, Greece, and South Korea). With this awareness, Somalis in the UAE pay little attention to challenges Somalis may experience in North America or Europe. The allure of the West remains: it is in Europe and the United States, Canada and Australia, many Somalis believe, where their economic goals and personal dreams can be fulfilled, where they can access citizenship that will break down borders for them. These destinations are imagined as the new earthly jannah for Somali refugees, replacing the Gulf countries of yesteryear.

Class is clearly significant in the search for Western citizenship, as it is the poor who encounter the greatest obstacles and incur the highest costs migrating, and who are also the ones who most desire it. The routes to Western Europe involve dangerous, often deadly voyages across the Mediterranean or journeys through Turkey and Greece. It can take months or even years for a person to make her way to Western Europe, as she often relies on smugglers who charge thousands of dollars, depending on the destination.[68] Even leaving the UAE requires that a person show a valid visa that allowed him to stay in the country, which those who are undocumented cannot produce. Rukia, a Somali maid, stated,

> The truth is that I want to migrate from this country. I want to go to a country where my life and future would be different. But my current situation is not permitting this, because I may not be able to come back to it once I

leave. When I decide to leave here, they will take my fingerprints and they will also do eye scans. Because of that, the only way I will get out of here is if I decide I want to return to my own country. The only people who can leave this country with the option of getting back in if things don't work out elsewhere, are those with documentation. Those who volunteer for deportation can also leave. But I am not ready to go back to my country.

Women and men in this position have very limited options for migrating to the West. Even when they use smugglers to try to migrate, there is no guarantee of their successful entry to the desired destination. The potential to be returned to Somalia remains real. Such risk makes it attractive for some to accept their undocumented status in the UAE, which potentially can lead to deportation but can permit them to earn a basic income for themselves and their families.

For many others who are not in as precarious a position as women and men who are undocumented or have low-paying jobs, further migration is not just a monetary strategy but a way to boost their socioeconomic position within the UAE. Economic incorporation and access to financial resources are hence tied to flexible citizenship, which represents another form of security. Osman, a man in his late twenties who came to the UAE in his early teens and whose narrative opened the book, detailed his conviction that further migration might not result in a better income, as he now earns around $2,000 in nontaxed income. And yet, he stated, "We know Somalis are people without proper legal status and that is what drives us to go to all these places." Though Osman himself said he is not planning to pursue further migration, he expresses sympathy for those who do, given Somalis' lack of recognized citizenship and travel documents. Other interviewees also weighed the fact that naturalization documents from a Western nation that grants refugee status would enhance their social status, expand their economic options, and allow them to visit and care for families dispersed in many regions. For some, such as Faysal, whose visa, procured for him by his aunt, who also employs him in her store, stories of the challenges Somalis experience in the West are insufficient deterrence from undertaking an arduous journey to follow family members to the West. Others, such Osman, have decided that unless a more direct and easier route opens up for them, they are unwilling to risk all they have built in the UAE. Omar, a young taxi driver, quoted a Somali proverb, "geed walba in gubtaa baa hoos taal" (all individuals have their own struggles), to indicate that all Somalis—including those who have made it to the West and obtained citizenship—confront challenges and that it is futile to idealize those places. He said that many Somalis with whom he is in touch in the United Kingdom don't even make $1,500 per month, whereas he makes more than that amount. And yet awareness of the potential to spend months and even years in detention centers and the long process of naturalization in many Western countries is no deterrent to those Somalis convinced that their social and economic standings would improve with Western citizenship.

Two women, one in her late twenties and the other in her early thirties, who came to the UAE as toddlers and who now work for transnational corporations (one in the pharmaceutical industry and the other in marketing in a British department store), expressed their desire to migrate further if the opportunity arose. They acknowledged that their salaries would not necessarily increase much but that they would be able to continue their graduate education, which is impossible in the UAE. One of the women earned a marketing degree in Syria, the other a degree in pharmacy from India. India, China, Malaysia, Egypt, Sudan, and Syria all attract Somali students whose families cannot afford the high cost of UAE universities. Asked how she feels about living in the UAE and her legal status, the pharmacist—whose three sisters are nurses and whose brother is an engineer, all well established professionally—pointed to the insecurity intrinsic to being a Somali in the Gulf, regardless of education:

> We are Muslims, and it is true that we all know Allah is taking care of us. But we feel insecure.... It happened that my sister, who sponsored all my family members, lost her job. She lost her job and we felt like the earth shook around us; that was the first time we felt that way. Then, what's next? We can't go back to Somalia because, to be honest, we have never lived in Somalia and we would probably not be able to live there for a while given how bad things are there. Unless there is an improvement to the security situation, we cannot go.... I strongly believe that once there is security and they form a government, then I would go and do something to contribute.

But unfortunately, because of the legal paper issues here, this is the reason everyone is seeking to get out, get a [Western] passport and come back here. We are only here because of insecurity, and one feels bad because it is unfortunate we don't have a secure country. In terms of jobs, I think if you are an American or European citizen, you are paid better or even interviewed better here ... maybe because of ignorance, maybe they think these people are more educated than us, or maybe they think they know more than we do. I have no idea.

This sense of insecurity revolves around Somalis' temporary legal status, which shakes any sense of economic security in a highly volatile local and global economy and geopolitics. In the search for a master citizenship anchored in the global nation-state hierarchy, Somalis well understand the possibilities and prestige of Western citizenship as they confront a range of abuses in Kenya, Ethiopia, and parts of the Middle East as a result of their nationality.[69] Thus, though financially secure in their current positions, these two women desire migration to the West, based on the same rationale a young man from Mogadishu articulated: "If one goes to Europe and gets a passport, then he can easily exit the UAE even if his visa is canceled and he can reenter the country anytime. But if he is deported carrying a Somali passport, he will never be able to come back."

3 South Africa

Insecurity in Racialized Spaces

> Actually if it were not for Muslim business owners, Somalis would not have been able to accomplish anything in this city [Cape Town], and that is just a fact.
>
> —Hanad, businessman, Bellville

> We believe that they have a bad image of us. They kill some of us claiming that foreigners have taken what belonged to them. According to them, foreigners are driving better cars than they are, living in better houses, have shops and everything else they were supposed to have.
>
> —Yusuf, small store owner, Pretoria

Migrants' and refugees' continual search for conditions that fulfill their material, physical, and emotional needs complicates our neat categorizations of these populations, as we highlighted in the introduction. While refugees conjure forced displacement and persecution, migrants often bring to the fore the economic rationales for cross-border movements.[1] The case of South Africa further blurs these distinctions. We see how Somalis' initial forced displacement and refugee status in Kenya continue with subsequent crossings of four, five, and even six international borders.

The chapter also underscores two concurrent forces that shape Somalis' material and psychological well-being in South Africa: strong religious networks and economic opportunities accompanied by extreme levels of violence and vulnerability. These forces, like so much in contemporary South Africa, emerge from the legacy of apartheid and the country's complex ethnic and racial groupings. Though these identities can seem simple, with clear and obvious divisions between white, black, colored, and Indian, the identities of newcomers in the postapartheid era further undermine such boundaries. Somalis moving across the African continent into South Africa would at first glance fit into the "black" category, yet they rarely identify with the Bantu peoples who make up the country's majority black population. Instead, they consciously identify as northeastern, Muslim Africans to build alliances with a prominent minority group in South Africa: Indian Muslims. But highlighting the situational nature of identity and the malleability of their cultural tool kit, Somalis' African identity is brought to the fore only in times of crisis and violence against them in the hands of some black South Africans. This testifies to the malleability of religion and race and how newcomers position themselves within a society polarized and segregated on ethnic and racial bases. I argue that a calculated religious alliance and identification with and settlement among the economically more established Indian Muslims pay great dividends for Muslim newcomers and provide them with a launching pad to independence and opportunity in this postapartheid nation.[2]

This chapter also examines the making of the Somali merchant and his ascension to the category of "middleman minority," a category that Somalis only occupy in South Africa and that can only be explained by the particular historical and racial legacies of apartheid.[3] As such, Somalis in South Africa are one of the dominant entrepreneurial groups in poor, black residential areas, a feat facilitated by networks with Indian Muslims. Gender is also key to understanding Somalis' economic integration into South Africa. Somali men are most likely to work in these poor black areas, bringing them in direct contact and competition with the poorest sectors of society located on the margins of townships and informal settlements; the economic pursuits of Somali women, meanwhile, mostly remain in more secure, racially mixed areas dominated by Indian and colored populations. This bifurcated experience underscores the predicament of a group that is able to enter and even dominate a lucrative economic niche yet must simultaneously deal with the uncertainties of living and working in areas with some of the worst crime rates in the world.[4] As a result, quite similar to their brethren in the UAE, most Somalis in South Africa continue their dream of further migration, with Western countries still viewed as ideal destinations. As we shall see, limited mobility due to difficulties in securing travel documents and physical security concerns hinder Somalis' ability to settle and imagine a future in South Africa, even amid the opportunities for economic success in this postapartheid nation.

Historical Fissures and Racial Polarization

Southern Africa has long been a meeting place of diverse peoples and cultures.[5] In recent centuries, however, the movement of people within this region has been largely shaped by a single force: the rigid and intrinsically racialized efforts of European settlers; that particular colonization has dominated migration since the 1670s. Through wars of conquest, Dutch and British settlers in particular have deeply shaped South Africa. This history of colonization culminated in the apartheid regime, which came into power in 1948, a historical trajectory fundamental for our understanding of the political, economic, and social relations of the peoples of this nation at the beginning of the twenty-first century.

Apartheid laws restricted blacks and colored peoples to residential areas outside of economic and political centers exclusively deemed "white areas." But the labor of these blacks remained essential for the functioning of white farms, mines, and homes and thus brought out some of the contradictions of these policies. The ultimate objective of apartheid was to achieve the unattainable—to maximize the exploitation of cheap black urban labor while minimizing the presence of the laborers in white areas.[6] Through these restrictive and exploitative labor laws, the apartheid regime achieved its goal of coercing the majority black population to sell its labor to the white economy by working as farmhands, in the mines, or in domestic and factory positions in urban settlements.[7] Blacks increasingly poured into white urban areas in search of work, propelled by the absence of other ways to make a living.[8] Given the restrictive laws governing where blacks could live, townships emerged around white residential towns and economic centers, serving as "labor reserves" for the low-paying, low-prestige, and unskilled work required to guarantee comfort for whites, such as working as maids, gardeners, and drivers.[9] Those "ministering to the White man's needs" were temporary sojourners, nonresidents of the white residential areas where they worked.[10]

This segregation, and the stranglehold of apartheid between 1948 and 1994, produced a nation of terrible contrasts: a nation known for its powerful urban economic centers, dominated by high-rise buildings, a world-class financial sector, research hospitals, and universities, which in turn are surrounded by overcrowded townships and informal settlements made of flimsy shacks. More recently, these townships have been transformed by government-built homes, part of the Reconstruction and Development initiative implemented by the postapartheid African National Congress (ANC) governments to alleviate some of the key socioeconomic challenges inherited from the apartheid legacy. Generally known as Mandela houses, they have four rooms (two small bedrooms, a kitchen, and a sitting room) and are now as characteristic of the South African landscape as the shacks are. Though the postapartheid governments have spent much to try to alleviate the country's housing crisis, as of 2009, the proportion of South Africans residing in informal housing or shacks still remains high—at 13 percent of the population.[11] This population resides in these mostly poor and fragile environments, some of which are unconnected to electrical grids and lack sanitization facilities and paved roads. This can be explained by increasing urbanization and population size.[12] Thousands of South Africans migrating from rural areas and other provinces reside in these settlements. New immigrants must find both home and community within, or in between, these harshly divided areas.

Apartheid also shaped South Africa's immigration laws, with citizenship rights only conferred to those of European descent. Those from neighboring African countries, though long instrumental in the country's history of mining and farm labor, were categorized as sojourners under apartheid, expected to depart once their contracts expired. This was also the case for the Chinese mine laborers, who were recruited from China in the first decade of the twentieth century and who mostly repatriated, and the Indian indentured laborers who, until the 1960s, were expected to repatriate to India.[13] Under such policy, the hundreds of thousands of labor migrants in the mining industry from neighboring countries of Lesotho, Zimbabwe, and Mozambique were ineligible for legal, permanent settlement and occupied an ambiguous position very similar to positions of the many foreign laborers in the UAE today. These categories changed drastically with the fall of apartheid in 1994 and the subsequent immigration reforms.

These reforms now account for the high number of asylum seekers in South Africa, which received the greatest number of asylum seekers in the world in 2010 and 2011.[14]

Somalis who head toward South Africa have mostly all come through Kenya, where they had refugee status. But they again submit asylum applications with South Africa, which signed the Refugee Convention on January 12, 1996, following the collapse of apartheid rule. Because most Somalis already held refugee status elsewhere, and mostly undertook a long trek to South Africa for better economic opportunity, I also refer to Somalis as migrants, because their position within the South African landscape has all the characteristics associated with economic migrants, as demonstrated by the following discussion.

From the hundreds of Somalis with whom I have interacted in South Africa between 2007 and 2013, and from my interviews with Somali interpreters who work closely with refugees, it is clear that Somalis are rarely denied asylum. Though each person goes through individual status determination, South Africa grants this group a prima facie refugee status, based on the political situation in Somalia, which is still embroiled in conflict.[15] But each individual must present a narrative of persecution as part of her asylum claim. Despite opportunities for asylum in the other countries through which the Somali asylum seekers passed, the recognized failure of the Somali state provides legitimate grounds for asylum applications in South Africa, in distinction from the experiences of Somalis in the UAE.

Unlike in Kenya, where all Somalis register with the UNHCR, South Africa does not put refugees and asylum seekers in camps and permits them to settle themselves within the wider community. The initial documents given at the border are often temporary, fourteen-day permits, serving until a formal application for asylum is submitted at a refugee reception center, which are located around the country. In these centers, refugees fill out the Eligibility Determination Form (BI-1590) free of charge, have their fingerprints taken, and are provided with an asylum seeker's permit (Section 22 permit), good for one to three months, as proof that they submitted an application for asylum.[16] Some applicants may have these one- to three-month permits renewed a dozen times before they are summoned for the second interview for a status determination hearing. In a majority of Somali cases, this leads to a Section 24 permit, bestowing on the asylum seeker a renewable two-year legal permit. This is normally expected to lead to a permanent resident document, for which one is eligible to apply after three renewals of the Section 24 permit (six years), though the process is never as straightforward as it is on paper.

The rest of this chapter delves into the experiences of one of the latest groups searching for their fortunes in the new South Africa. How do Somalis who cross South Africa's porous borders benefit from the new immigration policies of the post-1994 era, and how do they negotiate their racial and religious identities within this highly segregated and racialized society?

Looking Out for Minarets

Afrah was in his early twenties when he arrived in South Africa in 1994. He embodied the aspirations of the first cohort of Somali men who, though traversing uncharted territory, carried a strong faith that wherever there were Muslims, there was a community, an umma. Afrah recounted the advice given to him by a friend who had studied in South Africa under apartheid:

> He told me that I can count on a strong and well-connected Indian Muslim population living in a separate area in South Africa. He told me I could only live among them and only there could I make a living. That was the main reason why I came to South Africa.

Afrah arrived in South Africa a few months after apartheid officially ended, keenly aware of the country's racial segregation. With no contacts in Johannesburg, he initially stayed at a white-owned hotel but felt lonely and unanchored there. He said he stopped the first Muslim he saw in the street, recognizing him by his long robe *(khamis)* and Muslim cap *(taqiyah)*, and asked the stranger to take him to "where the Muslims live."[17] The Indian brought Afrah to Mayfair, a suburb of Johannesburg now home to the biggest ethnic enclave of Somalis in South Africa.[18]

Somalis, as we saw in the discussion of the UAE in chapter 2, share a strong belief in being part of a global Muslim community. As a diverse and dispersed people, they hold a common worldview that is bound by "virtue of a shared commitment to faith and brotherhood."[19] Faith was especially instrumental for the settlement and survival of the first wave of Somali refugees, those who came to South Africa around the end of apartheid in the early 1990s to about 2000. The mosque served as means to mediate a connection between Muslim strangers, who used this shared space to overcome the cultural, linguistic, and economic distance separating them. Contrary to the important role of Muslims as a compass in a new land, a shared racial identity with South African blacks was absent in these early Somali accounts of settlement; in fact, the belief that a Somali could "only live among Indians" was stressed by these early arrivals.[20]

As more Somalis came, these newcomers too asked for directions to the mosque in whatever town or city to which they first arrived. These mosques served multiple purposes. First, houses of worship were the first places where Somalis could access water to wash their exhausted and often dirty bodies following crossings through bushes, mud-filled ponds, rivers, and border controls, as detailed in chapter 1. Some men reported how their bodies were filled with lice, having worn the same clothing for as long as a couple of months at a time. Many had to dispense of the suitcases they'd packed, as these had become a hindrance over multiple border crossings with smugglers. These border crossings often involve hiding in obscure shacks and

FIGURE 11. Trekking to South Africa: migrants experience perpetual policing and brokering as they cross five or more countries from Somali to South Africa.

houses established by smugglers along the trails over which they take their human cargo. Arriving in Tanzania, Malawi, Zambia, Mozambique, Zimbabwe, or South Africa, the mosque became the first place where Somali refugees cleansed their bodies and clothes (Figure 11).

Second, mosques provided these refugees spiritual reconnection with faith as well as fellow Muslims. These spiritual needs were as imperative as basic necessities such as food and shelter following stressful voyages.

Finally, the mosque provided, not only a space for congregation for the umma, but also a space where Somalis could meet others from their country. Newcomers felt sure that any Somali man in a given town would eventually visit the mosque.[21] And even if a Somali did not find these compatriots, the Muslims of the town or city were expected to extend a hand to any Muslim stranded in their midst. This sense of umma, a community with obligations toward each other and a compulsion placed on all Muslims to bail out their brethren, bore fruit for these Somali travelers. Consequently, the country's mosques, and the Indian Muslim communities in general, served as a first stop for Somalis arriving in South Africa in the mid-1990s, providing them with a basic anchor and extending to them charity that fundamentally shaped their subsequent experiences.

Charity in the Fold of the Umma

Many of these Somalis arrived at the borders with empty pockets, unable even to afford the shared transportation to Johannesburg in the Gauteng Province, the first stop for the majority of new arrivals. Ahmed, an interviewee who came in 1996, captured the toll the trip took on these travelers:

> When we first come to Johannesburg, you know that we were travelers who had the harshness of the road trips on our faces. A Muslim man looked at our condition and he took us to his house. He gave us lunch and also twenty rand each.

I asked Ahmed how this Muslim man recognized them and asked if he and his colleagues wore taqiyah.

> No, we were not, but I had a beard and we recognized each other anyways, through our faces and so on. Furthermore, the Somali person is understood

that he is a Muslim. I thought that this man had seen our faces and recognized that we were very hungry.

Two others also recounted their experiences in mosques in Nelspruit, a city close to the Mozambican border, where each of the dozen or so Somalis in this group received R200 (more than $50 at that time) as support to get them to their final destination. Though the earliest cohort benefited from this charity, this support was particularly indispensable to the small number of women and children who arrived prior to 2000.

New legislation enacted with the collapse of the apartheid regime instituted old-age pensions for all South Africans, removing the racialized access to state welfare.[22] This new legislation benefited those at the bottom of the socioeconomic ladder, mostly blacks and coloreds.[23] The government expanded small grants for single parents or kin caring for small children. This maintenance grant was R160 ($21 in 2007) per month, a meager but important income only accessible by South African citizens and legal residents.[24] Though Somalis, like many other Africans, saw great promise in a postapartheid South Africa, they encountered an endemic economic inequality and poverty. As a new South Africa was birthed, it was a country where "18 percent of black households had internal piped water, and only 37 percent had electricity—compared to 100 percent of white households."[25] The astonishing accomplishment of the ANC's election could not transform the massive social problems faced by the South African majority.[26] Nevertheless, progress was uneven but palpable. The new constitution the ANC drafted in 1996 is considered by many to be one of the most progressive in the world, a "state-of-the-art" document.[27] This constitution recognizes the protection of the civil, social, and political rights of all, including migrants and refugees, sexual minorities, and the poor.

The first cohort of Somalis mostly consisted of single men and a small number of single women. I documented only one large family whose needs were covered by the Indian Muslim community and its charities. This family first settled in a Malawian refugee camp and became well known among Somalis in the region after they accepted land that was distributed to refugees willing to farm. Most Somalis going to Malawian camps were fleeing from the insecure and overcrowded Kenyan camps and also hoped for resettlement in the Western world. But this family successfully farmed in Malawi for two years before deciding to move on to South Africa. Both parents cited education for their nine children as the rationale for moving.

Once they arrived in Mayfair, they located a woman they had known in Somalia who took all eleven of them to her two-bedroom house, which she shared with her husband and their four-year-old child. The parents called a niece in Seattle, United States, to inform her of their situation, and she offered to send them $200 per month until they found their footing. Though this was helpful, it was inadequate to meet the needs of such a large family. The small Somali community shared the news of the plight of this family at the mosque, reporting how both the mother and the father were ill and unable to work. Ebla, the mother, recounted how they were struggling to pay the rent with the $200 sent by the niece and to feed such a large family until

> an Indian Muslim man came to us. He took us to a charity center and told us to get donations from there . . . they gave us food twice a month, the beginning and the middle of the month. They would give us good amount of sugar and oil, but also little amounts of tea, carton of milk for the tea . . . the sugar was about twelve kilos and five liters of oil. The oil and the sugar would last us the entire month. We would even have leftovers that we would sell at times or exchange them for whatever else we would need. Also, we got soap. Every few days he would come and visit us. He would ask us to open the cupboards so that he could see what was missing. Eventually, the food was partly reduced because there were many Somalis coming.

This "blessing" from a Muslim charity, as Ebla put it, was "Allah's grace," extended to them in a difficult period, when the mother suffered from malaria and high blood pressure and the father had a displaced disk. These infusions of charity lasted for longer than a year, allowing the family to establish a sustainable life. With the family's most basic needs taken care of, the mother started a small project with another woman. They pooled a few hundred dollars and opened a small store serving the increasing Somali presence in the Mayfair neighborhood.

Except for this type of charity from Indian Muslims, this initial cohort never accessed any welfare or public assistance. Nor did this group encounter

UNHCR intervention as Somalis do in Kenya, as we have seen. The role that humanitarian services like UNHCR play, and that the welfare state provides in many Western countries, was in South Africa filled by Muslim charities that permitted Somalis to establish themselves in their new country without fear of destitution. Connecting with this Muslim community quickly emerges as a wise strategy in a place where de facto racial segregation still prevails, a segregation that newcomers cannot avoid.

Upon arrival to Gauteng Province and, more specifically, to the Johannesburg area, two of the three main residential options are closed to Somalis: settling among the masses of black Africans segregated in townships and informal settlements and settling among middle- and upper-middle-class whites in their own segregated cities and towns. This racial and religious distance between blacks and whites meant that the group with whom Somalis identified most was South African Indians, whose socioeconomic, racial, and residential positions also fell between the black and white extremes. The umma connection with Indian Muslims thus overrode the "racial" identification of Somalis as Africans. Somalis' historical self-perception as Arabs and non-Bantu Africans, demonstrated by the discriminatory treatment of the Somali Bantu minority in their midst, explains this lack of common racial affinity with the majority black South African population.[28] As a result, Somalis (and Ethiopians) remain distinct from the other low-skilled African migrants and refugee groups, many of whom settle within the larger black population in the segregated black townships around the country. Instead, it is within Indian residential areas that Somalis establish their bases.

With the arrival of more Somalis in South Africa and in the Mayfair area in particular, some started to work and pool their incomes and were able to rent apartments in Muslim Indian residential and business areas (Figure 12). Seeking rental homes in white areas would have been impossible owing to cost, racial segregation, and Somalis' own fear of religious and racial alienation in these settings. But living in the townships and settlements where most black South Africans live was equally undesirable for Somalis for many of the same reasons.[29] Somalis sought, and continue to seek, housing among Indian Muslims, with whom their sense of racial and religious identity is most aligned.

Newcomers were directed to the houses that Somalis had rented, and dozens of people often shared one room, until some secured jobs, moved out, rented their own places, and started hosting other newcomers. Being part of this system required all to accept overcrowded conditions as rental costs were high, the community small, and wages low. Newcomers were granted a few days, a week or two at most, to find jobs, with the expectation that they would contribute their share soon after. Such a cycle guaranteed, not only that everyone strived to enter into the labor force, but also that new arrivals always benefited from those preceding them in meeting their basic subsistence and shelter needs. This closely knit support system involved both Somalis and Indian Muslims and created a channel through which these newcomers could find work in diverse sectors of the economy but also share resources for collective success.

The Search for Employment:
Muslim Networks and Twenty-First-Century Peddlers

Whereas families mostly relied on Muslim charities, the majority of the earliest Somali cohort arriving between 1994 and 2000 were young, single men who were expected to fend for themselves after a few days of hospitality.

FIGURE 12. Somali families pool resources and share accommodations to make ends meet. Eastern Cape, South Africa.

Though bolstered by the emotional and financial support extended to them in their initial contacts with the mosques, it is easy to see how newcomers also benefited from the generosity of fellow Muslims, Somali and Indian alike, who were already in South Africa. These new arrivals strived, and were expected by their hosts, not only to promptly seek employment but also to repay the support extended to them. To achieve this, the Muslim Indian community incorporated these workers into their businesses, with most working in clothing stores, wholesalers, grocery stores, bakeries, gas stations, and electronic shops in major urban areas.

This initial contact was between strangers who, except for a shared religious affinity, were ignorant of each other's cultures. Most Somalis were uninformed of the history of Indians within this land, and most Muslim Indians were unfamiliar with Somali culture in the Horn of Africa. While Asians found themselves in a middle-status position within the racial hierarchies in the South African nation, between the poor, marginalized black South African majority and the still economically dominant white minority, Somalis viewed themselves as outside of this hierarchy altogether. This disjuncture was not sufficiently problematic to hinder Indian Muslims' efforts to support the Somalis' entry into paid labor nor the Somalis' appreciation of the instrumental role that South African Indian Muslims played in their settlement experience.

For example, the first job Hanad held in South Africa in 1997 was for an ice cream factory, owned by an Indian Muslim, in the town of Bellville. He started at a wage of R180 per week, the equivalent of $40, which was a favorable wage at that time:

> My boss gave me a place to sleep at his house. I and another girl who worked for the company would leave together in the morning, we would start the machines for the ice cream, and while she started up the machines, I would make sure that the ice cream trucks were ready for all their deliveries.... I had to make sure that their orders and delivery routes were planned, and make sure they had gas money. I would have to do that before the first workers came in at 7:00 A.M., and by 7:30 all the trucks had to leave.... I didn't have to pay for rent, or food, and my clothes would be washed, and I was getting paid well.

A few years later, Hanad was in his mid-twenties when he started running one of the earliest Somali money transfer companies in South Africa. Hanad's initiative to start his new business was only possible because of the jobs that other Somalis found within the Indian Muslim economic niches and their need to find ways to remit to families they had left behind.

Another man, Kayse, who is now in his mid-fifties, discussed his first job at a halal butchery:

> I used to go to the mosque and pray for a decent job. After a couple of days in the mosque a man approached me and asked me what I was doing in the mosque. I told him that I was looking for work. He asked me, from whom? I answered him, "From Allah." He left me and after a few days he saw me again in the mosque and employed me. I started earning money but nothing for the first few days. Then he paid me two hundred rand and also gave me five kilograms of meat. I shared the meat with the approximately thirty men who were living in the same house with me. . . . I was earning forty-one rand per day for five days a week, plus bonus money that I saved and requested to be paid to me at the end of the year. . . . I worked for him for one year and four months. Then I realized that working for someone else would not allow me to succeed the way I wanted to and I decided to start my own business. I spoke to the employer and I told him that I was getting older and that was finding this type of work difficult to do. He asked me what kind of work I would do. I told him I wanted to work as a hawker. He wished me luck and handed me five thousand rand.

The generosity of the employer to give close to six months' wages for someone working in his butcher shop was exceptional. But others also discussed developing very intimate, familylike relationships with their Muslim employers, who at times offered them donations and loans for them to start their own business ventures.

But working for these Muslim Indians was not without its challenges. For instance, a middle-aged woman who also arrived in Johannesburg in 1997 recounted working for an Indian Muslim–owned factory folding clothes, for which she was paid R120 per week. Asha complained that the wage barely allowed her to survive. As she put it:

I had back pain. I feared that working in this sector would damage my health. We would stand all day. If the Indian sees you sitting, he will ask you why you are sitting. He will only allow you a short time for tea.

Asha later quit this shop and joined others she knew in Port Elizabeth to work as a peddler, a line of work I'll discuss subsequently.

Although working for Indian Muslims in Johannesburg and Cape Town was initially very attractive to Somali refugees, some found the wages inadequate to meet their needs. But considered against overall employment in South Africa, such wages, though low, were better than what the majority of South African blacks made, even ten years after the collapse of apartheid. For example, 55 percent of the African (read black) population earned less than R400 ($50) a month in 2004, with 16 percent of this population making less than R100 ($13) per month;[30] in contrast, the first cohort of Somalis earned from R150 to R200 per week to just over R800 per month in the late 1990s. Whereas the majority of low-income, black South Africans live in substandard housing in townships and informal settlements, typically paying about R100 for rent, or build makeshift shacks for themselves, Somalis renting housing in the Muslim Indian areas often paid R1,000 for a two-bedroom apartment, sharing housing to reduce costs.[31]

Those I interviewed still found these wages too meager to survive in Mayfair or Bellville with high rents, let alone to cover family commitments elsewhere. Interviewees all expressed that their experiences in South Africa and the harsh and painful trek through four, five, or six countries, and the abuse by smugglers and immigration officials over the course of these journeys, were not commensurate with what they have encountered in South Africa. Hence it is clear that these Somali migrants' reference point in terms of how they are faring in South Africa is never the poor South African black population but rather the Jannaalle notion that migration should always lead to remittances to family left behind and eventual asset accumulation for those who migrate.

As Somali newcomers worked in wholesalers, gas stations, and other Indian-owned retail businesses, they became enfolded in the country's complex class and racial relations. Many of these workers had never held paid employment and were unfamiliar with the standard expectations of a relationship between employer and employee. Some commented on their shock of having someone looking over their shoulders, watching how they worked, where they sat, and when they ate.

Two interviewees reported their shock by the treatment that South African black employees got from some Indian business owners, which they viewed as condescending. They reported that the South African black workers, as well as migrants and refugees from Malawi and Zimbabwe, accepted this treatment and acted very "docile." A young Somali man who worked and lived with an Indian Muslim family recounted witnessing his boss slap a Malawian house servant for not cleaning the car well enough. For this Somali, whose understanding of the racial structures of South Africa was minimal, this treatment of the servant was stunning.

Class and cultural differentiation between Somalis and Indian Muslims became more salient in a highly racialized South African socioeconomic and cultural context. Though Indian-owned businesses were essential for Somalis as they acclimated to their new country, disappointment with the working conditions as well as low wages led these newcomers to explore other ways to make a living.

Most Somalis were low skilled and unable to break into the formal economy, especially when unemployment and underemployment were the norm for large segments of the native black population. Peddling and hawking in urban areas emerged as an important niche that propelled Somalis into full immersion into the informal economic sector. As in most countries, the realm of business that is conducted off the books, that blurs the line between formal and informal, is a complex web that stretches across all facets of most of the economies in developing and underdeveloped regions of the world. South Africa's informal economy was mostly small when apartheid collapsed, and new opportunities opened up with this major political transformation, which coincided with larger African migrant and refugee arrivals in South Africa.

One of the initial strands of this web for Somalis involved the sale of religious recordings. Somali men who initially worked for Indian businesses realized, sometime in the mid- to late 1990s, that there was a market for selling Koranic recordings to the same Indian Muslim community. As one of the earliest religious tape hawkers explained, they would purchase new cassettes for R5, record Koranic chapters on these tapes and duplicate them, and then sell the tapes for R15. Three men who worked in this sector equated the work to hitting the jackpot, as one individual could sell hundreds of tapes per week. One man reported making R700 profit within a week, an income fourfold what Somali employees of Indian Muslim businesses made.

As was common for these liminal economic efforts, however, too many Somalis went into the sale of these religious tapes, as they found it more lucrative than working for someone else. "It has reached a point where Somalis were equated with those tapes and Indians would ask any Somali they see if they had those cassettes. The Indians also benefited from us because we taught them the Koran," reported another of the earliest men to sell these tapes. This niche not only expanded economic opportunities for Somali men but also permitted them to travel around the country, especially in the Gauteng and Western Cape regions, explaining the current Somali geographical spread in South Africa.

Somalis also started selling the long robes worn by some Muslims as well as skullcaps. Many in this cohort used the money they made selling these wares to diversify into other informal economic pursuits, whereas others went back to the same stores that initially employed them and sought credit to establish themselves as peddlers and hawkers in the streets of urban centers.

Though most eventually left Muslim Indian employment, Somalis have not abandoned their reliance on native-born Muslims and continue to recognize the assistance, credit, and trust this community bestowed on these strangers that set the stage for the economic integration of Somalis into South African society. A Somali man who arrived in 1998 articulated the role of this credit in propelling Somalis into new sectors:

> V. owned a cash-and-carry. I wish we were in Cape Town now for me to introduce you to him! We got along very well! We took the stock from him in the morning and we brought his money back in the evening. He would count the money with us. He would take his share and gave us our share. You could skip with all the money if you wanted, but you wouldn't, as your integrity would not allow you to do such a thing. When he did not have the stock we needed, he lent us cash and told us to buy our stock from Panorama. Panorama was expensive and we were not their clients, though they

were also Muslims. So we would take the money and buy stock from another shop, then pay him back that same evening.

The South African cash-and-carry model necessitates a cash payment up front. Some Indian business owners bent the rules for these Somalis, offering them goods on credit, not only because of religious solidarity, but also because of the profits that they both drew from this transaction. These Somali newcomers are ultimately an extension of a tradition that extends back to the early twentieth century, especially in Johannesburg, manifested in a "symbiotic relationship existing between many informal hawkers and formal retail outlets."[32]

Somali women also benefited from these religious and entrepreneurial networks. Nura, a woman who arrived in Johannesburg in 1996 with her husband, also detailed how credit from Muslims got them into the informal sector:

> I went to see some Indian Muslims and told them that I am a Muslim woman, a Somali woman, and that I needed help as I had children to feed. I asked them to assist me in any way they can. They gave me sandals on credit.... I took the sandals and went to the streets. I got kicked out from every place I spread my things, and I just moved on to another place. I probably got kicked out of thirty places before someone finally allowed me a spot to sell the shoes. I ended up selling those shoes. The locals were still not used to people selling things in the streets; it was a new experience for them.

Nura used her status as a Muslim mother in need of assistance to draw sympathy from an Indian Muslim business owner. But such credit was mutually beneficial, with Indian Muslims gaining new markets for their goods and Somali peddlers and hawkers opening up a new ethnic niche and securing a living, however hazardous, in their new country. As Nura highlights, the earliest Somali arrivals portray themselves as pioneers in hawking in Johannesburg, Cape Town, and Port Elizabeth. Though an exaggeration, research confirms the underdevelopment of this sector over the course of the colonial and apartheid eras, a fact observable to these early Somali refugees.[33]

Though underdeveloped, hawking or peddling had always existed in urban South Africa. However, blacks could not legally hawk goods in white cities and towns, where they were considered sojourners and were mostly confined to unskilled wage labor.[34] Surveys conducted in Johannesburg in the late 1970s reported 200 to 250 regular hawkers in the city center, whereas this number surged to 15,000 by the mid-1990s.[35] These street traders confronted the acrimony of city inspectors checking licenses and the wrath of the stores in front of whose doors they set their wares.

Somali hawkers typically chose an intersection with substantial traffic, such as a bus or train station, or a food market, where they spread their wares. They roamed street corners as well as bus, taxi, and train stations and often traveled miles from where they lived carrying on their bodies their wares, ranging from potato chips to candies, from belts to hats and gloves. Though all operated without government licenses, these hawkers arrived at an opportune period, a period of optimism and transition from apartheid rule. They mainly targeted the poor and mostly black workers who flocked to urban economic and residential centers for unskilled work, leaving just before sunrise from their township and informal settlement residential areas. Migrant men and women selling cheap goods in these bus and train stations provided an alternative to the high-end stores that were out of reach for the majority of South Africa's working poor. For Somalis, this informal sector provided an attractive alternative to earning R150 to R200 per week from an Indian employer. Similar to earlier twentieth-century Indian laborers in South Africa who went into this sector as an alternative to wage work for whites, Somalis' experience of wage work with Indian Muslims convinced them that street trading was a better alternative.[36] The contrast between the going wages from Indian stores, which amounted to less than $200 per month in the mid- to late 1990s, and the opportunities they found on urban streets is illustrated by Ismail:

> I was initially working for an Indian in a supermarket. At that time, many people started selling things around the streets. So, I left my job at the store and I decided to become a hawker in August 1995. People hawking were still small in number. I left for Johannesburg on a train with fifteen hundred rand that I'd saved. I bought several boxes of shirts, trousers,

and shoes that were Chinese products. I started from there. When that year ended, in the span of about four months, I'd made a profit of sixteen thousand rand.

To explain how one could make a profit close to fourteen times the amount he invested in such a short time, Ismail continued to describe South Africa in the first year after apartheid:

> It was a transitional period. The black Africans and the colored were interested in these hawker clothes. We were selling for fifty rand the trousers that white and Indian shops were selling for two hundred. So whites, blacks, and all the poor shopped from us. You put your goods on the table and end up selling everything the same morning.

Yet the new openness of South Africa did not mean that street trading was easy. Foreigners required a thick skin to bear the daily resentment they faced from some locals. Most Somalis' inability to converse in English, Afrikaans, or any of the other nine African languages spoken in the country made communication difficult and rendered their otherness salient. Somalis portrayed targeting clients whose language was completely unknown to them as a testimony to their acumen in this setting. Their narratives often carry a self-portrayal of fearless survivalists who struggle to establish themselves in a new country.

The earliest experiences of these vendors also included a sense of shame, as many had no idea as to the economic niches that they would find in South Africa. Just as those in Somalia never knew what the Jannaalayaal in the Arabian Gulf did for work, the migrants themselves entered these sectors unprepared for the nature of the only jobs they could access. As such, Sahal, who is now a hotel owner in Mayfair, gave an example of how street trading contradicted his migration imaginings, resulting in internal self-conflict:

> I once had a horrible experience while selling my wares in the streets. Some friends told me that I should sell my goods in front of bars as the clientele of these bars spent a lot. I then started going to these bars. My first day there, I was standing in front of a bar where I displayed my goods to the customers.

Suddenly I saw two Somali girls that I knew in Kenya walking toward me. I felt nervous, as I did not want to meet them while I was carrying belts and hats on my shoulders. I run toward the back of the building where the bar was located. Suddenly robbers grabbed me and took about half of the things I had.... This was a very critical experience for me, a horrible scenario. As a matter of fact, I think I would have returned to East Africa that day if I'd had the money to do so. It was also Ramadan and I was fasting. I almost cried not knowing what to do!

The hawking sector remains a key entry point into the South African informal economy for many Somalis. But its nature, in its being outdoors and exposing hawkers to uncertainties including verbal and physical abuse and robbery by customers, thugs, and even law enforcement officials, pushed most Somalis to consider this niche as a stepping-stone to more secure trade. From employees of Indian-owned businesses to peddling their own wares around the country, Somalis ultimately combine what they have learned from these two sectors to further establish themselves in South Africa.

Making Money in the Margins: Township and Informal Settlement Economies

The concentration of migrants in particular sectors of the economy is nearly always the result of a complex historical process. Some migrants transfer the skills and crafts they brought from elsewhere, such as Jews in the gold and diamond economy in New York.[37] Others are often attracted to areas where they feel they can achieve the most socioeconomic mobility and least discrimination in a new country.[38] In the Somali case, newcomers initially sought their livelihoods in the low-wage, unskilled labor market within the Muslim Indian community, as we have seen, and moved up to become independent street vendors (Figure 13). Within the latter sector, they often achieved higher incomes and were able to save more money. But the nature of street vending and the physical and emotional costs it demanded from individuals necessitated that Somalis branch out from this sector. The niche that Somalis discovered next was a product of the unique economic structures of apartheid and the underdeveloped economies on the fringes of townships.

FIGURE 13. First step of a Somali entrepreneur. Bellville, Western Cape, South Africa.

Such underdevelopment remains intrinsically tied to the wage labor concentration of blacks in South Africa and their marginalization from the capital-intensive formal sectors of the economy. Historically these black areas were without an established economy, except for informal, small-scale trading activities, which were policed and repressed.[39] These areas are served by major department stores mostly found in white urban areas. Major stores, such as Pick-n-Pay, Shoprite, and smaller Indian grocery shops located in white, Indian, and black residential areas, meet the daily consumption needs of most South Africans. The dominance of non-black-owned shops means that newcomers and the majority black South Africans rarely break into this sector and thus do not pose much of a threat to established businesses. But on the margins of black townships are millions of poor blacks who incur additional costs to access township-central commercial areas or white urban areas.

An increasing constituency within the township populations resides in shacks made from corrugated iron, in areas lacking police presence, sanitation, electrical services, or paved roads (Figure 14). Millions of these people on the margins still depend on major city centers and township centers to shop from established businesses. This is where Somalis, Ethiopians, Bangladeshis, and Mozambicans, among other newcomers, penetrate for economic survival. These newcomers discovered a gold trove, albeit an intrinsically insecure one.

Ismail, a business partner in a group that opened a small grocery store in the township of KwaNobuhle, just outside of Uitenhage in Port Elizabeth, articulated the impetus for entering these black residential areas:

> We got to know some Africans and some Indian wholesalers well. We benefited from two factors: the black African men took us to the townships and showed us some shops that were in risky areas. Blacks are usually lazy and if they open a shop, it usually ends up getting closed. They told us they have shops and they are willing to rent them to us. We subsequently went to the Indian wholesalers and asked them for advice about our trading in these shops. They encouraged us to open them and said they will be happy to supply our stock.

FIGURE 14. Informal settlement in Gauteng, South Africa.

Here we see this Somali man reproducing a racist depiction of South African blacks, positioning himself as an industrious newcomer able to do what the "blacks" fail to do—run a profitable business in these poor residential areas. In fact, this contrast between Somalis and South African blacks was common, with the distinction put not only in racial but also in cultural terms, with "they are lazy" bestowing on the whole group an ailment that explains their social location within the larger South African population.

Asked why he consulted with Indian business owners to open these stores in townships, Ismail replied,

> We were afraid of them; also we needed to get stock from them because we knew it would be a headache with no stock and support. That is how we started. And I was the first person [among Somalis] to open a shop in the townships. . . . I was actually the first in the whole country to enter this sector.

The year was 1997, and the place where the first Somali stores—known as spaza shops—opened was in the KwaNobuhle township in the outskirts of Uitenhage. The Somalis in South Africa consisted of a handful of young men. After working in stores and factories owned by Indian Muslims and eventually trying their hand in street vending, this small group of men spread quickly into the economy on the edges of townships. Contact established with other blacks working for Indian businesses was key to Somali businesses within the black South African areas. Ismail articulated Somalis' grasp of the pecking order: with South African blacks at the bottom, living in poor, crime-ridden areas, as "lazy," lacking an entrepreneurial knack; the Indian Muslim wholesalers as the role models; and his fellow Somalis as striving to rise up in such divisions. Ismail acknowledges his strategizing to build alliances with the dominant Indian group, whose support, approval, and credit emerged as the springboard for Somalis' economic pursuits. At the same time, he doesn't acknowledge the stereotypes embedded in this vision of the pecking order and in fact reproduces a racist portrayal that justifies why black South Africans occupy the bottom position in this hierarchy.

Another businessman, Sahal, who opened a shop in 2000, highlighted how Somalis were also warned of the sector as volatile and as outside the rule of law:

We were even more afraid than we are now because at that time no one used to intermingle with the black community and for that reason we believed that our safety was only assured about 80 percent of the time. Also we were advised by some local Muslims not to go into business in these dangerous areas. However, we still decided to do so to survive and to save money within a short period of time.

I suggest that Somalis in South Africa have become the latest occupants of a long-standing social category: the middleman minority. These newcomers have thus achieved what Bonacich called "an intermediate rather than low status position" as a migrant ethnic group.[40] The sharp division of South African society, between a small, white elite and the poor masses of black Africans, fits the historical pattern that encourages the emergence of a middleman minority as a group of people who facilitate transactions across the great divide of class and race. Starting in the preapartheid era and continuing to this day, Indians have been the dominant occupant of this middleman minority role and have endured a history of resentment and riots as a result. In the late 1940s, for example, deadly clashes erupted between Indians and blacks in Durban.[41] Particularly in moments of social unrest or economic instability, permanent "foreigners" like Indians can easily be seen as usurping the country's limited economic opportunities and thus blocking black people's aspirations. South African Indians are usually scapegoated for the exploitation of the natives and sometimes even accused of receiving preferential treatment from the country's whites.[42] Somalis now find themselves enduring similar tensions.

A Success Story: From a Refugee to a Merchant Haji

Kayse came to South Africa in 1998, but like many migrants, his trip to the southern edge of the African continent was not his first journey. For most of the 1980s he worked as an unskilled laborer in Saudi Arabia. After being deported back to Somalia in 1989, and the subsequent collapse of the country in 1991, he headed to Yemen. He returned to Somalia in 1994 and promptly moved on to Kenya. For two years he traded between Somalia and Kenya but then decided to come to South Africa. We saw earlier how Kayse secured a job at a butcher shop owned by an Indian Muslim he met at the mosque. With the money he earned from the butcher and a generous donation from his employer, Kayse spent the next few years as a street vendor selling cheap Chinese goods in the streets of small towns all over Gauteng and Western Cape. He subsequently saved enough to establish a small corner store with another Somali man in 2002. Kayse's first partnership ended in disappointment, as the other man left town and returned to Somalia without telling Kayse that he sold the store to other Somalis, fleeing with the money. Eventually, another business partner came into the picture:

> He assured me that he is nothing like that guy who robbed me and finally persuaded me to become his business partner. We pooled about twenty thousand rand each and we started a small wholesaler in Claremont and it thrived. A friend of mine from Nigeria who owned a kiosk asked me if I wanted to rent his kiosk. I brought my nephew from Somalia. I gave him about fifteen thousand rand and told him to stay here close to me. But he preferred to go to Port Elizabeth. After a year of not accomplishing much, I called him back and told him to join me in Cape Town and to run the kiosk. I then opened another shop in Haut Bay in a container.

Despite the failure of his first partnership, Kayse's second venture succeeded. After the first successful venture, Kayse developed a number of small stores all over the Cape Town region using the same formula. This success triggered a chain migration of his young male relatives. The "container" to which Kayse refers is a metal cargo container, normally used to ship freight but, in South Africa (and many other countries), often transformed into a corner shop by carving out a door and small window in its sides (Figure 15). These containers are placed on land in poor townships or informal settlements with rents of R300 to R500 for the space. The cargo container cost R7,000 in 2009 (about $1,000) and it was filled with basic retail groceries that the locals needed for their everyday living.

> The sales of the shop progressed day after day. In the first day we sold fifty rand and one hundred rand in the second day and so on. . . . We were three shareowners in this new shop. We employed someone to keep the shop running. After six months we saw that the shop was doing extremely well and

we decided to add an extension of up to sixteen meters to the original container. We told the locals that we were Indians from Port Elizabeth and they believed us because Somalis were few then and not as familiar as they are today. That was in 2003. We then decided to rent an open space from one of the locals for ten years and we erected a two-story house made of bricks.

Kayse spent about R100,000 (around $13,000 at the time) for the brick house.[43] For these Somali entrepreneurs, a combined R40,000 not only launched one business in a central location of Claremont, a multiracial urban center, but also instigated a rapid expansion to poor black residential areas. Kayse, along with a small group of similarly determined and lucky Somali migrants, progressed from being a low-wage laborer to an independent street vendor to an employer. He is one of a small group of major Somali entrepreneurs whose employees include both family members and nonfamily all over South Africa. His successful business strategy embodies the most prevalent model of successful Somali entrepreneurs and explains how Somalis are now one of the dominant groups in these small shops in townships and informal settlements all over South Africa. Here, then, the self-employment practices of Somalis can be compared to those in the UAE, except that these two cases target different clientele for their business. In the UAE, it involves business dealings with Somali clients around the world, whereas South African Somalis' businesses mostly depend on black South African clientele.

Kayse now owns or co-owns fourteen shops. With the exception of the first two shops, which he started with partners, his business ventures involve only male relatives. By 2009 he had brought into South Africa eleven close relatives—nephews, uncles, and cousins—all initially working for him and earning from R2,000 to R3,000 per month ($300–$400). These workers sleep and eat at the stores and thus save most of their wages. Those in Claremont and Wynberg in the Cape Town suburbs sleep at Kayse's home in Claremont, where his wife and a maid prepare their meals and also do their laundry. These young men often remit around $50 to $100 a month to their families. With discipline and thrift, a young man can save around R10,000 to R20,000 a year. Kayse discussed how he encourages them to partner with him. He keeps their savings for them and "when their money becomes enough to open a shop, I arrange one for them provided that they give me a

FIGURE 15. A shipping container turned into a corner shop outside of Cape Town, South Africa.

share." He suggests a 75 percent share for him and 25 percent for the young man. Through a partnership solidified by blood relationship, Kayse is proud to recount how hard these young men work on these ventures. They strive to protect their own investments, which guarantees that they also protect the investments of their older relative and guardian.

Such networks of kin and community account for the integration of Somali newcomers into the South African economy. As is true for other middlemen minorities, thriftiness, long hours of work, and a strong sense of solidarity within the group are evident.[44] In fact, workers in the spaza shops in the informal settlements may not come down to Somali ethnic enclaves such as Bellville, Korsten, and Mayfair for weeks at a time. A term utilized by Somalis in the diaspora to refer to men in South Africa is *shaar gaduud,* or "those whose shirts have turned brown or reddish." This term acknowledges the toll on their bodies and stresses how the pursuit of money overrides all else, including personal hygiene. But this hiatus from the community enclaves is also portrayed as being part of the cost of making a living in South Africa, as the only profitable and accessible enterprises that can be opened in these areas require little capital but also much sacrifice and risk.

Somalis create shareholding schemes to start these small businesses. Two, three, or four men often pool their savings, with each shareholder drawing profits in proportion to his investment. In addition, those running the stores are salaried. Thus shareholders staying in towns where they may pursue other economic interests get their stake of the profit minus their portion of the labor cost for paid employees.

Kayse's success made him a leader serving as a respected mediator and elder throughout the community. His pilgrimage to Mecca earned him the title of "Haji," which further enhances his position within the community.[45] He and others like him pay emergency funds for the aid of Somalis in financial need and for community projects, in essence playing the role that Indian charity organizations previously occupied for the first Somali cohort.

But the largest portion of Kayse's spending is dedicated to the family he left behind. When asked what he remits, he reported that he sends about $3,000 per month, with half going to his sister and her large family, who now live in Uganda. He also sends smaller amounts to his uncles, aunts, cousins, and other relatives in Somalia. Kayse now owns a residential villa in Claremont and also invests in land properties in Mogadishu and its surroundings, where his extended family still lives. His businesses, which are located in main, nonblack urban centers as well as in poor, residential black areas, permit Kayse to weather the uncertainties experienced by those reliant only on marginal residential areas, as discussed next.

Spaza Sector: Contact, Competition, and Conflict

Somalis utilize the old nomadic strategy of *sahan* to enter into the South African spaza economy. Sahan is what nomadic Somali men must undertake every so often, as families move from a settlement where water and pasture are becoming scarce to a place these men have identified as a potential settlement site to which the family or larger social grouping may move. Sahan, then, is an exploration for a location that can sustain the family and community and often represents a move from scarcity to abundance. Typically in South Africa, a few Somali men drive through multiple settlements to identify particular housing blocks lacking access to retail stores. Men may undertake this sahan to set up their own shops or as middlemen who sell their information to others looking for business venues.

To translate the sahan into an actual business enterprise, these Somalis approach a South African individual or the head of a family residing on the land they desire for a shop, which leads to a rental negotiation. The majority of black families living on the margins of townships reside in one- or two-bedroom shacks on land they themselves may not own. Others with government-built housing rent out spaces either in the front of the house or in the backyard. Somali entrepreneurs then construct a one-room brick shop or place a container on the property that serves as a spaza shop. Some locals also rent out one of their own rooms (whether in a shack or a room in a government house) to make extra income for the family.

To explain why and how Somalis started entering this spaza sector, Magan, one of the earliest shop owners in townships, put it this way:

> You see, Somalis see with one eye and hear with one ear. They followed our [the first few Somali pioneers] example and flocked to the locations.[46] Indeed, there are two major factors forcing Somalis to go to townships. One is that they don't have enough education to enter into the mainstream workforce and they don't have enough capital to establish formal businesses. So capital scarcity makes it attractive to aim for small shops, where you can manage things, can know the price of the stock and the profits. Also the general unemployment in this country is a major issue; even if you have enough education, the income you can expect is low and cannot cover all your needs. And jobs are very scarce anyways. So these are factors that are forcing Somalis to seek alternative ways of making a living.

Magan highlights what fuels "replication" in a given portion of the economy, where the initial entry of a few Somalis into township spaza work culminated in an elaborate economic niche for this community.[47] Somali entry into this niche was of course partly facilitated by the collapse of apartheid. With the emergence of middle-class blacks with purchasing power, major retail stores such as Pick-n-Pay and Shoprite (all, of course, owned by nonblacks) expanded to these previously shunned areas and now dominate the economic centers of the major townships. Those living in the fringes of these townships, or in smaller townships, still travel significant distances to purchase goods from these retail stores. As a result, the spaza shops are an attractive alternative, which are increasingly owned and run by non–South African migrants and refugees on their doorsteps.

Omar, who co-owns two stores in Attredgeville, a township outside of Pretoria, further explained why Somalis flocked to these marginal areas:

> An informal settlement has more customers than the average town. It has more customers because the person who lives in a good house in the town often has a car.... The majority of the people living in that area are people who work and earn a decent wage.... They go to Shoprite and buy what they need on their way back home.... But the others [in informal settlements] receive some social grants by the government and they may also work in low-end jobs. That person cannot afford to come home in a taxi, carrying all the stock he needs. So he comes home with his money still in his pocket. Before he goes to his home, he passes by your store and spends that money with you. Many others who do not work stay at home for the whole day. These buy from you one or two rand items all day. So this area is better for us in terms of sales.

Those residing on the edges of townships are portrayed as captive customers whose everyday needs are met by the small spaza shops. Both desperate, refugees and migrants unable to break into formal employment and economic sectors and poor informal settlement residents dependent on the convenience of these spaza shops converge in an intimate yet tenuous relationship.

Most Somalis begin with limited language skills beyond their own native tongue and have a hard time communicating in English, Afrikaans, Zulu, Khosa, or any other South African language. The few who are fluent in English work as interpreters within the larger community and assist other Somalis in negotiations for store spaces and the like. But once a store opens, the young men running it initially rely on sign language and often pick up bits of English and the most commonly used local languages. Nasir, a man in his twenties who previously worked for a relative outside of Cape Town, but currently co-owns a small wholesaler in Bellville, described the language gap on both sides:

> My customers were blacks and did not speak much English. If they wanted a specific thing, they just pointed to it and I understood them. They mostly call goods by their brand names. For instance if they want rice by Spekko, then they simply call it by that name and we understood them. We picked up their language in our everyday contact and ultimately learned it.

Except for these business transactions, however, Somalis reported limited interaction with the local population. The fact that some of the earliest Somalis entering this economic niche presented themselves as "South African Indians" illustrates the cultural and linguistic distance between these Somali entrepreneurs and the local, diverse black population as well as the distance between South African Indians and blacks. Lying by pretending to be Indians when leasing shops in the townships and informal settlement areas permitted Somali newcomers to avoid explaining the geographical, social, and religious distance they occupy vis-à-vis the local black citizens. But it also associated Somalis with the "exploitative trader" stereotype that had for decades been assigned to Indians.[48] It is unlikely that Somalis understood well that associating themselves with Indians would trigger suspicion. But Somalis deemed that being Indian, which is a racial group known to these black South Africans, was a better signifier than divulging their Somali nationality, which most of the earliest arrivals believed was unknown to these South Africans.

Sahal, one of these early pioneers who now runs a small lodge in Mayfair, detailed his eventual "outing" as a foreigner:

> One day, we passed an unused store space and we asked children playing in front of the building where the owners of this store lived. The children guided us to the owner's house and we expressed our interest in renting the shop. After that, they asked us what we were and where we came from. Of course we knew that they did not know Somalis. So we told them that we were from Durban and we acted as though we were South African Indians. I remember long after that initial contact, a man who was a member of the ANC who lived in the area asked us where we were from and we again repeated that we were from Durban and we were South African Indians. But he retorted that he thought we were either from Ethiopia or Somalia and he

added he was almost sure that we were Somalis. But we have never met anyone else who knew Somalia.

The correct suspicion of the ANC member may be due to ANC exiles' wider contact with the rest of the continent during the antiapartheid struggle and to greater pan-African awareness compared to the majority of the locals. But more important, Somalis racially distancing themselves from the numerically dominant but socioeconomically marginalized black South Africans speaks to their own sense of identifying as non-Bantu Africans who are racially distinct from most sub-Saharan Africans. Again, this is in line with what we saw for Somalis in the UAE, whose sense of affinity and identity with the Arab Muslim population in this nation anchored their sense of belonging and well-being in that country.

Instead of the sense of belonging articulated by Somalis in the UAE, the South African experience is characterized by a sense of physical insecurity. The security concerns migrant and refugee businesses confront can be divided into two broad kinds. The first involves petty criminals committing minor thefts. Young men and women trying to sneak candy or bits of food remains a common experience of small businesses everywhere but poses little risk to the lives of the locals and newcomer business owners. The second type of security threat Somalis and non-Somalis in townships confront involves gangs armed with knives or guns (Figure 16). Easy access to illegal guns remains a major security challenge in South Africa, which in 2006 had the third highest number of firearm deaths out of 112 nations studied.[49] Only Venezuela and Colombia had higher reported firearm deaths. Consequently, the majority of homicides in South Africa are committed with illegal firearms.[50] Guns, knives, and machetes are widely available to all, including Somalis and other foreign businessmen.

I heard several stories about Somali businessmen who drew their guns to fight back against robbers, with neighbors alerting the police, who then raided the businesses and incarcerated the owners for illegal gun possession. Somali business pursuits in marginal areas around South Africa thus involve intrinsic insecurity, exacerbated by simultaneous pressure from law enforcement, which is often ineffective at protecting anyone but which criminalizes Somalis when they protect themselves and their property.

FIGURE 16. Self-reliance for protection in the outskirts of Strand, Western Cape, South Africa.

Yet migrants' and refugees' entry into the spaza sector not only expands the limited economic activity in these areas but also heightens the competition that South African blacks confront in their residential settlements. Contact and communication between newcomers and the marginalized groups can at times become tense, as research in the United States also shows.[51] Somalis' entry into informal settlement and township businesses was thus accompanied by violence soon after apartheid's end, with the first violent confrontation with the locals occurring in Motherwell Township near Port Elizabeth in 1997. However, this violence did not deter Somali businessmen, nor did it lead to a search for alternative sources of employment. In a context of limited economic opportunity in the formal economy, the spaza sector in black residential areas emerged as a lucrative but risky niche for newcomers. As the following vignettes illustrate, a cycle of high risk and high returns characterizes Somali migration experiences in South Africa.

Asad, a partner in a spaza shop on the outskirts of the township of Langa near Cape Town, who also runs his own store at the center of the mostly colored township of Mitchells Plain, discussed the dangers of spaza work. He detailed a call from a neighbor:

> He said your brother was killed. I took some guys with me and we went there. When we reached the store, we found him wounded but alive. They shot him seven times and robbed the store; they took stuff. I called the police and they came. The ambulance took him to the hospital. He survived. As for me, I am still at the same place. The reason being, we are in a desperate situation. If you are a man who has three kids and you have no one else to turn to, what else can you do? If you tell yourself to give up on this type of business and you take your suitcase looking for a job, you cannot find it because they will ask for ID papers. There is no way to get another job. You are not allowed to get a job in South Africa! You have to survive. I slept at the store the second night while his blood was still fresh in the store. I had no other option.

Though Somali refugees often have refugee IDs, these rarely lead to residence papers—the ID papers to which Asad refers—which are necessary for job applications in mainstream sectors. Also, Asad referred to his business partner as a "brother," though this man was not a blood relative. In the face of adversity, these Somali businessmen commonly present themselves to the locals as brothers. In fact, this sense that all Somalis are kin was reinforced by a resilience necessary to confront the major security challenges all Somalis face in these settings. Thus constant communication among Somali storeowners in a particular area and alarm calls broadcasted when any shop is attacked serve as a collective protective strategy. Others with cars from surrounding townships or neighboring Somali enclaves rush to assist after a robbery and often salvage whatever property they can. In extreme cases, they just rescue the shopkeepers and flee the scene (Figure 17).

I asked Asad how the police dealt with the robbery. He replied, "We opened a case with the police but I did not hear anything from them or from anyone else. No one came to update us on whether anyone was arrested for the shooting. Nothing was done and the case finished like that." Asad also reported that it took three months for his partner to recover from his gunshot wounds and that he subsequently opted to return to Somalia, giving up on his hope of making it in South Africa. Many similar narratives highlighted

FIGURE 17. "Whenever someone enters your store, you are asking yourself, 'Does he have a gun? Is he the one who will kill you?'" Somali entrepreneurs live with this perpetual insecurity. South Africa.

the violence or the fear of violence in townships and informal settlements throughout South Africa. For South Africa's middle and upper classes, electric fences, multiple layers of metal barriers on doors and windows, and robust private security measures—everything from bulletproof cars to armed guards—are defining features of everyday life. Somalis, like the vast majority of South Africans, live outside the protections of such security and thus must find their way in these precarious conditions.

Afrah, a man who leads one of the two Somali advocacy organizations in South Africa, also shared his own firsthand experience of this pervasive violence, when three men broke into his home in the mostly Indian residential area of Mayfair, near Johannesburg, in 1999. He was at home with his wife and two children and a few family friends. The intruders separated him and the other man from the women and children. The criminals severely beat the two men and even burned them with a hot iron to force them to reveal where their money was hidden. Eventually the attackers fled, fearing that the neighbors would hear the children's panicked cries. After the men left, neighbors rushed into the house, got Afrah and his friend to the hospital, and also called the police. Such violence is rare in Mayfair, though all those residing in South Africa live with the real fear of violence and take great precautions, such as locking doors with very heavy padlocks when at home. But it is mostly women and children who remain in these areas and who benefit more from living and working in more secure parts.

Gendered Livelihood Niches

The violence endemic to South Africa has disturbing gendered implications; according to research, "South Africa has the highest reported rate globally of females murdered by shooting in a country not engaged in war."[52] Moreover, an internationally publicized survey conducted by the Medical Research Council in 2009 found that 28 percent of South African men admitted to raping a woman.[53] This gender violence continues to be underreported, and activists suggest that the data available, as shocking as they are, only touch the surface of the crisis.

The place of Somali women in South Africa also epitomizes the gendered nature of migration experiences. Somali gender norms take on added importance amid South Africa's many dangers. Women, for example, are discouraged from going into the townships and informal settlements at all and nearly always stay within the Somali enclaves owing to fear of sexual violence. Yet cultural preferences must also adapt to the realities of survival. The majority of Somali women in South Africa, after all, undertook difficult and expensive journeys and are just as eager as their brothers and husbands to better their family's future, just as they did in Somalia. Unlike the men who have moved up to spaza work, however, these women continue to search for work around the predominantly Indian and colored areas where Somalis first created their ethnic enclaves. In these areas, Somali women's dress does not appear so different, with many Indian and Malay Muslims also dressed conservatively. The three most important concentrations of Somali women's work are hence in Mayfair, an Indian enclave in the Johannesburg suburb; in Uitenhage and Korsten, near Port Elizabeth; and in Bellville and, to a lesser extent, Mitchells Plain in the Cape Town metro of the Western Cape. The latter are mostly colored and racially mixed areas (Figure 18).

Most recent arrivals sell their wares on street corners, often spread on the ground, just like many newly arrived men (Figure 13). But in addition, many women with licensed stands mostly cater to black South Africans. A small

FIGURE 18. Bellville market licensed clothing stalls.

number of Somali women also have small shops that mostly cater to Somali families and stock goods imported from the UAE and Kenya that meet the clothing, household, and dietary needs of the community. Though petty theft is common, the overall security concerns Somali women confront in nonblack urban areas are much fewer than what the men in the township and informal settlements articulate. This is not to say that killings and robberies cannot occur in these residential areas. Unknown assailants strangled a pregnant Somali woman in her ninth month in her home in the middle of the night, in the central business district of Uitengage in September 2012, while her husband was away in the township spaza shop where he spent most nights.[54] Nevertheless, the scale of lawlessness those in the informal settlement spaza sector often describe is absent in the areas where the Somali ethnic enclaves are established. These are the areas where women and children live, while the majority of men spend most of their time in the spaza shops away from their families and the larger Somali community.

This permits women, whether married or single, to engage actively in and around the Somali ethnic economy. As such, the largest Somali mall in Mayfair, which resembles the Somali malls found in Kenya, the UAE, and the United States (see Figures 19 and 20), is almost exclusively a women's space. Some women run small restaurants and lodges that cater to the thousands of Somali men who descend on these centers on weekends after a full week or two in their spaza shops. The South African experience is thus similar to what those in Kenya and the UAE experience in terms of the active and vital roles that Somali women play in providing for their families, a continuation of their productive and reproductive roles in Somalia.[55]

The married Somali women I interviewed detailed how they and their husbands always worked side by side as hawkers, but the women continued street trading or entered the ethnic economic niche while their husbands flocked to the lucrative but dangerous spaza sector. I have not documented any resistance among Somali men to Somali women working, except for one case in which a woman reported that her husband asked her to quit hawking after she gave birth to their daughter. She argued that his request was illogical because she left behind three other children and her parents, who needed her financial support. In the late 1990s, Hoda and her husband worked as street vendors, spreading out their goods on street corners or carrying socks and belts on their bodies to different bus stations. He also worked as a security guard for a few hours at night for an Indian Muslim store. She explained:

> He wanted me to stay at home and be a housewife and a babysitter. I told him I could not stay at home and I wanted to hire a babysitter and work because we have a baby here and we left children back home and it is imperative that we both work.

I asked Hoda if she stayed at home in Somalia, and she replied:

> No, I have never stayed at home in Somalia. I used to cook and sell incense and carry and sell clothes all over town.

This conflict led to the dissolution of their marriage. However, many community members who intervened in this marital conflict sided with Hoda, given the economic circumstances of Somalis in South Africa as well as the need to provide for families left behind. Community elders and religious leaders may have sided with the husband under normal circumstances, with the argument that Hoda, as the wife, should obey her husband and stop her economic pursuits if her husband can provide for her and her family. Yet that logic was undermined by the necessity of work for both husband and wife in the South African context. Hoda stressed, in addition, that her husband was incapable of managing his street trading without her assistance, as she played a pivotal role running the business.

Hoda's case highlights how housework, children, and paid labor all compete for attention. Somali women with children are able to combine outside work and family demands thanks to the extremely cheap domestic labor found in South Africa. Like for migrant women elsewhere around the globe, individual economic pursuits are contingent on other women providing affective labor, whether it is other migrant women or kin in the home country who undertake the emotional and physical family obligations toward husbands, children, and parents.[56] Thus many of the Somali women spreading socks, combs, and hats on street corners across South Africa employed other women to care for their toddlers and do the cooking and cleaning of their homes. The presence of a large number of African migrants from

Zimbabwe and Malawi, as well as the extreme poverty and unemployment rates for South African blacks, enables these Somali women to find others in a more desperate situation than they are. In 2007 and 2009, Somalis paid monthly wages ranging from R800 to R1,000 (around $110–$130) for domestic help. These wages were lower than the minimum wage set by the South African government, but no one I spoke with mentioned any difficulty finding women willing to accept such wages. The wages these Somali street traders paid amounted to 20 to 30 percent of their monthly incomes. But such a cost is deemed worthwhile as it allows these Somali women to earn enough to provide for families left behind in the Horn and still take care of their families in South Africa. In the UAE, by contrast, we saw that only the best-off Somalis could afford household help, testifying to the relative location of Somalis within each country's social strata as well as the relative wealth of these two countries.

Just like in the UAE, however, the majority of women interviewed reported that their incomes still permitted them to remit to their families. Women whose husbands were economically more stable were often exempted from financial contributions to the household, including rent, food, and children's schooling. When the husband was able to take care of the needs of the immediate family, that enabled the wife to remit an even larger percentage of her income to her extended family elsewhere. The obligation enshrined in Islam that the husband provides for the children and the wife is strictly followed by Somalis, both in the UAE and South Africa, but only if and when the husband's economic status allows him to assume all these financial obligations.

Though spaza ventures are nearly the exclusive domain of men, a few women have challenged this trend. Two examples provide us with a window into the dynamics of work, gender, and migration that Somali women negotiate in South Africa. Shukria, a widow who came to South Africa in early 2007, had a small food stand in Bakaara, the biggest market in Mogadishu, but left soon after Ethiopia invaded Somalia, amid the surge of shelling, fear, and instability. South Africa was an easy choice for her because she had a brother working there. She left her four children, the youngest just two years old, with her parents. Once she arrived, her brother brought her to the spaza shop that he co-owned, in a township outside of Cape Town. She told me about her unusual life:

> In the area that I live now, [Somali] women don't stay here. They are in the Bellville area, which is a central place. At the time when I arrived, there were not many work opportunities for women. The community was still small. The jobs that are available for women today like street trading and selling perfumes were not as common in those days. My brother told me that I needed to work with him and his business partners as he could not afford to rent a place for me and as I left children behind and needed to provide for them. Hence three guys and I worked and continue to work in this shop. One delivers the stock for us and the others remain running the shop. . . . Although we lived a dog's life because I lived with men who were not my brothers and not my husband—working together, physically coming into contact.

Shukria's claim that Somali women were not involved in street trading in 2007 when she arrived is somewhat of an exaggeration. But her claim that the majority of opportunities that attract Somalis were in the spaza sector is well founded. The spaza Shukria co-ran is about twenty-five square feet in area, with an adjacent small bedroom and bathroom. Given the limited sleeping space, the men gave the small room to Shukria, while they spread their thin mattresses inside the store, among the boxes of groceries. Shukria emphasizes how living in such close proximity to unrelated men was discomforting for her, an observant Muslim. Shukria's way out of this dilemma was to marry one of the business partners, a marriage she rationalized as one of convenience:

> If I tell you the truth, I got married because I was forced to marry by the circumstances. . . . I did it because I was spending all my day with someone who was neither my father nor my brother. You accidently touch each other all the time and you have even seen us eating together once. I cook their food, I wash their clothes, and I clean the place. We are together all the time. I am afraid at night. There are times when thieves climb the building, and we all hide in the small room with the guys bringing their mattress into my room. So I thought that instead of living in a sinful life, I may as well marry one of them. There was one that I got along well and we agreed to get married.

Asked about their economic arrangements in terms of who pays the bills, she replied:

> What bills? We eat the rice together in the shop. You cannot get anything from him. He will tell you that he makes the same amount that you make and that he also left behind a family in need! What will you get from him? He will say we get exactly the same wages and my family is also depending on me! You know how the pressure is. It affects us all!

Shukria's case illustrates the role that social pressure and Somali cultural norms play in how women navigate life as migrant workers while still safeguarding their and their families' reputation. Shukria's brother, though still a partner in their business, now runs another small spaza shop in an informal settlement in the Western Cape region. When I asked Shukria why she did not leave this shop to work with her brother instead, she reported that his spaza was a shack in an informal settlement in Strand. These shacks lack bathroom facilities and thus are unsuitable for women. Young men running these stores often use cans and bottles to attend to their bodily functions. Shukria, for example, joked about the comments she often gets from the township residents who find her dress *(jilbaab)* fascinating and who regularly comment on her unusual presence in the township.

Shukria explained her income from the store that she runs and also co-owns:

> If my labor is counted, I make about five thousand rand [per month]. My labor accounts for two thousand rand, and three thousand is from my share of the profit from the store. The income from my labor is constant, but the profits fluctuate. I may get four thousand, forty-five hundred, five thousand rand, depending on how well the business is doing.

An individual income between R4,000 and R,5000 a month, adding up to about R48,000 to R60,000 a year, placed Shukria in the higher end of the income bracket for blacks in South Africa. In fact, the median income in South Africa in 2011 was only R3,033 per month, lower than what Shukria was making in 2007.[57] Contextualizing this income further, the second and third quintiles of South Africans earning less than R30,164 in 2005–6 included 72.5 percent of black Africans, 45 percent of coloreds, 17.6 percent of Indians, and 3.3 percent of whites.[58] Racial disparities clearly account for the two extremes. If we assume that Shukria's husband made about the same income as she did, though in reality his share of the business was larger, then their household income would place them in the upper quintile (those earning more than R68,528 per year), again a position only 7.9 percent of blacks, 25.6 percent of coloreds, 50.0 percent of Indians, and 83.0 percent of whites occupied in 2005–6.[59]

Shukria's family income, though high relative to a large segment of the poor South African population, would barely cover all their needs if she were to bring her four children to South Africa. Her presence in the townships may change if she has children with her new husband. I have not documented any Somali family residing in black townships or informal settlements. Instead, most Somali families reside in Indian areas, such as Mayfair and Laudium, or mostly colored areas, like Mitchells Plain, Korsten, and Uitenheige, as well as the more mixed area of Bellville. Rent in these areas ranges from R3,000 to R7,000, and families often share a house with other families or rent out one or two rooms to single men or single women to reduce their share of the cost. Ebla, the woman who came with her children through Malawi, resides in a villa in Mayfair with her family that costs R8,000 ($1,000 in 2009) per month. But her family can now afford this cost, as Ebla and her husband run two stores in the Somali mall, and one of their sons also runs a small electronics shop in a corner of one of their clothing shops. Thus Shukria, Ebla, and other Somali families' incomes are high compared to very poor South Africans, mostly living in government-provided houses or self-built shacks. But even these incomes can be strained considering the cost of living in the areas where Somalis live as well as the number of family members each individual supports. Moreover, despite the economic success of all Somalis in South Africa compared to the plight of the majority of citizens, a sense of uncertainty taints their experiences in this country.

For women, this uncertainty is represented by the experience of the second case of a Somali woman who, against the advice of the whole community, chose to go into the spaza shop sector in the townships. The story of Saida Mohamed, who, with her three children aged thirteen, ten, and eight, was brutally killed in her home adjacent to her store in October 2008, now acts as a cautionary tale for Somali women. Ms. Mohamed was stabbed 113 times, while she and her ten-year-old daughter were both allegedly repeatedly raped.[60] This case as well as the general fear of violence in South Africa continue to reinforce the gendered nature of work in the Somali-run spaza shops, which defines Somali economic pursuits in South Africa but also Somali physical and psychosocial insecurity in the country.

The Underbelly of Economic Success: "Xenophobic" Violence and Permanent Insecurity

The death of more than thirty-four Marikana miners at the hands of South African law enforcement officials in August 2012 shocked the nation. These strikers were demanding better wages and job security from their employer.[61] The police claimed that they shot miners in self-defense, as the miners were armed with "dangerous weapons," including handguns, machetes *(pangas)*, and knobkerries (walking sticks with a knob at the top), among other weapons.[62] The heightened publicity of this lethal police reaction, as well the public debate on low wages in the mines, provided the momentum for workers in other industries in South Africa to voice their grievances.[63] But such protests in South Africa are often accompanied by attacks against migrants and their businesses.[64] During the recent Marikana strike, foreign-owned businesses in the vicinity of the mines in Rustenburg were looted, and some shops were burned.[65] In 2008, highly publicized attacks against migrant businesses in townships and informal settlements around the country led to the deaths of more than sixty migrants and locals, though the unrest itself had nothing to do with migrants. Such spillover persists alongside the problems endemic to life in townships and their surroundings—poverty, inequality, violence, and corruption in housing and the delivery of public services. Rage is an unsurprising result of these perpetual problems, and foreigners are a convenient scapegoat.

Two decades after the demise of apartheid, many South Africans see little progress in their economic and social exclusion. Feeling like outsiders in their own country, "South Africans quickly resort to violence as a means of solving conflicts—whether in the domestic, social or work environment."[66] The now iconic picture that symbolized the attacks against migrants in 2008 showed a Zimbabwean man who had a burning tire around his neck, a practice called "necklacing." This type of lynching is a remnant of the vigilante justice commonly suffered by those identified as selling out to the apartheid government in the 1980s, a deterrent for others tempted to serve as informants for the state against the antiapartheid struggle. In its postapartheid manifestation, alleged criminals and rapists continue to be subjected to this mob justice in many parts of South Africa.[67] In a 2011 recent necklacing in New Brighton, a township outside of Port Elizabeth, two men suspected of robbery were doused with petrol and set on fire with a burning tire around their necks. A local resident expressed the widespread frustration with the police: "We report these criminals to the police. They come out the next day and commit the crimes again, so we got tired of opening cases that never go anywhere." Another onlooker stated, "These boys had been causing problems in the community for a long time. They terrorized us."[68]

Such aggression against criminals would seem, in theory, to benefit Somali business owners, who are often the victims of theft and physical violence. Yet these vigilante attacks, far from comforting, ultimately contribute to a pervasive sense of instability and lawlessness. The majority of the poor population in townships feels excluded from the dreams of liberation and black rule; amid this deep frustration, migrants and refugees seem to realize their dreams at the poor population's expense. Proximity, in a context of seemingly permanent insecurity, inevitably impacts migrants and their enterprises as well as locals. Though black South Africans may buy things from street vendors, and may rely on spaza shops for much of their food and daily needs, the Somalis who sell these goods are still tinged with otherness; the linguistic, cultural, and religious distance between the newcomers and the locals can fuel resentment and thus make Somalis targets during unrest. Riots against county, provincial, state, or even private firms metamorphose into anger against foreign-owned businesses.

Although contact between new and old immigrants with natives does not always lead to violence, previous research shows that this can be the case in areas where drastic economic disparity and high crime rates previously prevailed. For example, studies of the United States' inner cities demonstrate the tensions that might erupt between entrepreneurial newcomers and long-segregated marginalized groups in urban areas. Koreans dominating the small-scale business sector in African American residential areas are a case in point. Jennifer Lee's work shows how African Americans lack some of the social capital that is available to minority immigrants who are attracted to fill the niches existing in these areas. Conflict between these two groups is often attributed to the structural conditions existing in poor black neighborhoods, which are said to be conducive to racial unrest.[69] However, as Lee rightly points out, conflict would be ever present in all inner-city settings, thus this approach "overpredicts" conflict when in reality violence is more the exception rather than the rule in the inner-city American setting.

In the South African context, violence in these areas is often labeled as "xenophobic" in mainstream media and public parlance, and Somali interviewees use this term in English to discuss the violence they confront. But I argue that such framing simplifies a complex social process. The everyday lives of many black South Africans are characterized by a continual structural violence; the refugees and migrants living and working in these settlements inevitably become incorporated into this normalized violence.[70] The attacks in 2008 are a telling example; far from a small number of criminals targeting a spaza store for robbery, these attacks involved substantial segments of the population in many informal settlements and townships. The trend often involved mobs scaring the migrant business owners by descending into the stores. After the death or flight of these migrants, the mobs looted all the property found in these stores, including the shelving material, and at times torched the constructions and everything in them.[71]

Apartheid policies have created an entrenched culture where "race" is still utilized as a basis to account for all social ills in South Africa. It is thus not surprising that the widespread attacks against migrants and refugees in 2008 and 2009 triggered a debate on xenophobia. This framing demonizes the black South African poor, who are viewed not to have emerged from the violent era of apartheid but are still using tools that should have been discarded once liberation had been attained.[72] Academics and journalists alike often ask why South African blacks can't appreciate the sacrifices that other African nations have made to support the struggle against apartheid, and why they respond to this generosity with violence now that these fellow Africans have been pushed out of their own nations by civil wars or political instability.[73] Yet the prevalence of violence and frustration in South Africa has a devastating impact on South African blacks. Resentment toward newcomers is part of the explanation but cannot wholly account for the insecurity both the poor locals and newcomers confront in their daily lives.

The Somalis with whom I spoke were, however, equally likely to use stereotyped, simplified notions of black South Africans. But they also emphasized the skewed competition between newcomers and natives for economic opportunities. In fact, Somali businessmen repeatedly acknowledged that they held the economic upper hand compared to locals. They expressed their perception of how these marginalized South African citizens were trapped even as they strove to free themselves, portraying them as unable to compete in their own land. Asad, one of the Somali men who has run businesses in these black residential areas for more than a decade, discussed how competition for customers contributes to the resentment toward Somalis:

> One factor contributing to the murders is that they [Somalis] open a store in close proximity to a local store. The person [the Somali] may already own another store in the neighborhood, and when he opens a second one, people think that he is expanding his domain. Somalis also don't engage in fair competition. They don't respect these black businesses. They would not work with them to decide on the prices of the goods they sell. They would instead set out to destroy the local store. It is possible that this black man has a family with many kids that he supports.... They [Somalis] would sell their goods at low prices, very cheap prices. Nobody would go to the black-owned store. All the customers would go to the Somali business and the black guy would go under.... What do you think this guy is going to do? He is going to murder one of the storeowners.

Resentment toward the success of Somali entrepreneurs in residential areas dominated the narratives on violence against newcomers. Interviewees widely acknowledged that Somalis had a competitive edge in this sector, in part because of the support they got from the Indian Muslim community and because of their strong community networks and their willingness to pool resources. But some, like Asad, also blamed Somalis for the resentment that they confront. In community meetings bringing together Somali and native business owners, one of the key assertions made by local entrepreneurs revolves around the lack of respect for agreements that the two groups signed, including a cap on the number of stores Somalis can open in a given area.[74]

But some interviewees also acknowledge Somali racism toward the local people. As discussed earlier, I heard a few adults saying that "blacks" are lazy and that if they open a shop, it usually ends up getting closed. Those espousing such attitudes included a Somali Bantu. Though himself belonging to a Somali minority group subjected to racism by the dominant Somali ethnic group, he still stereotyped South African "blacks" as inferior and unable to compete with him and other Somalis. Not only did some Somali adults discuss the "laziness" of blacks in this country, but even some Somali children with whom I had informal conversations categorized their teachers as "good" Indians or whites or "bad" blacks. This disdain toward the local black population, viewed to have been permanently damaged by apartheid, extends to the local police force, who are portrayed as corrupt.

Ali, a businessman running a large, successful clothing store in Bellville, explained why he viewed the South African legal system as dysfunctional:

> In this country, it seems that the criminal has more rights than the victim. Criminals that are caught are always out on bail and "innocent until proven guilty" is in use. But the question is how one determines if someone is guilty if the police don't do their work properly and there may not be witnesses to the crime. Also I have myself witnessed the police involved in robbery in both Cape Town and Johannesburg.

Somalis, who lived under a dictatorial regime in Somalia, distrust South Africa's more democratic court system, which is seen as undertaking long criminal investigations that rarely result in convictions. Moreover, bail for alleged criminals awaiting trial is something new to Somalis and often leads them to view the system as more aligned with the criminals than the victims. Somalis' distrust of the South African police force is further fueled by reports of police brutality and corruption toward marginalized communities.[75] But it is also anchored in their limited contact with a legal system where due process is the norm. In Somalia, the culture of legal representation for victims and the accused was unknown—very different from the South African legal system. This in part explains Somali refugees' frustration with South African legal processes.

Somali hiring practices also discriminate against South Africans. A Somali man running a spaza shop between 2009 and 2011 would start with a salary between R2,000 and R2,500. The small number of local blacks hired as support staff are paid around R800 working full time. One Somali co-owner of a medium-sized convenience store in Attredgeville reported paying R500 to one of the local community leaders who spent the afternoons in his store. The latter employment was a strategic one, triggered by the looting and expulsions of Somalis and other foreigners in townships and informal settlements. Somalis mostly hired local women for cleaning and at times paid what would amount to extortion money to community leaders to appease local animosity. Nevertheless, I have not found a Somali with a salary of less than R2,000, no matter what work they may do within the Somali ethnic economy or the spaza sector. Some Somali families who hire Somali maids for the care of their children pay them R2,000 to R3,000 in monthly wages, whereas the South African, Zimbabwean, or Malawian women who work in almost all Somali homes, as we have seen, often make less than R1,000 per month. I documented one live-in maid who was paid R1,500 working for a highly successful business owner and his family. But this last case was an exception, as she had been with this Somali family for more than eight years and even got paid holidays to visit her family in Zimbabwe. This kind of differential treatment further exacerbates the cultural, linguistic, and religious distance between migrants and refugee business owners and the local poor black populations.

In contrast to the persistent chasm between Somalis and black South Africans, the riots in 2008 further reinforced Somali connection with the South African Muslim community. Muslim charities came to the rescue of the thousands of Somali business owners chased out of the townships and informal settlements. Though the provincial governments in both the Western Cape and Gauteng established camps for these displaced populations, Somalis discussed their appreciation of the Muslim community's role in their darkest hour. As one man in Mitchells Plain put it:

After the xenophobic violence, Muslims in this country really assisted us. They visited the areas with the large displaced populations. They fed people. The Somalis refused the food that was brought by others saying they did not know what was in it and whether it was halal or haram.[76] ... Then, Muslims came and cooked food and gave it to them. They also brought blankets and brought milk for the children. So the Muslim community provided tremendous assistance to the Somalis during this time.

International refugee and human rights agencies also intervened following this displacement. This intervention further reinforced the notion that South Africa may not be suitable to host refugees and migrants given its inability to protect these migrants and their businesses. This led to the registration of some individuals from diverse African nations identified as vulnerable and qualified for resettlement. These included Somali families led by women with children, those with family members who were physically and mentally impaired, and men who suffered physical and psychological wounds deemed to be serious enough to warrant resettlement. As discussed earlier, however, Somali families rarely reside in these townships and informal settlements. Once the businessmen in the spaza shops were robbed and chased away, some of the families who lived in Mayfair, Bellville, or Korsten moved to newly created temporary camps for those displaced. The 2008 riots and subsequent violence against refugees and migrants led to a new role for the UNHCR in Somali affairs in South Africa.[77]

Some of these refugees registered with UNHCR with the hope of accessing resettlement opportunities in the Western world. However, similar to the experiences of refugees around the globe who now confront increased security checks and scrutiny before being granted resettlement, fewer and fewer Somalis and other Muslims are able to successfully pursue this resettlement option. For example, South Africa saw a reduction from 387 in 2010 to a mere 81 resettlements in 2011, though this number increased in 2012.[78] Moreover, as was discussed in chapter 2, only about 1 percent of the world's refugees are put forward for resettlement by the UNHCR in any given year, and only one-half to three-quarters of those who are put forward are actually resettled.[79]

Most Somali interviewees articulated two reasons for desiring further migration. The first revolved around South Africa's high insecurity, which made permanent settlement undesirable. The second underscored the difficulties of family reunification and legal documentation in South Africa. Though the majority of refugees can get permanent residence papers and, eventually, achieve naturalization in South Africa, the process takes years and even decades. This can result in a long separation of husbands, wives, children, and parents. The long, treacherous routes to the country as well as the extremely high cost of living in the secure areas that Somali families viewed as their only option rendered the separation necessary. The earliest cohort reported that getting legal refugee papers was often smooth in their first years after arrival, but all reported that the process has become more corrupt in the last ten years.

I have met a number of Somalis who have been in South Africa since the 1990s but who still renew their Section 24 permits every two years. For example, Hoda in Korsten complained that even though she arrived in 1997, she still has to renew her permit every two years. She stated, "I applied for permanent residence papers in 2004 and I am still waiting. I even have the receipt that I was given when I applied." This is in part the outcome of the large number of asylum cases the South African Home Office has to process, with a backlog of three hundred thousand cases still awaiting a decision in 2012.[80] But many interviewees also argued that it is also the result of deep corruption that only responds to bribes, thus shutting out those who do not pay up.

Given that many Somalis work for themselves or work for others in this community, seeking work permits was not viewed as paramount. Consequently, many neglect to put in the lengthy time and energy required to pursue these legal papers. Mohamed, who co-owns a small corner store in Bellville and has been in South Africa for more than two years, explained how the time and cost invested in obtaining these documents can discourage many:

> I have a permit that I renew every three months. We have a big problem with these permits. After so many attempts to get a proper document, I gave up. I have now been without a permit for a year. It is very difficult to get permits. One has to go and sleep in front of the Home Affairs office on Monday night, continue to line up on Tuesday and only a few people are accommodated that morning. You might be one of the lucky ones.

It normally takes one, two, or even three years before a refugee gets the two-year permit, but pervasive corruption within the Home Affairs office means that some migrants and refugees expedite their legal status without ever setting foot in these immigration offices. Such corruption is undermining South Africa's standing around the globe, as nonelite nationals are joining others with inflexible citizenship around the globe. Developed nations that previously did not require visas for South African citizens now impose such a requirement. For example, the U.K. government imposed visas on South African nationals in 2009 for the first time, following years of warning that curtailment of corruption within the Home Office was necessary to avoid this "embarrassment."[81] Moreover, the United States produced a damning report indicating that thousands of fraudulent South African passports are being issued to noncitizens, thus compromising its War on Terror on the African continent. The report's harsh portrayal called South Africa's immigration minister "an abysmal failure and a national embarrassment" in combating corruption in this office.

Given that Somalis were all too familiar with corruption in Somalia, Kenya, and Ethiopia, a Somali journalist suggested that they and others coming from areas where a culture of corruption is prevalent can also be partly to blame for the increasing cost of immigration papers in South Africa. The increasing scrutiny of South Africa's legal documents as a result of corruption in the Home Office has serious ramifications for all those hoping to emigrate from the country. I was told tales of Somalis who made it to Europe with their South African travel documents just before the turn of the century, when such paperwork was still considered credible for visas. But in a post-9/11 world, and with the decreasing integrity of the South African Home Office, even legally obtained South African passports no longer guarantee visas to the Western world, the destination most desired by Somalis.

With the exception of economically well-established Somalis, many of whom diversify their investments outside South Africa into Kenya, Somalia, Ethiopia, and the UAE, the majority of Somali men and women did not see a future in South Africa. Though most did not detail any immediate plans to migrate, I met a handful of men and women who repeatedly tried to get into Europe, Australia, the United States, or Canada through smugglers. Habib, for example, a man I interviewed in 2007, co-owned two spaza shops with his brother. He left South Africa that August and traveled via Angola to Brazil. I followed this case, keeping in touch with his wife, who was already in the United States. Once in Brazil, he eventually traveled through Latin America. Habib presented himself at the U.S.–Mexico border at the end of 2007. He subsequently spent two full years in a detention center, going through a lengthy immigration process requiring him to prove that he was not a member of the Somali terrorist group al-Shabaab. This South American route to the United States attracts a small number of young and mostly male Somalis willing to risk detention in the United States. Another route out of South Africa, though less popular, involves traveling to North Africa, then boarding rickety boats from Libya to Malta. If they arrive safely in Malta, the migrants then travel further into other European nations. Similar to entry into the United States, these trips entail a high risk of death and potential detention in refugee camps.

Asad, who was in his mid-forties and had a wife and three children in the Western Cape, recounted his multiple failed migration attempts:

> When you get the [South African] passport, you can go to a Latin American nation's embassy and you may get a visa. With that, you can just transit to the U.S. My younger brother who lives in Australia visited me twice. He wanted to help me. He gave me his passport and I tried to go straight to London. I also tried to take his passport and just go to Australia. Both times, I was stopped at the airport. My brother and I look very alike, but they figured it out because of my lack of language skills. It was odd that someone who has lived in Australia for twelve years could not speak the language. They asked me many questions, but I could not answer them correctly.

Another man in his mid-twenties recounted his failed attempts to get into Europe through smugglers who rent out valid European passports. Even though Raghe has now been caught three times, he still wants to pursue migration to Europe. Many women also expressed their hope to migrate to Europe or North America. Ardo, for example, got to Europe on her third attempt in 2009, after failing twice, as was discussed in the introduction. She thought she could do more for her family from Europe than from South Africa. Ardo acknowledged that she and her husband could afford to bring her sister and her children to South Africa, but the cost of maintaining this family would be very high. Ardo's rationale for further migration was consistent with many others, who appreciated what they have been able to accomplish in South Africa but who nevertheless imagine there would be better return from migration to the Western world. But the personal connections and the exchange of information across transnational Somali networks underscore both the relative insecurity that Somalis in South Africa confront and the potential for the internationally recognized travel documents and citizenship that many Western nations extend to refugees. The latter permit family reunification as well as safe passage to visit the Horn and stay in close contact with families left behind.

Asad, who discussed his attempts to go to England and Australia, articulated an awareness of the opportunities and challenges intrinsic to migration to the West, similar to those discussed by Somalis in the UAE. When I asked what he expected to accomplish with a European or North American migration, Asad replied:

> If you compare there and here at the economic level, it is better here. But there is no security here whereas there is peace there. Here, you are not safe and you don't have legal documents. I don't have documents I can use if I decide to visit my mother in East Africa. When you have legal documents, life becomes easier.... One of the main reasons why I want to migrate relates to security, to a place where I can wake up in peace. Even if I am not sleeping at the store, whenever the phone rings, you fear that someone will tell you that your brother was killed or your cousin or someone you know was killed. If you are at the store, you get scared at every crack or sound you hear because you are frightened and thinking, someone will break into the store right now. What can be worse than being afraid of every customer? Whenever someone enters your store, you are asking yourself, "Does he have a gun? Is he the one who will kill you?" ... I don't think that people in the U.S. or Europe are walking in the streets thinking that someone will kill them.

These pessimistic diagnoses of the barriers to permanent settlement in South Africa were expressed by Somali men and women alike. Security, family separation, and barriers to family reunification all contribute to their doubts about a future in South Africa. Beyond these universal problems, one successful businesswoman from the northern part of Somalia offered an additional gendered twist to why further migration was necessary. Saharla, a divorced mother of eight children, came to South Africa with her oldest son. He runs a spaza shop in an informal settlement near Cape Town, while Saharla operates a lodge and restaurant that serves Somali workers in Mitchells Plain. She described multiple obstacles preventing her from bringing all her children to South Africa, including the expensive and treacherous, long trip across half a dozen African borders. But Saharla also acknowledged that having her family in South Africa would mean prohibitive costs for schooling and housing in the Western Cape. Although Somalis have access to public education, which is mostly free or involves only small fees, those who can afford it choose to send their children to Indian Muslim schools. Public schools in nonwhite areas remain plagued by underperformance.[82] Some Somalis still send their children to mainstream public schools, though not without apprehension and only out of necessity.

Saharla registered with the UNHCR following the 2008 attacks against refugees and migrants. She had a resettlement case pending with Canada when I interviewed her in 2009. I asked what her expectations of Canada were; she stated:

> I know I will not make this amount of money, but I know my kids would get a better education and better future there. Life is very short and it is important to have your kids with you. Life is only beautiful when you live with your own children. And when your time comes, you die by their side. If they need anything, you stand by them. We are not concerned about accumulating money. If you have enough to survive on, but you are together, you can be happy. This is what it is all about.

What Saharla and her son make in South Africa enable the two of them to comfortably provide for the rest of her children and her parents, who are caring for the other seven children in Hargaisa. However, her case underscores the competing financial and emotional demands that all families negotiate in making migration decisions, as research on other migrant groups has highlighted.[83] Thus, though South Africa was admittedly economically better for her and her son, she insisted that this transnational mothering made it painful for her to settle for this economic success, which was only possible if she remained separated from the rest of her family. Her search for further migration was driven by the future well-being of her family; as with so many other migrants and refugees, settlement in the West seemed the ideal solution for her and her family's financial and emotional needs. But Saharla was also clearly aware that meeting her family's needs in Canada would require dependence on state welfare support and even that bringing her whole family would involve costs that were beyond her ability and that would involve Canadian charity organizations and government support.

Similar to the UAE, the South African Somali experience further illustrates the pull of the West for refugees and migrants around the globe. These men and women express an understanding of the instrumental role that Western citizenship can play in their physical, emotional, and economic security in a world where mobility and family reunification collide with borders that exclude the majority of the world's population. Moreover, a key distinction that the South Africa case highlights is the complex way that racial and religious identities are put forward in diverse settings. Somali interviewees frame their contact and relations with South African blacks in economic terms, as potential clients for their cheap wares, whereas their relations with Muslim Indians often connoted larger spiritual connections and even closer ethnic affinities. Somalis in the UAE, however, expressed no such affinity with Muslims from the Indian subcontinent. In both contexts, Somalis build alliances with numerically minority groups (Emirates and Indian Muslims, respectively) who enjoy socioeconomic power over large marginalized groups (South Asian migrants and South African blacks, respectively). Religious, ethnic, and cultural affinities that are strategically managed anchor Somalis' expressions of belonging and well-being within the Indian Muslim population, in a context where physical violence hampers any sense of belonging within the wider South African society.

4 United States

Slippery Jannah?

> I myself met a man who told me, "I am the head of the household. How can you put the woman's name on the file?" A Somali man! I explained it to him like this: I said, "This is the way it is in this state. The government is not going to run your household but this is how the system works." "So the government is interfering in our business; I demand that you put my name as head of the household. Why this woman, when I am the one who goes to the offices?"
>
> —Abshir, social services interpreter

As we have seen again and again, America is one of the most idealized destinations for Somali refugees around the world. It is also one of the hardest countries in which to gain entrance for refugees and poor migrants. Life in the United States is discussed, imagined, debated, and dreamed about by Somalis in the Horn of Africa and the Middle East. And yet, for those incredibly lucky few who do gain entry, life in America emerges as much more complex than most expected. The way life in the United States is portrayed, both by Somalis in the UAE and South Africa and by refugees and hopeful migrants the world over, is a particularly beguiling blend of reality and fantasy, built on both the real and exaggerated experiences of those who preceded them in North America and on the tales that trickle back across the oceans.

Unlike in the UAE and South Africa, where initial migration is made mostly by individuals, some of whom eventually bring their spouses and children, Somali migration to the United States is much more diverse. Somalis come to the United States mainly through humanitarian resettlement and family unification programs and thus include a large number of intact families. But even more consequential, these resettlement programs introduce Somalis to the essential yet all-encompassing world of public assistance, which produces unintended consequences that are shaping what it means to be Somali in the United States. New Somali refugees do not have the resources available in the UAE and South Africa, that is, the vibrant export–import sector dominated by Somalis in the UAE and the economically powerful Indian Muslim community in South Africa, offering employment, information, and charity. In the United States, basic subsistence, housing, and health needs of newcomers have to be met by the federal and state welfare institutions that accompany resettlement programs and the granting of refugee status. This initial refugee status shapes Somali settlement in the United States in major and irrevocable ways. In turn, Somalis are linked with the broad segment of the American poor, whose class, race, and even gender dynamics have historically been shaped by the ways they are "managed" by state institutions.

Somalis underscore how their migration experiences are shaped by gender dynamics produced by America's radically different socioeconomic opportunities and challenges. As such, this chapter pays particular attention to how Somalis navigate the new contours of gender, class, and race as they strive to maximize their and their families' life chances while safeguarding key components of their cultural tool kit.

The laws of eligibility for public assistance, which prioritize women with children, challenge the Somali dominant gender ideology. Moreover, the opportunities open to most refugees in the lowest tier of the American economy do little to challenge women's social location, while it forces men into occupations with little prestige. Finally, whereas entrepreneurial pursuits in the informal economic sectors were possible for Somali women in the UAE and South Africa, opportunities in such sectors are limited in an advanced economy such as that of the United States. We witness tensions between resource needs and identity constructions, between structural conditions and available strategies.

This chapter also critiques the celebratory tone often used in discussions of transnationalism and remittances, a particularly prominent concern for Somalis in the United States. The demands on Somalis who have migrated to the western hemisphere are greater than those felt on the African continent or even in the Middle East. I suggest that transnational demands undermine the settlement process and also feed a heightened nostalgia for the home country.

In the Land of Immigrants

Mahamed Abdullahi Sangub, a prominent Somali playwright who until recently lived in the Twin Cities, popularized the widely held belief that Somali women in the diaspora refuse their traditional and religiously ordained position as "housewives" deferential to their husbands. In *Qabyo,* a 1998 play satirizing the dynamic and novel challenges of Somali migrants and refugees in North America and Europe, a social worker comes into the house of a Somali couple; he only addresses the wife, who speaks better English, while the husband is present but is unable to follow the conversation. The social worker tells the wife, "In North America, the rights of women, dogs, children and cats are protected. . . . He cannot touch you . . . you are the head of the family and the checks will be in your name."[1] When I interviewed him in 2005, Sangub discussed how his migration expectations were so very off when compared to what he and other Somalis actually encountered in North America. Discussing the reception of this play by Somali audiences around the globe, he stated,

> It was the most watched play ever; every Somali I have met, including those in Somalia, say they have seen it. It was a small project, but it exploded because it touched a sore spot with people. Its inspiration was something I personally believed. I believed that if I went to America, I would make tons of money. I even believed that once I stayed there for three months, once I accumulate three or four million, I would then just return [home]. And this was something that they made people believe. . . . They [Americans] exaggerate everything. For example if they advertise a cream, they will make it something else, even though it does nothing; they advertise tablets, and they make it amazing but it really does nothing. So people have swallowed propaganda that these people released through mass media. I was convinced that I would become wealthy once I came here. So the play was about what I believed and what I have encountered here.

Needless to say, Sangub is far from alone in believing that everyone can make it in America. Sangub, a playwright and an artist, came to the United States in his late sixties at least, and without much English or any transferable skills. Even so, he insisted that he still imagined migration to America would lead to economic prosperity for him and his family. In retrospect, he attributes his optimism to a mirage that he thinks America sells to the rest of the world through its economic, political, and cultural global hegemony. This is, of course, a reading that Hollywood is America, feeding into the constructions of what America is for millions of people around the globe. But it is only after arriving in the United States that Sangub realizes that this is a mirage and that migration to America entails a far more complex mixture of great opportunities, as his play ultimately acknowledges, and also major challenges.

Promises of new opportunities for newcomers are also celebrated at American entry points such as Ellis Island. "Give me your tired, your poor, your huddled masses yearning to breathe free" has been inscribed at the base of the Statue of Liberty in New York since 1903.[2] In the poem, there is a line that refers to the Lady of Liberty's name as "Mother of Exiles." Though this statue is recent in the history of migration to the United States, it cements the United States as synonymous with migration but also with a haven capable of transforming the lives of those millions who come to this land.

The present American mosaic only emerged after centuries of contest and a slow, brutal shifting of racial, religious, and economic hierarchies. A key area of this contestation played out through immigration policies that determined who was eligible to come share this American dream, who was considered "worthy" of becoming a citizen.[3] Two laws most relevant for this study are the 1965 Immigration Act and the 1980 Refugee Act. The first act, passed at the height of the civil rights movement, eliminated the racially biased laws of the Immigration Act of 1924, a quota system for each region of the world based on census data of the groups already living in the country. The changes brought by this new legislation produced a seismic change in the American ethnic mosaic, resulting in a migration dominated by Asians and Latin Americans by the end of the 1990s.[4] This shift came about as a result of both the economic prosperity of post–World War II Europe, which diminished European migration to America, and the chain migration of persons mostly from Asia and Latin America, who brought children, spouses, and parents who have subsequently initiated their own sponsorship chains.[5]

Equally significant to the changing migration trends in the United States was the 1980 Refugee Act. President Jimmy Carter managed to pass this act, which reformed the country's narrow definition of a refugee as mostly applicable to those escaping from communism and adopted the United Nations's definition of a refugee. In the process, the bill established a far larger resettlement program aimed at refugees from around the world.

Most refugees arriving since 1980 have represented relatively new ethnic groups within the historiography of American migration studies, and this is particularly true for migrants and refugees from the African continent and the Muslim world. This refugee flow includes a vastly growing African migration, accounting for more than 5 percent of the legal immigrants in the United States for the year 2000.[6] This group is very diverse, though the census may at times not only lump them together as a category but sometimes even lump them with the African American population.[7] Somalis account for an important segment of the growing African presence in the United States, accounting for 5.5 percent of all refugees admitted to the United States between 1983 and 2000. That number has only grown; the African population as a whole nearly doubled in size between 2000 and 2010, from just over eight hundred thousand to more than 1.6 million.[8] And the Somali presence has grown accordingly: in the period between 2001 and 2005, Somalis accounted for 25.4 percent of all refugees entering the United States, with Cuba the only country to send more refugees during that time (31.4 percent).[9]

The majority of the Somali refugees in the United States come directly from refugee camps and urban centers in the Horn through UNHCR- and U.S. resettlement–facilitated programs, as detailed in chapter 1. Others come through family reunification, bringing their immediate family members (spouses, parents, and children). A small number, however, come through secondary migration from Europe or Canada, often making new asylum claims once inside the United States. Most Somalis land near wherever they already have family members or friends. Although there are small pockets of Somalis living in almost every state, Minnesota and Ohio currently boast the largest Somali communities in the United States.

Somali refugees have followed trends set by previous Southeast Asian refugees, such as the Vietnamese and Hmong, who resettled in the 1970s and 1980s. The large Somali refugee presence in Minnesota, for example, owes much to the strong voluntary agencies (known as volags) in the Midwest that settled earlier groups. These volags facilitate settlement, with earlier arrivals passing on the news of this resource to others who land in various states around the United States. Somalis thus access these volags, who cosponsor them and provide multiple types of assistance to refugees through their collaborations with government refugee resettlement agencies. These organizations, combined with Minnesota's exceptional economic prosperity in the early 1990s—a state the *Economist* called "the land of 10,000 opportunities"— acted as a magnet attracting Somalis to concentrate there.[10] New refugees reaped the experience and institutional expertise of previous refugee settlement programs as well as family and ethnic networks able to guide in navigating these programs.

Though the 2000 census listed only eleven thousand Somalis in the state, the Minnesota State Demographic Center put the number closer to twenty-five thousand using different measurements, including children enrolled in public schools.[11] Also, the 2010–13 American Community Survey gives an estimate of 21,120 Somalis in Minnesota.[12] If we use the underestimation of the 2000 census, it is probable that this population in 2013–14 is between forty thousand and fifty thousand. In fact, Somali community organizations in Minneapolis/St. Paul estimate the Somali population to be as high as seventy thousand. These figures are, of course, politically laden, and community organizations may inflate numbers for political purposes. These population estimation challenges also hold true for Ohio, where the Somali population is estimated at fifteen thousand to thirty thousand.

Using yearly statistical yearbooks of the Immigration and Naturalization Service, however, we can also get a glimpse of low migration numbers followed by an exponential increase in the two decades of the 1990s and 2000s. For example, the number of Somalis admitted for asylum was 277 in 1990, 3,555 in 1994, and 5,000 in 2001, but 13,331 at its peak in 2004. The most dramatic dip in these numbers is recorded in 2002, when only 237 Somalis arrived, following the September 11, 2001, terror attacks.[13]

The numbers from 1990 to 2010 add up to close to one hundred thousand Somalis, excluding those entering the United States through other programs such as work or diversity programs. These are really dismal in this case and won't significantly change the population estimates. For example, for the year 2000, the number of Somalis who came to the United States on an employment-based preference was eight.[14] Moreover, estimates exclude those born in the United States, who probably compose a significant number, given this community's high birthrate.

The analysis and conclusions presented on Somali settlement in the United States in the following sections represent reflections on the trajectory of this emerging community, its settlement experiences, and its relations with its diaspora.

In the Belly of the Welfare State

The majority of Somali refugees bring no monetary capital with them when they arrive and are thus completely dependent on family, friends, and resettlement agencies once they land at American ports.

U.S. Refugee Resettlement Assistance, often involving federal, state, and independent religious and civic organizations, thus plays a crucial role in the lives of Somali refugees in America. As the majority of these refugees are resettled from UNHCR-run camps in Kenya, the federal and state bodies responsible for refugee assistance have programs that ease these refugees' arrival and settle them within nearby Somali communities. The moment that refugees land in American airports, volunteer agencies, closely collaborating with the federal and state refugee resettlement agencies, receive them, often transporting them to housing already allocated for them. These volags essentially assume full responsibility for the initial settlement needs of newcomers, acting as guides to employment, providing educational and housing referrals, and also supporting newcomers in securing clothing, food, and other basic necessities.[15] The volags that were mentioned by interviewees and that remain instrumental for Somalis in the United States include Lutheran Immigrant and Refugee Services, Catholic Charities, International Rescue Committee, Community and Refugee Immigrant Services (CRIS), and Jewish Family and Children's Services. CRIS in Ohio and Lutheran Social Services of Minnesota are especially instrumental in Somali settlement support in these states.

Through the volags, new refugees whose legal status is guaranteed by their refugee-category admission access basic housing, financial, and health resources through two subsequent steps. For example, Ashkiro, who arrived in the 1990s with a large family, discussed how completely reliant on government assistance these refugees were:

> The government received us really well, because it was a good time to come. They provided us with good assistance, they moved us to two different homes and we are able to get assistance individually... every person was given an assistance of two hundred dollars cash and one hundred dollars in food stamps.

Bihi, a man in his thirties who came to Columbus around the same time as Ashkiro, reiterated the same experience with settlement agencies:

> When we came, Somalis who came before me were my biggest support because they knew things about the system that they needed to know, such as getting your license and state IDs. The first morning after we arrived, the family all got up really early for us to do everything that we needed to do. CRIS was able to resettle us, and they gave us a sum of money of about two hundred dollars per person, to help us with the initial settlement.

To cover these cash contributions, volags use funds from U.S. government Reception and Placement Programs as well as funds they raise from charity.[16] This cash assistance remains instrumental for migrant individuals and their families, which in some cases are very large.

Welfare provisions in the United States are also instrumental for new refugees. The Social Security Act enacted in 1935 forms the basis of public assistance programs. Though the evolution of this act over the last half-century is complex, most relevant for this study are the recent reforms the Clinton administration implemented in 1996, which promised to "end welfare as we know it." The Personal Responsibility and Work Opportunity Reconciliation Act (PRWORA) officially overhauled public assistance in America, ending the sixty-year guarantee of a safety net for the poor. Prior to this welfare reform, poor people were entitled to federally provided Aid to Families with Dependent Children (AFDC), which PRWORA replaced with state-run block grants, known as Temporary Assistance to Needy Families (TANF).

Clinton's reforms dramatically affected all those on the welfare roll, including noncitizen migrant and refugee populations. In the case of Minnesota, which hosts the largest Hmong and Somali refugee populations in the United States, for example, the Family Investment Program (MFIP) officially replaced AFDC in 1998. AFDC was restricted to single parents, mainly single mothers, and in rare cases was extended to two-parent households who might be unemployable for various reasons. MFIP continued these eligibility criteria, though changes were made to the conditions of access and also to the length of eligibility. Moreover, while single mothers on AFDC could previously collect welfare and participate in voluntary job training programs, the new MFIP program emphasizes the temporary nature of welfare provisions and promotes assisting workforce entry of both newcomers and the American-born on welfare. The central aim of the new program is in essence a gradual shift from government assistance to self-dependency.

In Ohio, TANF is implemented as Ohio Works First (OWF). The state implements compulsory self-sufficiency contracts; all work-eligible heads of household have to commit to seeking employment and closely working with state bodies in their search for jobs. Unlike MFIP's five-year limit, however, OWF has a thirty-six-month limit, with possible extension under extenuating circumstances requiring approval by each particular County Department of Job and Family Services. Thus Ohio's ultimate goal is to get as many people as possible off OWF, with the aim of encouraging people to pursue employment, without which sanctions are imposed on aid recipients. When a family reaches the program limit, the key sanction is to cut cash support. Cash receipt is the program state and federal governments mostly sanction, with food assistance and health care coverage often extended beyond the cash limits if a family falls under a certain income cap.

Newcomers, Poverty, and Public Assistance

Though government-run public assistance was and is still nonexistent in Somalia, and is also unknown to Somalis in the UAE and South Africa, its existence and its instrumental role in the survival of refugee families in the Western world are circulated widely. It is key to underscore that the availability of government assistance particular to the Western world is highly attractive for refugees caught in extremely precarious lives in refugee camps in Kenya or for those still living in Somalia. Similar to the earlier prestigious social location associated with the Jannaalayaal in the Middle East by those who remained in Somalia, the relative well-being of Somalis who found their footing in Western refugee-receiving countries is reinforced by the remittances to the families in Somalia, Kenya, and other Horn countries.[17]

Despite this prestige, the word for "welfare," *cayr*, now closely associated with Somalis in Europe, the United States, Canada, and Australia, translates as "destitute" in the Somali language. A family or community that is plagued by *cayr* has lost all its wealth, mostly as a result of a natural disaster, such as the droughts that historically wreaked havoc on nomadic Somalis. Thus the term now most exemplifying the Somali condition in the Western world has its origins in a nomadic life filled with uncertainties of nature; this current iteration is less a stigma and more an acknowledgment of the reality of Somali life in the West in the post–state collapse era.

Hodan, a woman in Minneapolis, expressed her image of America as a place of prosperity for all, contrasting it to the culture shock and sense of isolation that she confronted once she arrived:

> We previously thought that it [America] is a place where money can be made; people in Africa actually think that the ground is covered with money. When we got here, except for what you work, there is not much anyone gives you [laughter]. I came with a small child; there is no one to leave it with; you are isolated: except for me and that man I was married to, there were no other Muslims in the area where we lived. You cannot work and you cannot go to school. If you say "I have to work; I have left a family behind waiting for me to provide for them, or let me go to work," [my husband would say,] "You, working? You are not going to work; who is going to keep your child?" "You keep it the shift you are not working, and I work." "No," he says. I did not have any skills; I have finished only high school in Somalia, and he likewise; there was no other expertise that I had. I had a diploma in health care, but it was destroyed in the refugee camps when they burned down. So there are no skills that I can use to work here; and I did not know the English language well.

Hodan was aware of the availability of TANF in its abstract form, but her arrival in the Midwest, with its snow-capped landscape and majority white

Christian population, still led to culture shock. Hodan's narrative of being a mother lacking extended family support whose economic and educational pursuits were constrained was common among Somali women in Minnesota and Ohio. Though Hodan got support to feed her family, her claim that "there is not much anyone gives you" speaks to many Somalis' unrealistic expectations of what migration to America would entail. A key assumption within these expectations only applied to women, with a conviction that women's social location improves with migration.[18] But daily life in the Somali diaspora complicated their expectations, consistent with the complexity of the multiple demands and forces that shape the decision-making processes of refugee and migrant women.[19]

Somalis on public assistance shared many of the characteristics of Americans seeking government support. Most obviously, the majority of those on welfare programs are women with children whose lack of financial resources and recognized credentials limits their ability to meet their families' needs without outside help.[20] Illustrating this, Somalis on public assistance represented the highest proportion of eligible adults with no formal education in 2003: 29 percent of Somali MFIP participants had no formal education, a figure only surpassed by the Hmong. In 2010, only 32 percent of Somalis on MFIP had a high school diploma.[21] Education, closely tied to language skills, is key to migrants' chances for securing stable employment and any employment that pays above the minimum wage.[22] Of seven women on MFIP whom I interviewed in Minnesota, four had no formal education, one had completed elementary school, and two had dropped out of middle school. The four women with no schooling did not speak English, whereas the others had rudimentary English skills.

Time restrictions imposed on recipients by the 1996 reforms further exacerbate the difficulties beneficiaries confront in the skill and education development required for economic independence. For example, the Minnesota Department of Human Resources data show that those most likely to reach their time limit of sixty months' eligibility without having attained sufficient skills to secure above minimum wage often belong to disadvantaged groups, often minorities.[23] As Edin, Piven, and other scholars' work has shown, this setback for welfare recipients ultimately comes down to the incentives and disincentives of work and welfare.[24] The severe penalties to the assistance that these women receive for low-wage and unstable work force many of them to opt for assistance over insecure work.[25]

Somali elders in this study were also overwhelmingly reliant on public assistance, placing both elderly men and women in the same marginalized position. Migration has driven most Somalis older than sixty years of age to dependency on either SSI or MFIP, whereas they would have been working or been taken care of by their families were they in Somalia. Even those whose children are in the United States have to mostly rely on some form of government assistance, as their children and their grandchildren back home, as well as those in the United States, all have needs that must be met. Prior to migration, some men in this age group worked as small business owners, whereas others were in the military and one was a playwright and prominent member of the Somali national theater. The older women I interviewed in Minnesota and Ohio included a former midwife, a radio broadcaster, and many in petty trade. Some were also stay-at-home mothers. Some members of this group, such as the radio broadcaster and the midwife, expressed regret about the lack of recognition of their past training and reflected on their past professions and the important role they had occupied in their communities. But their discussions of these past accomplishments often dwelled on the dramatic collapse of their country and their condition as refugees in a nation where the language and culture are so drastically different from theirs that no options other than state support are open to them.

Benefits and Beneficiaries: Gender Power Recalibrated?

Unlike the perpetual search for visas in the UAE, or the constant sense of physical insecurity for Somalis in South Africa, gender dynamics emerge as the most salient topic in the Somali experience in America. Shifting relationships between men and women—alternately thrilling and terrifying—are invariably linked both to American culture in general and to the American welfare state in particular. Government welfare agencies have never existed in Somalia, and a citizen's relationship with the state did not include the provision of resources such as income and housing. Many Somalis have had some prior experience with receiving assistance, because stays in refugee camps included some dependency on international humanitarian organizations for basic rations and medical care. But this kind of international donor assistance in Dadaab and other camps, limited to bimonthly food donations and basic health care services, differed drastically from the public assistance programs available to poor households in America.[26]

All the people with whom I spoke acknowledged the crucial role that state and federal financial assistance plays in alleviating the financial insecurities refugee families confront in this new land. However, research participants also insisted that access to public assistance was not a neutral intervention but rather had gendered consequences for this particular community. There was consensus that access to welfare state resources had improved the position of Somali women. Most women claimed that the "system" had empowered them with the head-of-household designation. The "system" refers broadly to the institutions of government, everything from the welfare apparatus to the courts, and is a term now part and parcel of the Somali lexicon in the United States. The system was seen to strive to reverse gender roles within new refugee and migrant communities to bring them in line with the gender arrangements of the American mainstream. When I asked interviewees how this was accomplished, many of the male interviewees argued, "America is a country where women dominate." Ahmed, a university-educated Somali man working for a Minnesota social service agency, detailed the source of women's "ascendancy" within this new system:

> When families come here [United States], the head of the family is the woman by default. I can tell you the reasons why it is this way. The reason is that in the past, men would come to the house, abuse, and then leave. Many studies of people on public assistance found that these households are not stable. So since it is not stable, if the family file is registered under the man, for example, what happens? If the man leaves the house, and the case number is under his name, then the case has to be closed, and the mother has to file another application. This is a long process involving orientation, sitting in the office for a whole day, coming back for an interview! And she might not even get an interview for a week. So to avoid all that hassle ... nothing else changes except to add him or take him off the file. Since the person is a victim once, the government does not want to make her a victim again. So this is the reason behind this practice of putting women on the family file.

Women being granted the title of household head in fact doubly undermines the dominant Somali gender ideology: first, the man is no longer bringing in an adequate income for the family to survive without government assistance, and second, and more important, the state check is actually paid out to the woman, who can dictate how to spend it.

Safia, a female community activist, elaborated on the enormous consequences of this bureaucratic norm:

> In Somalia the father led the family, and the mother supported him. There was much mutual respect, which waned once people got here.... The responsibility that used to be on the father is now off his hands; because when they come here, and the family comes with kids, the mother and the kids are received by the state. The government settles them, provides for them, provides them with housing, takes care of all their needs, and assists the children to go to school. So as soon as the family arrives, there is no longer an economic need for the father. And when the family is registered, they are put under the mother's name. There are families where both are on the documents, but still in this country, most of the respect is given to the mother. So the father becomes someone with a limited role in the family.

Safia links migration with loss of mutual respect and family cohesion. The idea that a dramatic shift occurs in family dynamics with migration ultimately comes back to the shift in provision, control, and distribution of family resources, which in the Somali context were vested in the male breadwinner, with little acknowledgment of women's contributions to family survival, even if and when women worked.

This control of family resources was equated with respect, something that was usually the man's prerogative in Somalia. The wife's new role—as the primary family member dealing with state agencies when applying for housing, health care, and other services—contradicted the expected deference to the husband. Thus the male role was symbolically dealt another blow in the United States following the "idle" and "unproductive" period experienced in the refugee camps, where the family was in part fed by humanitarian agencies.[27] Migration in essence is presented as shaking the norms and the gendered patterns that were taken for granted prior to the Somali conflict and the mass displacement it triggered. Postmigration settlement in the United

States therefore challenges a core component of Somalis' cultural tool kit, which defined women and men in hierarchal fashion in terms of their economic roles in the family.

But welfare provisions, though very important, nevertheless leave many families living at substandard levels and even below the poverty threshold.[28] Some Somali women reported frequenting charity organizations, such as Food Shelf, that donate foodstuffs to low-income families, mainly bread, canned food, and sometimes meat. The poor resort to these organizations when their food stamps are insufficient to meet family needs. The inadequacy of public assistance for Somali families was particularly startling for those without subsidized housing. For instance, Nabila, a single mother of three young children between the ages of three and seven, reported receiving $621 cash and $415 in food stamps from MFIP. The two-bedroom apartment she shared with her three children, in a run-down, cockroach-filled building in a very poor area in the Phillips neighborhood of Minneapolis, cost her $670 per month. Her welfare check went to her landlord, and she had to raise the difference in rent through contributions from family and friends. She reported that she never had any money for transport or for other activities. She stopped driving because of lack of money for gas and car maintenance, which further hindered her ability to seek employment. Nabila eventually found a part-time babysitting position, permitting her to gain extra cash to supplement some government aid.

The persistent stress that women such as Nabila confronted in their attempts to make ends meet on public assistance was contrary to how certain Somalis discussed this arrangement. My conversations with numerous men often returned to the same concept: that public assistance is tantamount to financial independence for Somali women. Such claims are usually more reflective of how Somali men feel threatened in the United States rather than of real economic gains for women.[29]

Bihi, a young male activist and interpreter who also runs a community organization in Columbus, detailed how the particular rules of public assistance further alter relationships between men and women:

> One of the things that is shameful in Islam and to Muslims is a woman with children saying that she doesn't know where the father of her kids is. This is happening very much and it is becoming common mainly because of

financial hardships. For example if she wants to access health care coverage for her children, she needs to hide her husband. Her husband could be a truck driver or taxi driver or something else. If he is a taxi driver in this city, for example, there is no way he can afford to pay for all of their health care costs when he is making about one hundred dollars a night! So they need to do this to hide his income and work out ways to make ends meet.

Though disapproving of this practice, and bemoaning its "shameful" nature in religious and cultural terms, Bihi ultimately underscores the necessity and the inevitability of some women claiming to be single mothers while they are actually married. The socioeconomic position of such women and welfare regulations that penalize families even if the income from employment does not meet the family's needs necessitate bending the rules at times.

The Minnesota Department of Human Services data for 2003 give the "never married" category of Somalis on public assistance as 35 percent, while the "married but separated category" is at 32.3 percent. Given that only 3.6 percent of Somalis on welfare have no children, these "never married" and "married but separated" categories account for the bulk of Somalis with children on welfare.[30] Moreover, Somali MFIP recipients without children only account for 1 percent of those enrolled in this program for 2010, but the "never married" category with children was at 29 percent for the same year.[31] Despite the far more liberal norms of American culture, it is still uncommon for Somali women to have children outside of marriage. It is thus very likely that these "never married" and "married but separated" figures are widely inflated as a result of families' constrained economic options.

Contrary to the claims of empowerment for Somali women, a young woman who assists other Somali women in navigating the public assistance application process reported on its inherent humiliations. Discussing her experiences accompanying hundreds of women with children to the welfare offices in Ohio, this Ohio State University graduate reported,

> It is frustrating to go to the welfare office where there are so many people in need. It is really frustrating for them [the applicants], for me, and for the people that are working at that facility. At times, this is due to misunderstandings. But I mostly feel like my people are not respected and I feel

like they are treated negatively, just because of the way they look or their ethnicity.

The welfare office staff is said to talk to these Somali applicants as well as their interpreters in condescending ways. The frustration the applicants and those supporting them experience was not detailed much by other interviewees who portray public assistance as economic independence and empowerment for Somali women. The latter often focus on the acquisition of benefits, rarely mentioning the process that women and their children go through to prove their need for this support.

Despite feeling disgruntled with the ways that the state intrudes into the family in America, Somali men reluctantly accept the new rules of the welfare regime. They thus agree to live with women who control or disburse the welfare check, while loudly and vehemently condemning this new arrangement as contrary to Somali culture and religion. Abshir's epigraph to this chapter about the man dismayed that his wife's name is on the family welfare file hints at the humiliation that some men feel.[32] Amid the upheaval that public assistance creates, the irony is that the initial income these refugee families access through state and federal funding is inadequate for new families to make ends meet. Welfare regulations, restricted access, and the meager amounts ultimately necessitate combining work and welfare. The latter strategy is vital given the multiple familial obligations in this new land and obligations toward immediate and extended families left behind.

In this discussion of the role of government financial assistance within refugee families, we witness how American welfare policy affects Somali gender power dynamics. With the symbolic designation of women as heads of household, Somali women gain economic control of some of the family finances. Though Somali women have often worked in Somalia, this new designation, which is explicit in terms of how the welfare offices interact with the family, emerges as tantamount to contesting the role of men within Somali families and thus leads to new family tensions that we did not see in the UAE and South Africa. This phenomenon has also been reported within other Western countries (Canada, the United Kingdom, and Scandinavia) that provide welfare support to refugees.[33] Whether we can interpret new gender arrangements arising in these contexts as benefiting women by undermining

Somali cultural patriarchal relations is, however, complex. Women definitely gain by this new support, but their articulations of increasing demands on them by family in America as well as families left behind, and male resentment of the new rules, add to the challenges of settlement in a new country.

Refugees at Work

Let's now examine the position of Somali women and men in America's labor market, following their initial contact with and access to public assistance. The economic opportunities open to refugees and migrants in America are dictated in part by the skills, or the human capital, they have brought from their country of origin as well as the needs for such skills in their new country. In addition to a migrant's particular skills, his number of years of schooling remains a reliable predictor of his ability eventually to integrate into the labor market.[34] Consequently, the variety of educational attainment between different groups emerges as a key explanatory factor for the income disparity among immigrants.[35] A classic example in the immigrant literature illustrating the importance of prior skills and resources contrasts the experiences of Asian communities in the United States: the Indian, Japanese, and Filipinos versus Laotians, Cambodians, and Vietnamese.[36] The latter groups continue to confront many socioeconomic challenges. In addition to the differences in their modes of exit, with Southeast Asians being mostly refugees displaced by war in their countries of origin, the most significant difference between the two groups is education. As such, "23.3% of the total male population had a college degree or higher, 48.7% of Asian Indian men, 41.6% of Filipino men, and 35% of Chinese men were college graduates; among Cambodians, Hmong, and Laotians, only 3% of men had a college degree or higher."[37]

Historically, the jobs most available to refugees and many migrants are those in the lowest tier of the economy.[38] But over the last several decades, fewer and fewer of these jobs have been available. Refugees and migrants arriving since the 1980s have entered a very different economy, where the blue-collar manufacturing jobs that were a mainstay of America for multiple generations have evaporated, thanks to mechanization, globalization, and a host of other factors. The contraction in these sectors has impacted racial minorities more severely than any other group.[39] The latter shifts also benefited low-skilled women compared to low-skilled men.[40] Migrants and refugees thus join an American a society that is itself very divided, with a "high degree of polarization and segregation" between the poor and the rich.[41] In addition, refugees also join immigrant communities bifurcated into haves and have-nots, with those with the least education bringing the least transferable resources with them.[42] Because of these developments, newer arrivals fare worse in the labor market than earlier migrants, and the refugees among these newcomers are likely to face even poorer prospects.[43]

Somali Women: Contested "Empowerment"

Unlike in the UAE and South Africa, where the majority of Somali women work in the informal economy, Somalis in the United States mostly enter the formal sector, where they are wage laborers. This is mostly the result of the structure of the American economic system, where the types of informal economic niches that Somalis accessed in South Africa, for example, are limited. The initial legal status of Somalis as refugees who mostly come through U.S. government–assisted programs also further constrains their options.

With very limited education and English language skills, the employment opportunities open to Somali women in their thirties, forties, and fifties were mostly as janitors or as factory and assembly line workers. Somali women often work in the late afternoons and evenings cleaning private and public buildings throughout the Twin Cities or commuting to assembly plants or clothing warehouses in and around Columbus, Ohio. For single mothers with smaller children, these jobs are not as accessible because of child care commitments. Consequently, women in these sectors often have no children, have older children, or have spouses or relatives willing to watch the children during their absence. Because of the high concentration of immigrant and refugee women in these sectors, women gain limited language skills through their employment as they are supervised by other Somalis with better English language abilities, who act as intermediaries between employees and employers but who communicate with the women in their mother tongue. Their experiences can be compared to the experiences of women working in the Somali import–export sector in the UAE, for whom the acquisition of local language skills was hampered by their immersion into their own ethnic economies.

A small number of the Somali women with whom I talked found their way into the health care industry, working as nurse's aids or as attendants to the elderly. This sector is, of course, part and parcel of what Rhacel Parrenas has called the "international division of reproductive labor" or the "care chain," involving the concentration of migrant workers and women of color in sectors such as domestic work, child care, and elderly care.[44] Contrary to janitorial jobs, a position in the latter two categories requires some schooling; only those with some fluency in English and basic certification of at least a three- to six-month course in aid work secure employment in the elderly care sector, for example. Somali women going into this field are typically younger and often have some American education.

The Somali women I interviewed identified a consistent set of barriers to successful integration into the American labor market. For some, conforming to dress requirements was identified as a key challenge. Women with visible religious emblems, such as a *hijab* or *jalaabiib,* report being denied work in light of their dress. Interviewees as well as employment councilors working with refugee women report that employers sometimes view these clothes as a safety hazard. The majority of Somali women coming from East Africa wear jalaabiib, long, flowing dresses that cover the head and arms, going down to the ankles (Figure 4). Mohamud, a man employed in a hospital as a Somali cultural liaison officer, but who previously worked in factories with Somali women around the Twin Cities, confirmed this barrier:

> When Somalis went to these places [factories], the first issue they confront was regarding the safety issue. Girls working would encounter prejudices. Because the Somali man is wearing pants and a shirt, he could go anywhere.... But the girls, I would see girls wearing the jalaabiib, and we would be called in at times, those of us who spoke the language: "Tell this woman she cannot work in this place dressed this way; the machine will catch her clothing." And the women got discouraged, and they had major problems obtaining work.

A young Somali female interpreter in Columbus reiterated this challenge for women whose dress habits conflicted with employment requirements and regulations. When asked to comment on her experience of the employment sector for Somali women, Anab, who supports women in their job searches, replied:

> The thing about many of them [women] is that they don't have work experience and their attire is also an issue. I have really been having challenges with this. Many of these women may have found jobs in earlier days, but with the economic situation being very bad now, there is just too much competition for these positions. Their attire further exacerbates this, because some of them are unwilling to accept uniforms that may be required by the job due to religious reasons.

Women asked to alter their dress for their job requirements at times interpret this request as a way to undermine their religious piousness. Thus, though most employers don't require women to remove their head scarves, for example, requirements that impose any changes to the jilbaab that many women wear feed into some Somalis' belief that work and life in America threaten their religious identity. Such perception affects a core element of the identity and faith that these women used to survive a brutal war in their home country and a precarious life in refugee camps.[45]

In addition to the challenges stemming from Somali women's dress practices, some interviewees argued that the welfare apparatus itself is an obstacle to women's socioeconomic mobility. These argued that the welfare agencies' objective to push beneficiaries into the labor market often clashes with the educational and vocational needs of people on assistance, causing women to be pushed back on public assistance after short periods of employment. Asha, a woman working with community organizations, highlighted this dilemma using her sister's case to support her argument:

> When they [state welfare] paid her the first month, they called her in for a meeting and said, "You have to start working." I said, "This woman still does not know the directions to step out of the house." I am bringing her out of the house; I take her back to the house. This woman first needs to learn the basic A, B, Cs of English so that she can communicate with her supervisor. The woman [social worker] said, "No, my job is that she brings me proof that she has applied for many jobs, that she finds a job." "But how will she go

about this? She does not have a car; she does not know the bus system." So what happened to my poor sister? She started a janitorial job at a hotel, and she cries, saying her back is killing her. She works for eight hours in a hotel. That is very painful. She is twenty years old but she has a child. As a twenty-year-old, she is denied high school. Since she cannot attend high school, she has to work. She is told that she is too old for high school. So she goes to night school, ESL [English as a second language], and she goes exhausted. She is lucky that her mother watches the child for her. But this shows you how the system further destroys women who come here. So everything has its own consequences. America has not helped these women; if they said, "You are illiterate, first get some education and bring us proof that you have gone to school every day and that you have learned something," they [these women] would have gained. So the new society that they came to did not help them.

Asha further underscored how financial imperatives often override long-term investment in the human capital of many Somali women:

Work seems to be compulsory, since the man's income cannot cover the family. So the woman is forced to work. But though the woman works, she does not have sufficient education. Somali women are laboring in janitorial jobs [said with pity]. They all work in janitorial and assembly work. Because women came here illiterate, and continue to be illiterate . . . they are all earning eight dollars, six dollars in janitorial work; those who work in chicken factories go outside of town, in areas where there are factories. So though education is available in America, these individuals only think of working. This hinders many women who would have liked to get some education. I have seen many in that situation.

The constraints that these Somali women experience in the American labor force are in part rooted in their backgrounds and their low educational attainment in the home country. In addition, however, U.S. government welfare policies at times hinder the economic prospects of refugees as well as the native-born poor.[46] The goal of getting people off of welfare faster has the unintended consequence of further marginalizing newcomers and even potentially prolonging their need for public support. Of course, the resource limitations the states and counties confront in meeting the needs of the poor require acknowledgment. But the long-term costs of not supporting women's educational and skill development to get off welfare ultimately outweigh any savings from pushing women into the workforce for short stints.

Some of the Somali women who lived in the United States for five to ten years could still barely communicate in English, rendering employment paying above the minimum wage near-impossible. The instructors in an ESL program with whom I spoke in the Twin Cities reported that many students cycled through their program, often coming in and then dropping out. Though structural barriers might not be the sole factor explaining the poor language skills of these refugee women, such barriers represent systemic challenges for newcomers in their search for viable skills and successful integration into the mainstream labor force.[47]

High fertility rates also delay language acquisition for some Somali women and thus their labor force participation. In the case of three women I interviewed who had been in the United States between eight and ten years and could still barely communicate in English, language classes were often disrupted by childbirth. It was not uncommon to hear women report that they had attended ESL classes on and off for five or six years but still had difficulty communicating in English. Hodan, who previously lived in Nairobi, reported speaking more English when she first arrived in America than she did seven years later. She came to the United States with one daughter in 1998 but had two more children and one miscarriage between 1998 and 2001, when she separated from her husband. She had never attended English classes, had worked as a cleaner for only a few months in 1999, and has been on some form of public assistance ever since. Another woman, Farhiya, a thirty-two-year-old woman with five children, reported that she attended English classes for only two months when she first arrived in the United States in 1996, then worked as a kitchen helper for a few months just before she got married; she has had five children in less than a decade and has not worked since. This woman, who exhausted her five years of cash eligibility, was exempted from the requirement to show proof of employment search as a result of health issues from the Somali civil war. Women without such exemption, however, are required to secure employment after their five years of eligibility and lose their cash benefits once they reach their limit.

Beyond the disruptions of childbirth itself, the ceaseless demands of children and a lack of help with reproductive labor are further impediments to steady employment. The definition of the nuclear family used by the refugee resettlement process means that those accepted for resettlement only include a husband and wife and their biological children. But Somali definitions of family always included siblings and cousins, and a household nearly always consisted of multiple relatives, including women, who participated in child care and housework. These extended female family members played a vital role in women's economic pursuits in Somalia, and their absence is a key challenge for Somali women in their employment pursuits in the diaspora. Contrary to the situation in South Africa, where even Somali mothers at the lowest tier of the economy could hire South African, Zimbabwean, or other African migrants to attend to their children, Somali women in Minnesota and Ohio who work in low-paying sectors cannot afford private child care and still meet their family's needs. These women still search for and sometimes access government-subsidized child care programs. The latter, combined with the low wages for the few jobs these women secure, means that some Somali mothers opt to stay on public assistance and remain full-time stay-at-home mothers, at least until they exhaust their eligibility.

Unlike women with children, younger women in their twenties or early thirties whom I interviewed rarely worked in the janitorial sector. Being younger means that their ability to learn the English language is easier than it is for their older compatriots. These women found it easier to enter the service industry, for example, by working as cashiers in the chain stores that dot Minnesota and Ohio. Some of these women also worked in assembly plants while continuing their education. These young women's dress style was often distinct from the dress of the older generation: the jilbaab was replaced with a long-sleeved shirt, long skirt, and hijab over the hair. The latter accommodation to dress that is more acceptable to employers was also a sign of how younger refugees' settlement is aided by their age. Of the eleven women in their twenties or early thirties whom I interviewed in Minnesota and Ohio, only one collected SSI, for a health-related condition, and none collected MFIP or OWF. The rest either worked or combined work and school.

Some young women who did not acquire formal education in Somalia also took advantage of the available educational opportunities for younger refugees. Some with limited education at times secured decent-paying work within the community. For example, Dega, a twenty-seven-year-old woman from a rural background who had no formal education in Somalia and who barely spoke any English, recounted that she babysat for her aunt who has six children and for other mothers in the neighborhood who attended ESL classes as a condition of their welfare eligibility. Dega also worked as a cleaner in the evenings and reported making more than $30,000 in combined income from her two jobs. This woman built a house and also bought a truck for her family back in northern Somalia. Another young woman who had no formal education in Somalia but who attended adult education in Minneapolis worked for a major bank doing data entry, earning $11 an hour. These women were economically independent, despite coming to America with very low human capital. But their age permitted them to seize opportunities in the labor market. Clearly, then, women without children, even those with very little education, can take advantage of economic opportunities unavailable to women with young children. This flexibility was in fact also true for younger women in the UAE and South Africa. But married women in South Africa also pursued work (hawker, small stores) with the support of hired help that was not as accessible for Somali mothers in the UAE or the United States.

The postmigration opportunities for women as income earners through either formal employment, as discussed later, or public assistance in the American context present new challenges. As we have seen, women working mostly in the informal sector in Somalia, the UAE, and South Africa did not generate the types of gender conflict that we see in the United States. It is therefore clear that migration to a country where sociocultural practices greatly differ from those of the home country and where a previously unknown welfare apparatus plays a dominant role in the family finances of refugees creates an unintended disruption to the Somali gender order. Concerns about this gender disruption are most often articulated by Somali men.

Somali Men: Labor Market Experiences

I documented a handful of doctors, lawyers, and professors who constituted the country's tiny population of upper-middle-class Somalis now living in Minnesota and Ohio. These represent the Somali elite, who own their own homes and who typically stand apart from the refugee Somali majority in both Minnesota and Ohio. These are employed in their fields and are well integrated into larger American society in terms of language, residential areas, and income levels. Many in this group remain very active in facilitating the settlement of the larger refugee population that has arrived since the mid-1990s, and they are at the forefront in bridging the gaps that newcomers confront in areas such as public health, education, and the American political process, such as voting. Though very important, these professionals only number in the hundreds at most, and thus their experiences are not representative of the experiences of the estimated fifty thousand to seventy thousand Somali refugees living in Minnesota and Ohio.

Contrary to the elite group of Somali professionals, others with college education often worked in the social service sector serving the Somali community. Many of these social workers, including one community leader with a PhD from a major research university in the United States, were underemployed and had salaries not commensurate with their educational levels. For example, one interviewee in Minneapolis who had an accounting degree from Somalia worked as an employment counselor for a Somali community organization.

With the arrival of thousands of Somali refugees from Kenyan camps starting in the mid-1990s, many of the first waves of Somalis around the United States moved to Minnesota and Ohio to fill the numerous employment opportunities in the social service sector. These earlier migrants and refugees often worked as interpreters, employment and health counselors, and teacher assistants. Of twelve service providers I interviewed in Minnesota, six came to the United States in the 1970s and 1980s. Of these, one man held a PhD from an American university, whereas two men and one woman had MA degrees from American universities. In Ohio the situation was similar, with many of those having university educations clustered in interpretation, teacher assistance, and cultural brokering in the social service sector. Thus Somalis working in community organizations were often some of the highest educated members of the community.

As I've discussed in earlier sections of this chapter, U.S. resettlement agencies dispersed the refugees to different states around the country. However, many of these refugees eventually found their way to Minnesota, where they had family or friends. Similar to the community connections and networks that anchored employment searches in the UAE and South Africa, networks with other Somalis who preceded them enabled newcomers to secure employment. However, "the help ethnic networks can provide for securing employment in this situation tends to be constrained by the kinds of jobs already held by more established members of the community."[48] Many—including university graduates like Abdiwahab, who found a job in a meat processing plant in the mid-1990s—accepted what the market offered and started working in low-paying, low-prestige sectors such as in assembly plants. The chain continues to this day, with many Somali adult newcomers starting their entry into the labor market in meat processing and assembly plants. Because most factories are located on the outskirts of major cities, some job seekers either move to small towns closer to these plants or commute. In the Twin Cities, for example, plants in towns such as St. Cloud, Faribault, Anoka, and Marshall employ thousands of Somalis, along with Mexicans, Liberians, and members of other refugee and migrant groups.

Somali male interviewees working in the meat processing plants dwelled on their initial disbelief at working in the meat industry, a sector that had negative clan connotations in Somalia. Minority clans who were looked down on and discriminated against in Somalia were associated with this type of work, though in reality poor people of all clans performed these jobs.[49] The grueling physical toll meat processing plant work takes offered a particularly brutal contrast with refugees' long-held dreams of what was possible in America. To bridge the chasm between their expectations of migration and their far more bleak reality, Somali men working in a chicken processing plant in St. Cloud recounted how they mocked each other. In a small Somali café close to the plant, a handful of men who were working the evening shift had coffee with me and told me how they satirized their situation: one man might say to another, "hey, you, what will you tell the women you will court once you return to Africa? That you worked in the most renowned chicken factory in Minnesota? That you worked in an assembly line manipulating a flying chicken coming your way, cutting it dexterously this or that way?" Self-deprecating statements were very common among the half dozen men with whom I had informal conversations at this café, with a keen acknowledgment of their American socioeconomic reality and the imperative to take any job available.

The salaries these meat processing plants paid were often sufficient for one- or two-person families but not for most men and women who had to provide for large families. As we have seen, the majority of Somali families' economic obligations go beyond their immediate members in the United States, as almost all Somalis remit money to their families back in the Horn. Thus the low salaries paid by meat processing plants in Minnesota, for example, are inadequate to fulfill the full breadth of a family's economic obligations. Some of the strategies Somalis in the UAE and South Africa use to reduce their living costs—renting out rooms to other families—are uncommon in America, with landlords and community organizations explicitly discouraging this practice on health and safety grounds. The information sessions provided to refugees before and after resettlement portray this as impermissible. These newcomers fear state scrutiny and penalties for breaking tenancy laws, a fear that was never mentioned in the UAE and South Africa.

With the lack of the cost-saving methods that we documented in the case of the UAE and South Africa, reliance on different forms of public assistance emerges as a common form of making ends meet. But in extreme cases, eligibility regulations also necessitate that families resort to arranging their lives to meet these requirements. I heard that women who work or whose husbands work in the meat processing plants or other factories opted to claim single-mother status to qualify for public assistance. The incomes that families earned from low-skilled work supplemented aid such as food stamps and cash assistance, when qualification for the latter was still possible. In these situations, some couples reported their actual incomes and collected what they were eligible for based on their total family earnings. But in a minority of cases, couples claimed to be separated when they were still married and living together. In the latter cases, women would collect assistance as if they were single mothers separated from the fathers of their children, as was highlighted earlier.

It is no surprise, then, that a combination of welfare and work is the norm for most Somali families, in complete contrast to Somalis in the UAE and South Africa, where the role of state institutions in economic survival is nonexistent, where welfare is not an option, but where religious and ethnic membership supports those unable to provide fully for themselves. In contrast to the latter, then, Somali families who can cover all their expenses are a minority in America. If nothing else, the families depend on the state for health care (usually in the form of Medicaid) and housing (either via Section 8 vouchers or government-subsidized apartments). As such, the United States census data for Somalis in Minnesota show that 62.6 percent of this community accesses public health services, while 20.1 percent had no health care coverage, with only 19.8 percent able to purchase private health insurance.[50]

Hibak, a key informant working as an employment counselor in Minneapolis, explained the necessity of government support for family survival:

> When the man is uneducated, and he is working in odd jobs, the most he can earn for the family is a thousand dollars. When the family has six, seven kids, plus the father and the mother, and the rent alone is a thousand dollars, the mother is obligated to ask for some kind of assistance from the state. So that is often why they go on welfare, because the income that the family earns cannot cover their entire expenses.

The figures that Hibak gives are only illustrative and not applicable to all men. But her argument that those men earning low wages are unable to cover the combined costs of housing, health care, child care, and other family needs is applicable to the majority of the Somali refugees in the United States. For instance, two men I interviewed in the Twin Cities had wives who worked, one in an assembly plant for a company that made boxes and the other part-time in a clothing store. Both these families still collected some public assistance because of their low incomes. Some men also reported that their wives cared for small children at home. Another man who worked as a school bus driver reported that his wife previously worked in an assembly plant but that he asked her to stop to care for their three young children full time. This family had subsidized housing and still received health care coverage and food stamps from the state.

Clearly the need for public assistance is an indication that the man, who traditionally has the responsibility to provide for his family, is no longer able to assume this role alone but instead requires either government support in the form of cash, food stamps, subsidized housing, or health care or the wife's earnings, and often a combination of the two. Stretching low incomes to meet multiple needs has created much stress for these families. For instance, Omar, whom I interviewed in St. Cloud, reported that his wife once worked at the same chicken plant he did but had recently quit her job in the late stages of pregnancy. Once she stopped working, she demanded that he pay the rent for the house, which was just over $600 a month, in addition to $500 a month for food and utilities. He protested, saying that was too much for him, as he also had to support another wife and five children in Kenya. In addition, he needed to pay for his own car insurance and gas, necessities for his work. All this was to come from his income of about $1,500 per month. He claimed that he told his wife he would provide part of the rent as well as the food and utility costs but that she should go on public assistance to cover the difference. The wife refused this arrangement, arguing that it was his religious obligation to provide for the family. This family eventually separated. The wife ended up collecting public assistance, though Omar reported that he still provided part of the rent and also some cash for her.

This kind of conflict was said to be common among Somalis, as resource distribution became more prevalent in the new country. But the men I interviewed often focused more on women's lack of accommodation of the new reality, where the male income does not suffice to meet the needs of the family in America and family members left behind. Blaming the new institutions Somali men encounter in the United States that provide women and children assistance as well as Somali women who are said to feel empowered by these institutions is one significant way that men protest against what they see as a demotion of their social status in America.

Unlike those working in the meat processing plants discussed earlier, which serve as an entry point for many Somali newcomers to Minnesota, Somalis in Ohio were clustered in clothing warehouses located on the outskirts of Columbus. Abdirashad, a Somali teacher in middle school, put it this way:

> This city, this state, is actually known for its working class; it's a warehouse state! [Geographically] it is a transit for trucks from east to west, exchanging [loading and unloading new goods] here as well. . . . For many Somalis, even this industry is difficult because they don't know how to drive and they do

not have a license, they don't know the roads and how to get around. Because of all the obstacles it seems that they have no choice but to turn back to the government for assistance.

Stacking shelves in a warehouse did not carry the same cultural stigma that chopping up chickens did; yet the essential problems were quite similar for the men scattered across Ohio. Although they were grateful for work, their earnings were rarely adequate for meeting their families' economic needs. Similar to women's labor force participation, age was a key factor in male labor participation. The younger men with whom I spoke (in their twenties or thirties) were either in school full time or worked in a wider array of jobs, especially as security guards, car rental agents, or cashiers. Some also opted for assembly plants.

Some of these young men mentioned that they experienced more discrimination because of the September 11 attacks on the United States and found it harder to secure stable employment. Sa'ad, a community activist in Columbus, Ohio, who works with youths, argued in 2010 that the community was currently confronting racial profiling:

> One of the big issues is that youngsters feel they are being targeted because they are African American, black, or whatever it is. This is a big issue we learned through our engagement with the youngsters. We cannot be sure, but people feel they are profiled when going through the airports by the TSA or Border Protection when they return from trips to other parts of the world.

Younger men in their teens and twenties were most likely to bring up issues of racial profiling and Islamaphobia. For example, the terrorist attacks on Kenya's Westgate Mall in September 2013, triggered a media frenzy in ascertaining whether Somali youths from Minnesota were involved. MPR's "Renewed Focus on the Somali Community" and Public Radio International's headline of "An Unwelcome Spotlight Falls on Minnesota's Somali Community because of Nairobi Attack" are examples of this negative media attention and the apprehension that this community felt following the attacks.[51] This apprehension has become the norm in the post-9/11 scrutiny of Muslims in the United States, but especially of groups like Somalis, whose transnational relations with the home country locate them within local and global discourses of America's War on Terror. A more recent *Time* magazine opinion sums up young Somali men's sense of being found guilty until proven innocent. Jessica Stern's claim that "We Need to Worry about Somali Terrorists in the U.S." served to increase the profiling of Somalis as potential terrorists.[52] Such scrutiny has increased since 2008, when around two dozen young Somali men left Minnesota to join al-Shabaab, now listed as a terrorist group based in Somalia.[53] This scrutiny is disconcerting for many young men and women, who now feel that being a Muslim in America is to be misunderstood and stigmatized. Nadine Naber's discussion of how "Arab Americans are racialized according to religion (Islam)" is very relevant for Somalis.[54] Thus Somalis' "Arab" identity and their Islamic faith, both assets in the UAE, become bases for their otherness in the American context, an otherness further exacerbated by their racialization as black Africans.

Some Somalis' articulation of racial and religious discrimination also coincides with a downturn in the U.S. economy since 2008, which has often translated to unstable, more seasonal employment. Somali employment counselors reported high rates of unemployment in this community. The high turnover inherent to the types of jobs in which refugee and immigrant communities were clustered partly explains this unemployment. Although no data are available on exact labor participation rates for Somalis, their employment experiences are possibly consistent with the experiences of other refugee groups with similar educational levels: "Southeast Asian refugees are persistently 10 to 15 percentage points less likely to be in the labor force than the U.S. population. Once in the labor force, like other ethnic minorities, they also experience considerably higher levels of unemployment."[55] More recent research also shows that "Southeast Asians—primarily Vietnamese, Lao, Hmong, and Cambodian immigrants—represent the largest per capita race or ethnic group in the country receiving public assistance."[56]

This economic marginalization holds true for Somalis in America, as the earnings of the majority of these families remain secondary to state assistance. As a result, a vast swath of this community is both marginal and reliant on public assistance. Although women contributed to family income in Somalia, their contributions were often viewed as marginal compared to the male breadwinner's income.[57] Dominant gender ideology in Somalia placed men in a superior social location, regardless of their socioeconomic positions vis-à-vis women.[58] Women's position of working in the lower tiers of the labor market in the American setting was nonetheless consistent with the marginal position women occupied in Somalia, whereas male occupations in meat processing plants, for example, were perceived as a demotion to a stigmatized work sector. We see how these occupations become tangled in perceptions of self and in the balance of power within the family. Male income contributions have been made secondary in the American context, superseded in importance by public assistance. This marginal socioeconomic location has led a small number in this community to try to increase their incomes through self-employment.

Self-Employment

Research shows that migrants have higher tendencies to work for themselves than the native population.[59] Though most refugees bring less human capital than some migrants, self-employment is more common for Somali women, who own women's clothing stores throughout the Twin Cities and Columbus (Figure 19). As we have seen in the UAE and South Africa, Somalis establish small shopping complexes in all the countries in which they settle. Minneapolis has a few such complexes, including Al Karama Cedar Mall, the Village Market (known as Mall 24), and Karmel Mall, and in Columbus, Ohio, are Global Mall and Benadir Mall. Stores in these malls are predominantly owned and run by women and specialize in women's fashion and home decorations. The stores within these malls run by men are mostly money transfer companies *(hawaalado),* halal meat and grocery stores, restaurants, and shops selling music or religious books and tapes (Figure 20). This gender division is found throughout Somali diaspora communities. As such, out of about twenty restaurants in the Twin Cities, only two are female owned and run. Conversely, over 80 percent of stores in the Karmel Mall sell women's apparel and are women owned.

Two women who own small stores in Karmel in Minneapolis suggested that clothing stores, *bacadlayaal,* were in fact a male-dominated specialty in Somalia. However, the women reported that this has changed since the civil war, with women taking over the sector, at least in the diaspora. This

FIGURE 19. A Somali shopping mall in Minneapolis, Minnesota.

FIGURE 20. Ethnic malls as one-stop service centers. Minneapolis, Minnesota.

is consistent with a trend I also noticed on my trips to Kenya over the last decade, where women dominate small clothing stores in Somali enclaves, even though the wholesalers who import and distribute the goods are mostly men. To account for this phenomenon, the two women with whom I spoke at Karmel Mall suggested this sector was not as profitable in the diaspora as it was in Somalia, with men no longer caring to be involved in businesses that require long hours of work for little profit. Older women who were used to working back in Somalia but had difficulty securing formal employment in mainstream sectors dominate this sector to stay active, even if profits are small.

Most of these Somali businesswomen do not seek credit from mainstream banks because of Islam's prohibition on paying or receiving interest. But these women would have had much difficulty securing such loans, as they have very limited assets and lack the skill to put together the business plans major lenders require. Regardless of this, women often find the capital to start small enterprises. Ambaro, a woman in her late fifties who runs a clothing store in Karmel Mall informed me that she started very small, often taking merchandise from other Somali women on credit and then paying them back once she sold the goods. She eventually saved enough money to fill most of the store but continued to get merchandise on credit (Figures 21 and 22). In a sense, this model of small business ownership that Somalis in the United States use is a smaller-scale model of that Somalis in South Africa practice, though the clientele and the networks from which they draw are more expansive in the latter case compared to in the United States. Other women also informed me that they joined rotating credit associations where they collected a lump sum of money to launch the business and then paid it back in small installments. Some of the money used to open these businesses is also raised through family and friends.[60]

These small businesses are located in areas where Somalis are clustered and serve both economic and social purposes in the community. They provide many of the specific ethnic dietary and dress requirements of Somali Muslims living in a Western country. But catering only to Somalis limits their market reach and thus their profit margins. Most Somali businesses are clustered in areas of Minneapolis and Columbus where the Somali community is concentrated and are small-scale businesses run by one or two people

FIGURE 21. Early-morning lull. Cedar–Riverside neighborhood, Minneapolis, Minnesota.

FIGURE 22. All that glitters is not gold: a shop in Karmel Mall. Minneapolis, Minnesota.

FIGURE 23. A halal market in Karmel Mall. Minneapolis, Minnesota.

within the same family, rarely employing other workers. These restaurants, clothing stores, and halal meat markets serve exclusively Somalis and rarely attract mainstream American clients, thus limiting economic flow from the mainstream community (Figure 23).

More important, I estimate that these business opportunities permit about 500 to 1,000 Somali refugees to be involved in 250 to 500 businesses in Minnesota and about half that number in Ohio.[61] Though just an estimate, this could represent just over 3 percent of Minnesota's Somali population, even if we use the low end of recent population estimates of about twenty-one thousand.[62] Despite the relatively small number of jobs that these businesses create for the community, they are vital for women and some men, who find income-earning opportunities in these Somali sectors where they do not confront language barriers (serving Somali-speaking clientele) and new dress requirements.

However, a lack of expertise in business planning and financial projection, market saturation, and avoidance of mainstream financial institutions all result in isolation and high rates of failure among Somali business ventures.[63] Moreover, Somalis who are self-employed in the United States represent a minority when compared to South Africa and the UAE, where self-employment is the *only option* for the majority of the Somali population. I would argue that this is the case even when we include those involved with economic transactions that are "off the books," comparable to what Venkatesh finds in poor African American neighborhoods.[64] Thus services, from child care to tailoring to food catering and carpet cleaning, that some Somalis provide to the larger community are provided without any set business address or official recording of the economic transactions. These economic services are often performed in concert with more formal employment or as an additional source of income for families getting government assistance.

In conclusion, Somalis in Minnesota and Ohio constantly strategize how to survive in their new land, using a combination of working for themselves, working for others, and collecting public assistance. Despite these perpetual efforts, the 2000 U.S. Census found that Somalis had the highest poverty rate of all groups in the United States. The poverty rate among refugee groups such as Somalis and Hmong was in fact double that of the poorest groups within the native-born population. The highest poverty rates in the United

States were among blacks and Hispanics, with 24.1 percent and 21.8 percent poverty rates, respectively.[65] Somalis had double this poverty rate, with 59.1 percent of Somalis earning incomes below the poverty threshold. That rate of poverty is largely unchanged a decade later, with 57.7 percent of all Somali families living in poverty according to 2010–13 data.[66] These figures illustrate the socioeconomic position of Somalis and their need for creative ways to enhance their sources of income and their access to public support, not only to meet their subsistence needs, but also to secure adequate housing for their families.

Affordable Housing: Neighborhoods and Neighbors

Many Somali families live in subsidized housing located in inner-city neighborhoods in the Twin Cities (Figure 24). Of all MFIP recipients, "Somalis had the largest proportion of cases with housing subsidy, 67 percent for 2003 and 60.7 percent in 2010."[67] In comparison, 33.7 percent of African Americans and 32.8 percent of Hmong on MFIP had subsidized housing.[68] These findings testify to the marginal position Somali refugee families currently occupy within the greater Minnesota community and the challenges these families face.[69] These factors also lead to the necessity for some form of public assistance for many Somali families, a finding consistent with the experience of refugee groups in other states.[70]

Consequently, most refugee new arrivals seek affordable housing from the state once they settle down. The quest for affordable housing is shared among the poor. As a result, the search for this most basic of human needs brings two of America's most marginal groups—refugees and the native poor—into intimate contact, in neighborhoods, schools, and public assistance offices.

An example demonstrating the urgency of the search for housing was highlighted in a recent incident in Columbus, Ohio, when the Mount Hermon Missionary Baptist Church sponsored an information session allowing individuals an opportunity to put their names down for subsidized housing. The *Columbus Dispatch* reported:

> Columbus police used pepper spray to control and disperse a larger-than-expected crowd of people who had gathered at a Northeast Side church yesterday to sign up for a subsidized-housing waiting list.

FIGURE 24. Cedar–Riverside high-rises: first home to generations of new and old migrants and refugees. Minneapolis, Minnesota.

Authorities said the crowd that gathered at Mount Hermon Missionary Baptist Church, 2283 Sunbury Rd., numbered more than 1,000 and consisted mostly of local Somalis.[71]

That a crowd of more than a thousand people showed up with the hope of be among the two hundred people permitted on this housing waiting list is a potent testimony to Somali migrants' need for housing. Market-rate rentals in both states, often affordable for those with stable and well-paying jobs, are often out of reach of those surviving on government support or those combining low-wage work and public assistance. As such, securing subsidized housing, which can accommodate the fluctuating incomes of these new refugees, guarantees that their rental costs remain affordable in times when they may be struggling.

Ida, an activist working with the Somali community in Columbus, who had a daughter in her twenties still living with her, discussed the importance of housing subsidies for all refugees. I interviewed Ida in her apartment located in the suburbs of Columbus, an apartment that was tidy and elegantly decorated with IKEA furniture. As an assistant teacher, Ida reported that her income from working with new refugee students in Columbus did not permit her to afford market-price rent. She therefore applied for and eventually got a Section 8 housing voucher. These vouchers permit individuals and families to seek rental units anywhere they choose, for which they pay 30 percent of their incomes. In this program, Ida paid $180 toward her rent, with the rest of the $600 market-price cost shouldered by the government. Tenants of Section 8 housing are required to report any changes to their incomes to the local Public Housing Agency to ensure the continuation of the subsidy. Getting a Section 8 voucher is not guaranteed, however, and can take years of waiting. Still, for Somalis, like most other refugees and native-born low-income families, it remains preferable to public housing, which is often in inner-city neighborhoods with high crime and poverty rates. In 2013, approximately 2.1 million families received Section 8 vouchers around the country; that figure is nowhere near the number of people in the United States needing housing subsidies.

Though desiring and aggressively pursuing these subsidies when they can, Somalis still recognized the class and racial dimensions of poverty in

America. Roble, a Somali high school teacher who himself owns a home in the suburbs of Columbus, discussed what he viewed as an unintended consequence confronted by Somalis living in public housing:

> Many Somalis believe that they are riding a high horse and accomplished something great once they receive government housing. For these people it's a great assistance as it allows them to afford the rent. But when you look at it closely, it has become a great disadvantage for them. This is especially so for their children and the way these kids are being reared and the negative part of the [American] culture they are being exposed to.

Somali men were particularly likely to disparage public housing, despite acknowledging the need for such housing for families unable to afford market-rate prices. Another man, Yusuf, a tall, gray-haired man in his mid-fifties whom I interviewed in the Global Market in Columbus and a respected leader in the Somali community in Ohio, recounted how he himself worked for the post office and also lived in Section 8 housing. He lamented what he viewed as the downside of living in public housing:

> It [public housing] is something that always puts the family values down. A Somali saying goes, "Once a frog said, if water is really wonderful, I don't want it reaching my lips, as I have my bottom immersed in it for 24 hours!" So if public housing is there to uplift people, it would have done so for people who came here before us and people who were born in this country.

Yusuf is referring to the poor African Americans living in public housing in Columbus. Yusuf argues that public housing provides short-term relief for Somali families but potentially creates a long-term nightmare. Similarly, Roble's reference to "the negative part of the [American] culture" is an implicit reference to poor African Americans. Similar to those in South Africa, Somalis in the United States persistently attempt to distinguish themselves from the native-born blacks. The racial inferiority that Somalis assigned to the Somali Bantu minority mentioned in chapter 1 is extended to African Americans. Many Somalis thus accept and reproduce the racialization of African Americans, while rejecting such racialization for themselves.

Somalis' attempt to distinguish themselves from African Americans is a common feature of discourses asserting the "cultural distinctiveness" of African and Caribbean migrants vis-à-vis pathologized African Americans, as illustrated by Jemima Pierre's work,[72] and this is consistent with how Somalis distinguished themselves from black South Africans, the group most excluded and racialized in that country.

But despite this resistance, Somalis' position as refugees, Muslims, and poor within the United States locates them with the groups who are most marginalized. Indeed, Somalis and African Americans are often lumped together by bureaucratic institutions. But Somalis see vast differences in culture, language, and race between themselves and African Americans. Such a gulf often produces distrust between the new Somali community and the mostly black and poor American, inner-city residents in subsidized housing.

Notice how the social status of Somalis in the United States is different from that of Somalis in the UAE and South Africa. The latter two cases showed how Somalis' socioeconomic and racial and religious locations straddled majority and minority groups, with Islam and their concentration in ethnic economic niches allowing Somalis to physically, socioeconomically, and symbolically separate themselves from those at the bottom of the socioeconomic ladder in those contexts. But in America, their religion does not grant them the networks it did for those in the UAE, nor does their socioeconomic location and religious identity separate them from poor native blacks, as they did in the South African case.

Lamenting the consequences of the Somalis' entry into public housing, several interviewees in Columbus cited Capital Park to illustrate the dangers they identified with inner-city America. This is a residential area previously exclusively housing African Americans, but over the last decade, it has turned into a Somali neighborhood. The arrival of a few Somali families in the late 1990s was followed by a miniature version of chain migration. Those early Somalis would tell their friends and extended family members as soon as a unit became available in the neighborhood; by 2010, a long waiting list of Somalis searching for public housing replaced the previous concentration of African American residents. Such displacement led to tensions between African Americans and Somalis, tensions that occasionally erupted into physical altercations in the public schools and on the playgrounds.

Warsan, a Somali university student in Minneapolis, discussed the same types of clashes in the Twin Cities and argued that the issues that anchor some of these clashes boil down to conflict over identity and belonging:

> I don't identify myself as an African American or black only because there are certain connotations to those references. When filing applications I put "other" and "Somali American." I do this because I consider these two [African Americans and Somalis] as different communities that should not be lumped together. So, I consider myself Somali or African or someone from sub-Saharan Africa. I consider this to be different than being African American.

The "connotations" that Warsan mentions refer to the stereotypes associated with African Americans in the United States. The lower status that African Americans occupy in American society is not lost to these Somali newcomers, who, as discussed in the previous chapter, had their own cultural perceptions of inferiority of other black Africans. This is consistent with other research showing that Somalis view American racial categorizations as inconsistent with their own identity.[73] In addition to these Somali youths self-identifying differently in their encounters at schools and public spaces, then, African Americans see Somali families and Somali businesses coming to their neighborhoods and schools, a contact that at times leads to cultural clashes between them. There are numerous documented incidents in the Twin Cities and Columbus areas where teenage Somalis and African Americans fought, requiring police intervention as well as follow-up discussions between community leaders to prevent escalation and reoccurrence of such conflicts.[74]

The analysis thus far, on settlement issues, economic pursuits, and gender relations, brings to the forefront questions of belonging. As with previous groups, Somalis' settlement process occurs in parallel with social, economic, and political transnational ties with their home countries and the families left behind in the Horn of Africa. As such, the challenges and opportunities detailed here inform the relations maintained with others left behind as well as attitudes, dreams, and actions taken or foregone toward home and kin.

Transnational Ties:
Nostalgia for and Relations with the Homeland

Family dispersal is a major consequence of civil wars and forced displacements all over the world. Muna, a twenty-four-year-old college student in Minneapolis, reported that her ten siblings were living in six different countries on three continents. She had five brothers and sisters in the United States, one sister in Canada, another in the United Kingdom, a brother in Sweden, and another in the UAE. She insisted that it would be too complicated to map out the number of countries where she had close family members, such as cousins, aunts, uncles, and other relatives. Burhan, a thirty-five-year-old small business owner, also stated that his parents and sister were in Somalia, while he had three siblings remaining in Kenya. He had just sponsored two other brothers to come to the United States, while another lives in Saudi Arabia. Farah, a man in his sixties with whom I often conversed in one of the main Somali community organizations in Minneapolis, where he spent much of his time socializing with other elders, also reported having a son in the United States, his wife and another son in Sweden, a third son in New Zealand, and the rest of his children in Somalia and Kenya.

Family dispersal created scattered relations spanning the world. In addition to economic links, refugees also maintain social, political, and religious ties to kin and community networks (Figure 5). Refugee settlement in countries of asylum has therefore occurred in parallel with continued relations with family and kin in other locations.[75] Though dispersal makes communication a challenge, it also increases the need for that communication. Continued interaction, whether through travel, telephone and Internet communication, business investments, or political engagement with those in the home country, is the norm for Somali refugees. This experience is, of course, not unique to Somalis but rather is common among most migrant and refugee groups.[76]

The financial dependency of those in the Horn on those who found a foothold in the diaspora is a poignant responsibility and has great consequences for the lives of the latter.[77] Many of my interviewees emphasized that they confront excessive financial demands from families in Africa, which contributes to the stresses and household conflicts those in the United

States experience. As we have seen, the Somali family structure is built on strong bonds with both immediate and extended family; the result creates higher demands for remittances than many can meet. The socioeconomic position of most refugees in the West and their financial obligations to families left behind raise the dilemma posed by the Somali proverb "laba qaawan isma qaaddo" (two starving people cannot provide aid to each other). This dilemma also exposes the contradictions intrinsic to transnationalism and to the constant calibration and negotiation between financial resources and financial obligations (Figure 25).[78]

Religious leaders and elders who mediate in family conflicts cited resource distribution as a key source of family conflict for Somalis in the United States. Imam Osman, for instance, who reported that he regularly mediates family crises, gave the example of a couple where the man worked while the wife collected welfare. He said the man expected the woman to use her assistance check to care for the family here and also to remit to her family

FIGURE 25. Cedar-Riverside neighborhood, Minneapolis, Minnesota.

back in Somalia and Kenya. But the wife argued that it was the husband's religious obligation to provide for her and the children and that her income was hers and not negotiable. This imam also highlighted how some men tried to keep their incomes for themselves, neglecting their traditional obligations toward their in-laws, thus exacerbating household tensions.[79] A few other men with whom I spoke insisted that they support both their families and their in-laws. They stress how they negotiate with their wives regarding how much each side should receive, taking into account the particular needs of each family. One of these men even reported supporting his in-laws from his student financial assistance income while attending college.

The scale of the stress caused by remittances for Somalis of all ages in the diaspora can be inferred by the percentage of an individual's or household's income that is sent at the end or in the first few days of the month. The elderly men and women who sent from $100 to $300 provided one striking example. They were often on SSI, and the total amount most of them received was around $600 cash, with another $100 or so of food stamps. For example, Hawa, an elderly woman in her early seventies, sent $200 to her son who lives on the outskirts of Las Annod, Somalia. She commented, "I send $200, spend $200 on my rent, and pay $50 for the phone. What is left?" She remitted this amount to her son and his nine children every month. She said she sent small amounts to other family members, though these were irregular. Asli, another elderly woman in her mid-sixties, also sent $150 dollars and reported sending this amount every month: $100 to her son in Kampala, Uganda, and $50 to her daughter in Mogadishu, Somalia. I got to know the latter elderly woman well as I often attended a religious women's gathering at her small apartment in a public housing complex in Minneapolis, where I met women of all ages coming together to recite prayers and Sufi chants. Asli got food donations from the other community members, given her leadership position in this group. An agent who runs one of the main money transfer companies in the Twin Cities informed me that there were other elderly women who sent their whole checks to their families. Such women often lived with their adult children and hence were not paying rent. Subsidized housing, where many elderly women and men resided, permitted them to remit a high percentage of their incomes. Accessing food and household items from charity organizations and community members also increased these refugees' ability to remit.

Interviewees expressed widespread belief that those back in Somalia did not appreciate the sacrifices made by those in America, lamenting the discrepancy between how they were perceived by those left behind and their actual socioeconomic reality in the United States. The image that all Somalis in the United States were fountains of financial resources for those left behind was juxtaposed with the "dirty" jobs in which Somalis were concentrated, such as in janitorial work and meat processing plants. Interviewees underscored the increasing and long-term effects of these demands on their ability to settle in America.[80] As Bashir, a male social worker, framed it,

> Once the person pays for lodging and covers the subsistence needs of the kids, he/she sends the rest to his/her family. He/she shares the little they have. This encumbers your child's education and well-being.... So about five or six families [elsewhere] with no other source of income are dependent on the income of each family living here.

Remittances potentially entail grave consequences for future generations when their parents' resources are mainly spent on the home country and families left behind.[81] Like other migrants, many Somali refugees remitted most or all of their surplus cash rather than utilizing it to consolidate their lives in America. This exacerbated refugees' precarious socioeconomic position, hindering their children's mobility and integration as well as their own. One could alternatively argue that women and men supporting families left behind are teaching their children about values and obligations to the family. However, this was not what was underscored.

Instead, the parents' lack of resources to spend on children's needs after limited incomes were stretched was a poignant point many made. A few discussed how these remittances meant that Somali children felt deprived of the privileges their non-Somali peers had, potentially pushing them to fall prey to gangs and drug pushers, if for no other reason than a bit of pocket money needed to fit in with their peers. A recent newspaper article discussing East African refugees in Seattle underscored how an increasing number of boys from this community are enticed to join gangs and deal crack cocaine in the streets, with many ending up serving long sentences in prison. Though this article focused on Ethiopian and Eritrean youths, a number of Somali and Sudanese refugee youths were also involved in these gangs. This is not to suggest a causal relationship between Somali families' financial obligations to their families left behind and the fate of their children in America. Rather, it is to underscore the economic strain that these refugee families experience and one potential ramification for the second generation, who are mostly raised in inner-city America.

The perceived link between remittances, poverty in America, and Somali children's future prospects led Ismail, a Somali poet who works as a taxi driver in Minneapolis–St. Paul, to equate remittances with "blood money," or *diya*. In Somali culture, this money is what the family of a culprit pays to the family of a victim. Ismail elaborated on this, saying that the remittances Somalis in the diaspora sent were "our and our children's" *diya*:

> Those who migrated to the Middle East returned home and built homes a year or so after first migrating. How was the person capable of doing this? Because he was only responsible for his wife and children! But now, uncle, mother-in-law, father-in-law, aunt! Each person [in the diaspora] provides for a hundred and fifty people! Now let us see if those in the Middle East build homes in Somalia. If all your family, brothers and sisters, are in Somalia, you are not going to be too concerned about your kids here. A whole community is kept afloat. But they don't know that they are surviving on our blood money and that of our children [*magtayada iyo magtii caruurtayada*]. That is my opinion. It is the blood money of these children being absorbed deeper and deeper into the inner-city culture, those we have lost to this culture; the two hundred dollars sent is the blood money of those with no hope and future here.

Ismail compared the earlier Somali migration to the Middle East during the oil boom of the 1970s, when Somalia was relatively stable and when migrant remittances contributed to asset accumulation of the migrant's family, and what Ismail called "now," referring to the Somali migration since the civil war, when remittances are used for basic survival of families displaced around the Horn region. This comparison shows migration outcomes of different eras. The logic is that earlier migrations often permitted the accumulation of some wealth, enabling family advancement. In contrast, the current financial demands meet the basic sustenance of immediate and extended families caught in the Somali political crisis, resulting in remitters often having little to show for all the struggles they experience in the United States. This pessimistic conclusion—that remittances are compromising integration in America as well as the potential of future Somali generations—is one of many factors that lead many Somalis to idealize home and return.

Gendered Motivations: Dreams of Return

Most migrants in America express a dream of returning, especially in the first years after arrival. For the majority, however, these dreams are overridden by the urgent demands of their lives in a new country, leading to permanent or at least long-term settlement.[82] Because most Somalis have arrived in America since the mid-1990s, the dreams, or the "myth," of return were prominent in their discussions. This dream of return to Somalia, or at least to countries in the Horn region, drastically differs from the westward looking migration dreams that we saw in chapters 2 and 3.

The idea of return was assumed by most of those with whom I spoke to be not only desirable but also inevitable, and settlement in America was considered transitional. Though those in South Africa and the UAE also portrayed their migrations as temporary, the interviewees in those two settings articulated desiring further movement toward the West in search of flexible citizenship, permitting the mobility and transnational life necessary for refugee families dispersed around the globe. Thus this insistence on return by Somalis in the United States takes on a particular irony: these were people who had yearned to come to America for years. They had fulfilled the dream of many, as they were already naturalized Americans or were waiting for that process to occur. But then, once that goal was achieved, they yearned to go back home.

The rationales for return often revolved around irreconcilable religious and cultural differences with the new society. One key factor most expressed related to the fear of "segmented assimilation" of their children, in this case, being assimilated into America's lowest socioeconomic and racial groups.[83] Such integration was viewed as a threat to the ethnic and religious identities of Somali children. Though such an apprehension shaped refugees' consolidation of transnational linkages with the home country, as well as other countries in the Horn and the Middle East, the rationales men and women articulated for return drastically differed.

Men and Return: Nostalgia for Tradition

The majority of men whom I interviewed for this study, including some who came to the United States in the 1970s and 1980s, reported having every intention of saving up money to return to the Horn or the Middle East. Staying in America was often discussed as temporary and as a way of buying time until peace was achieved in Somalia. A few interviewees who still had not acquired American citizenship cited this as a prerequisite for their return. Citizenship would grant them an American passport, which would permit them to travel around the world, explore economic opportunities elsewhere in Africa and the Middle East, and still return to the United States if and when they so desired. Thus American citizenship bestows not only prestige on those Somalis returning to the Horn but also the mobility only possible with Western citizenship.

These men argued that their incomes in America only covered basic subsistence needs and that prospects for social mobility were meager due in part to their limited social capital. Despite these bleak prospects, most men expressed their goal to save up "here" so as to invest and achieve success and status "back there." "There" was, however, undefined. Owing to the continuing political limbo in Somalia, return to regions thought to provide an environment akin to Somalia in terms of religious and cultural practices was often prominent in these imagined journeys. Return thus becomes a strategy to maintain a stable sense of self, a way of minimizing disruptive changes to refugees' cultural tool kit (faith, gender relations, child rearing) that migration inevitably entails.

Travel narratives of friends or relatives who visited the Horn or the Middle East described how Somalis living in those regions lived much better lives than those in the United States. Such travel narratives in part fueled the dreams of return, as they juxtaposed the pressures the household experienced in America with a perceived higher status still possible for Somali men in Somalia and neighboring countries. Return for these men seemed a salve for all the problems embedded in life in America, including both their socioeconomic marginality and the gender power struggles epitomized by women's "empowerment" and economic independence.[84]

As was true for the earlier Jannaalayaal who went to the Middle East in the 1970s and 1980s, discussed in earlier chapters, Somalis dispersed in Africa and the Middle East considered Somali men in the Western world as ideal marriage partners. Of course, this view is closely tied to the status attached to migration to the West, which is also reported for many other migrant-sending regions.[85] Thus men in search of marriage partners find women eager to take them as husbands, and families in Somalia are often willing to marry off their daughters with or without their consent. Throughout my travels where Somalis are dispersed, I found that men of all ages, including those in their sixties or seventies, could marry women in their teens if they were from the diaspora. This also held true for men still in the Horn, for example, who have the potential to eventually migrate to places such as the United States.

A case from my first fieldwork in Dadaab in 2001 illustrates this situation. Amina, a woman in her mid-fifties when I met her in the market of the Hagadera refugee camp, recounted how her sons in Atlanta sponsored her and her husband to come to the United States.[86] A short and compact woman with a big smile, Amina was a tireless businesswoman. She owned a clothing store in the refugee camp and also received remittances from her children in Atlanta. She said that she had been involved in the clothing business since the 1970s and had always been the main provider for her family, as her husband was "just a soldier," barely making enough to pay for his khat habit. She and others in the community who knew her underscored how she was really the "man" in the family in providing for all her family's needs. The husband did not work in the camps, spent most of the day in the market socializing with other unemployed men, and only came home to eat prepared meals and to sleep. Despite the indispensable role Amina had played in the economic survival of this household since its formation, her husband, who was in his early sixties by then, was "given" a fifteen-year-old girl in marriage once this family's sponsorship proceedings were under way. Amina argued that the girl's father was already counting on the future remittances his friend, and now son-in-law, would send and did not care about the age difference between the young woman and this older man. Nor did this family mind that the new husband would not be able to take his second wife with him to the United States, as the sons' sponsorship only included their two parents and U.S. immigration does not recognize polygamous marriages.

Sitting on a mattress in her room with me beside her and her sister with us, Amina expressed her disappointment with the situation, stating her inability to do much in the refugee camp setting, where she had no male kin to support her in protest against her husband taking on another wife. She stated she did not want to allow anyone to see her as jealous, as the larger community would blame her, taking her husband's side by citing religious verses to justify how Muslim men are allowed to marry up to four women. She spoke about her pain in this situation, dwelling on how lazy and useless her husband has always been and the multiple sacrifices she has made to make up for his failures for three decades. But most important for this discussion, she asserted that she would take her revenge on him once she reached the United States, where she would have the protection of her sons and of the American legal system. I was able to follow up on this case, as I am still in contact with Amina, who settled in St. Paul with her family. Amina divorced from her husband as soon as they arrived in Minneapolis in 2003 and remarried in 2010. Her ex-husband continues to support his young wife in Dadaab but also recently married a middle-aged woman in the Twin Cities.

Clearly the transnational connections between those in the United States and those in other regions involve more than material exchanges, and Amina's conviction that the "American system" would protect her from her husband once they reached the United States represents the exchange of social remittances. This refers to migrants' transmission of practices and norms as well as social capital and identities to their homelands through travel and different types of communication.[87] New gender discourses within the Somali community are an excellent example of such social remittances. The woman in a refugee camp in Kenya already counting on the protection provided by American institutions was an example of transnational information and ideological flows among different settings across which the community was dispersed.

For many Somali men in the United States, dreams of return to Somalia, or elsewhere in Africa or the Middle East, were also linked with "the claiming and valorization of social status" and the regaining of authority or masculinity within those more traditional Somali communities.[88] Jeffery, studying Pakistanis in Britain, reported that return "'home' to lead the gracious and leisurely lives of the newly rich" was idealized, and surely because of the concentration of Pakistanis in low-status menial sectors within British society.[89] Similarly, as we have seen, the mere fact of being an American citizen or resident regardless of occupation granted Somali men status and respect within their communities of origin, making return desirable.

Although many Somali men expressed the desire to return, they were cognizant of the constraints of realizing this dream. Only two out of thirty-three men whom I interviewed in Minnesota, and two out of sixteen men in Ohio, had even visited the Horn in the last five years. None of the men I interviewed have so far moved back. Somali male idealization of the "idea" of return to Somalia, the idea of home, where they would regain their status, speaks of their sense of dislocation in the American setting, Their imaginings of what migration to the United States would entail and what they have encountered reinforce these reimaginings of home.

But as much as the men dreamed of return, the prospect of return for their wives and children was even more desirable. One interviewee reported that his wife and two sons moved to Nairobi in 2003 and had been there ever since, while he stayed behind. He reported not having any plans to have them move back to the United States until the children completed high school. He stated that his wife agreed with this arrangement and that the family visited him during the summer vacations. His rationale for the move was related to the children's schooling, disciplining, and religious and ethnic identity, all of which he saw as undermined in the United States. This man sent monthly remittances to his wife and children. Though he could afford to do this because of his position as the head of a community organization, many others who reported wanting to return their families could not do so. Though the return of one's wife and children to Africa or the Middle East was idealized, only a few could afford to commit to sending more remittances than they were already sending to their other family members. For the majority, then, limited financial resources necessitated living with the reality of a cultural dissonance between the Somali cultural tool kit and that of mainstream U.S. society.

Not all men, however, idealized return to overcome this dissonance. One interviewee in Minneapolis claimed that return was out of the question for him and his family. This man was in a higher socioeconomic position than most of those whom I interviewed. He held an MA and worked for Hennepin County, where his wife also worked as an interpreter. They were one of dozens of families who had bought a home in the Twin Cities metro area. Their settlement and integration into the middle class were more secure than what the majority of Somalis living in Minnesota and Ohio had experienced. This couple's siblings were also mostly in North America and Europe, and they rarely had to remit to their extended families, which permitted them to focus on building their lives in America.

Rabi, a man in Columbus, Ohio, who operated a Somali educational program, was adamant that return was out of the question for him:

> I don't think I will go back to Somalia at all, I don't have that vision and I don't think Somalia's problems will ever be resolved. I think that only 1 to 2 percent of us will go back home, but the majority of us will make America our home.

The preceding cases may indicate that those most idealizing return were those most struggling socioeconomically, as they were more likely to fear their integration into the bottom rungs of inner-city America. They therefore perceived return as an escape from a sense of marginalization, a fear that many women also shared.

Women and Return: In Search of Social Mobility

Similar to Somali men, Somalia's protracted conflict did not prevent women from imagining and idealizing the prospect of return. Women in this study discussed their dreams of return, depicting an idealized Africa and Middle East where life would not be as difficult as they found it in the United States. These women stated that the main reason they have not already left was financial constraints, arguing that they would return tomorrow if their husbands were able and willing to support them financially. Many of those who were divorced or separated also claimed they would go back if they had someone providing for them and their children. A married woman who had six children in 2005 explained why return was not only desired but absolutely necessary for those who could afford it:

> I am leaving for Kenya by December. I am moving. Can you keep a Somali man and six kids in America? To tell you the truth, you cannot. You need help. I don't have the time to help my kids with the homework.... Now I cannot even talk to them. I have lost it. It is a lie if someone tells you that they are raising six children in America and they are giving them attention. But I feel guilty. I feel that I don't do the homework with them; they don't get good marks, Bs, sometimes Cs.... So due to that I decided that if I move to Nairobi, I will get someone to help me with the kids. My husband will send us money and he won't be expected to help with them, since he has never done that anyway. So I will find someone to help me with the kids. While someone is watching the kids, I will give these two [her oldest kids] attention. I will take them to a private afterschool program.... So those here who can struggle with them might do so, may Allah facilitate this for them. But those who can afford to take them away, I would say take them there and build them up.

Asha moved to Nairobi twice in the 2000s but moved back to Minneapolis, where her husband continued to live during those periods. She made her third move to Nairobi in 2012, with her husband also relocating as part of the latest reshuffle of the Somali government.[90] She had two more children since my first interview with her in 2005. She moved with her six youngest children, leaving the two older kids attending community college in the Twin Cities. She and her husband bought a house in Nairobi, though they kept their family business in the Twin Cities, which is being run by paid employees.

Asha's emphasis on the stresses big families experience in the absence of kin highlighted the reasons why many Somali women idealized return to the Horn or the Middle East. Asha, in fact, was in a better socioeconomic position than most other Somali refugee women, because her husband ran a private agency providing services to the community. She was also university educated and worked part time as an activist and an interpreter, all while raising eight children. Nevertheless, she shared the experiences of most other women: lack of assistance from her husband and absence of female kin, leading to increased productive and reproductive demands on women. Thus a return to the Horn, with the availability of hired hands and the presence of other female relatives, became an idealized alternative to living in the United States. Those women such as Asha who could rely on a husband to send remittances contended that they would be able to meet their children's increasing educational and emotional needs in Somalia or Kenya, which they felt unable to do in Minnesota. Remittances from husbands remaining in the United States were considered more than enough to cover basic family needs, tutors for the children, and maids to help with housework. The women argued that the small amounts sent to them could easily be stretched to permit them to lead a middle-class life in Africa or the Middle East.

Beneath these monetary possibilities, however, was a much larger, more audacious hope: that return to "my country" would enable these women to fix the problems in their lives, to lead the lives that they intended. Hodan, the unemployed mother of three, declared:

> I am taking my kids back. I will take them back to my country. Educated people are opening schools there though there is still no stable government. I can also go to other places, where children will listen to you, where you can reprimand the kids, where you pay for good quality education, and your children will not confront racial discrimination. Now my daughter goes to school, she finished grade one, moved to grade two. She studies with whites. There are only three blacks: another Somali girl and another black boy. They are segregated from the rest. You see the racism in the children's play. All the others are together. The whole neighborhood is white, no blacks. We are the only black family. We are not well liked and the little girl feels it.

These homeward looking articulations had some elements of the grass always being greener elsewhere. But those who have migrated to the United States are still perceived as being the ultimate Jannaalayaal by those still in Africa and the Middle East. What Somalis in Minnesota and Ohio experience is in a way counter to their expectations of a land where they would access great opportunities, thus engendering new discourses on return.

Such return rhetoric was based on different rationales. One expressed by a few women dealt with a great apprehension about their children growing up as a racial and religious minority in the United States, especially since the terrorist attacks of September 11. Hodan, for example, was a single mother of three children living in Section 8 housing in a middle-class neighborhood in Minneapolis. As we have seen, women like Hodan consistently voiced their concerns that their children were not treated fairly in schools, curtailing their future chances of success. Mothers feared that the religious and ethnic identities of these children were in jeopardy, as their children were pinned into America's reductive racial grid, with Somalis lumped into the black–Muslim–refugee underprivileged category. Most women insisted that they escaped the civil war to build a better future for their children.

But the prospects of success in America looked bleak: the combination of racism, low parental human capital, and the transnational financial drain imposed on those in the diaspora contributed to pessimistic forecasts. Return was desired as one way to escape this "racial categorization," which research shows that other non-native-born people of color, such as those from the Caribbean, struggle with.[91] Some resist being lumped into the African American category, perceiving that America's rigid racial hierarchies would impact them and their children in ways that would hinder their life chances.[92] But as Jemima Pierre demonstrates, this resistance does not problematize racism, thus further reinforcing the "racial inferiority" of African Americans and, by extension, of all those identified as black and even as minorities.[93]

Other women also cited the challenge of disciplining children in America as another incentive for return. They articulated fears about losing the children to child protection agencies. Many referred to families who had lost one or more of their children who had accused their parents of mistreatment. A few cited their fear of a reversal of power dynamics between parents and children, with children aware that they can call 911 to protest against corporal punishment. Kibria's research with Vietnamese Americans found that women often supported traditional gender arrangements for exactly this reason: fear that disturbing the gender order was tied to disruptions of the power women had over children, something women were reluctant to cede.[94] Some Somali women also viewed life in America as threatening to their children's Somali and Muslim identities. Parental strategy thus went beyond support for patriarchy and included drastic measures for removing the children, and the whole family, if possible, from the pernicious possibilities of the American environment. These women asserted that it would be preferable to raise children in a Muslim setting where they could grow up with a positive sense of self, where parents could discipline them, and where the greater environment supported this form of discipline. Returning these children thus serves as a way to avoid too much discrepancy between Somali families' cultural tool kit and that of the mainstream community, which is what Somalis experienced in the United States. I heard about some families who had already left for Somalia, Egypt, Syria, or Kenya, often with three or more children.[95] Some of these families, not coincidentally, had teenage boys; Somali families at times take teenage boys and girls to Somalia for cultural education *(dhaqan celis)*.[96] Parents allegedly ship home those they fear might join gangs, have problems at school, or drop out.

The idealization of return by some Somali women contradicted findings on Latin American women migrants. For example, research shows that women from Mexico are less interested in return because of fear of losing the gains they had made in the United States.[97] The latter did not want to become "dependent" on husbands and made concerted efforts to consolidate their new lives by investing in household goods, which would make return more difficult. Mexican men, conversely, saved every penny for eventual return. In contrast, I found that the Somali women in the United States were as likely as men to idealize return. None of the women interviewed expressed fears of becoming dependent after having had economic independence in America. On the contrary, many idealized the "male provider" able and willing to fulfill his religious obligations toward his wife and children. These were therefore willing to exchange the opportunities they had found in America if their husbands were committed to fulfilling their role as providers. Other research showing that some Cuban women voluntarily withdraw from the labor market once their husbands are able to meet household financial needs is akin to the Somali women's case, except that most Somali men could not afford to fulfill these obligations, a fact blocking actual return for most.[98]

One can, of course, question whether this idealization of return is just a reflection of disillusionment consequent to how migration was initially imagined, or whether those who return in fact do overcome the challenges Somali women have confronted in the United States.

Though I am not able to answer this question fully, one example that I recorded during a visit to Nairobi, Kenya, in October 2013 may give us a window into how a belief that the grass is always greener elsewhere does not always hold up. Hani, a woman in her early forties, moved to Nairobi in 2011 with her five children while her husband continued to drive a cab in the Twin Cities. Hani and her kids have two maids—a Somali who cooks for the family and a Kenyan who cleans and is often preoccupied with hand-washing clothes for five young children. During my three-week stay in Nairobi, I had many conversations with her about her decision to leave the United States. Hani discussed the extreme expenses that the family incurred in Nairobi relying only on her husband to provide for her and the kids. Hani's husband remitted about $1,000 each month. But this was insufficient for the combined rent ($600 for a house in Eastleigh, a Somali enclave in Nairobi), food, and educational costs for the three oldest boys. Consequently, it was only because of the rent she collected from her mother's property in Nairobi that Hani and her family were able to afford living in Nairobi, with tutors and maids helping her manage her family's needs. The high cost of living in most major metropolitan cities, including those in the Horn, which also held true in the UAE and South African cases, contradicts women's claims that returning to Africa and the Middle East would be more affordable than living in the United States. But despite the realities of high cost and family separation that Hani articulated, when asked if she planned to return to Minnesota in the near future, she expressed some ambivalence, insisting that she wants her children to learn the Somali language and Islam, while also being cognizant of the difficulties of family separation.

Somali women's idealization of return and their exaggerated expectations of that return are embedded in the alienation that Somalis, as African Muslim refugees, experienced in the United States. This is to say that challenges to their economic incorporation and their sense of belonging define Somali settlement in this context. This marginalization produces common interests for men and women. Living transnational lives where both the home country's and the place of settlement's demands, norms, and values inform migrants' lives offers opportunities to diminish gender inequalities; but clearly some of these disparities continue as a basis for solidarity and identity.[99] Some women concurring with men that return was best for Somalis thus represented identity politics, promoting solidarity between men and women in a context where both feel marginalized and alienated from mainstream society, despite the norm of unequal, patriarchal gender relations.

Despite these hopes, most women in the United States also acknowledged the difficulties of returning to Somalia in its current state of political instability. This is consistent with what women in the UAE and South Africa expressed. But unlike those in the UAE and South Africa, and men in the United States, women in this case mentioned Muslim countries such as those in the Middle East and African countries neighboring Somalia as viable options that would provide the desired conditions for them and their children. Definitions of "home" were therefore expanded beyond the country of origin to include a broader region. As we saw in the two earlier case studies, Somalis in the Emirati and South African regions experience little shock to their religious and cultural identities. Although many Somali women in the United States expressed plans to return to those regions, only a few had a concrete timetable for doing so. Of the forty women whom I formally interviewed in Minnesota and Ohio, only five had visited the Horn in the last five years, highlighting the discrepancy between ideals and lived lives.

CONCLUSION

Muslim African Refugees in Perpetual Passage

The diasporic condition reveals much about migration today and its complex contours of opportunity and challenge, of hope and loss. "To be diasporic, at least in the present, is to be uprooted from one's place, detached from one's nation, and searching for both. A prime subject for historical inquiry is how the diasporic sensibilities of a given migrant people vary according to the places where they reside. In the end, diaspora and comparison are inseparable elements of migration history."[1] Historian Kevin Kenny's assessment of how uprootedness and detachment are concurrent with a search for home, or at least for the psychological comfort and contentment we associate with home, captures the permanent mark that displacement leaves. As we have seen throughout this book, those people who are displaced embark on, more often than not, a perpetual search for physical, economic, and cultural security.

When violence erupts, or when political instability threatens, our most fundamental need is for basic physical security. Once that initial concern is met, by crossing a border into a neighboring country, most refugees seek other foundational needs no less important but often far more complex, such as economic, social, and cultural community and stability. But such aspirations must then be negotiated, to varying degrees, with the host country's government, the people of the host country, and the international humanitarian organizations that often manage refugee camps. The experiences of Somali refugees who have fled just over the border into neighboring

Kenya illustrate the many difficulties that can emerge. When a poor nation aids refugees, conflicts are nearly inevitable, especially when many people within the nation are struggling themselves to access basic rights. Such conflict often pushes refugees, both Somalis and others, to continue on, crossing still more borders in search of better opportunities elsewhere.

It is easy to reduce the path of the migrant or the refugee to an origin–destination binary. But as we have seen with Somalis, that binary doesn't capture the complexity of this journey, with stops in two or three or even more countries on the way to the refugee's destination. The first type of step-migration is often driven by barriers that render certain countries inhospitable but is also driven by the pull of other destinations in the refugee's imagination. As such, current Somali settlements in the UAE, South Africa, and the United States may be viewed as only one step from another imagined migration, whether realizable or not.

The second type of step-migration involves a migrant or refugee moving to a new place and eventually sending for siblings, children, and spouse to join her.[2] For those refugees in the UAE and South Africa, this type of step-migration is only possible once they can fully cover the initial needs of their family members. In the United States, however, new refugee families can access government financial support for basic needs. But the distance to the United States and the difficulties in securing a visa, including visas for family reunification, amid the heightened security since the September 11 terrorist attacks have slowed this legal route for all nationalities, thus pushing some to pursue alternative and often criminalized ways to reunite their families.

A rosy imaginary of destination countries propels millions of migrants and refugees to leave the familiar behind to start new lives in new lands. The destinations imagined inevitably consist of a blend of fact and fiction about what is possible. Such blurring is a risky but necessary asset for these migrants, steeling their willingness to undertake a costly leap into the unknown, one that may culminate in imprisonment and, in extreme cases, even death. The dramatic stories of refugees and migrants leaving their birth nations and crossing seas and deserts and war-torn lands to seek their "fortunes" exemplify the potency of that imagined destination. The neoclassical explanation for migration, which emerged in the second part of the twentieth century amid a time of major intensification of global economic interconnectedness, still remains key for migrants and refugees at the beginning of the twenty-first century.

The pull of destination countries resides, in part, in the real economic opportunities they offer. But that ability to earn a living is often accompanied by exaggerated expectations, which translate, in many migrants' minds, to the attainment of an earthly jannah. As we have seen, the prospect of access to economic resources is only one facet in a complex set of needs that the migrant or refugee seeks. The fact that migration is the exception rather than the rule around the globe, as evidenced by the small number of people who migrate relative to the global population—even from the regions with the fewest economic opportunities and the most intense political turmoil—shows that the rationales informing migration decisions go far beyond the economic realm. And this is where the dichotomy between resources and identities found in much of the available literature is misleading. Ultimately, I believe that the search for a reliable income is inseparable from the many other aspects of a migrant's sense of self, sense of belonging, sense of community.

In addition to stressing the importance of resources, then, a key contribution this book makes is its emphasis on migrants' and refugees' search for flexible citizenship, a desire that is facilitated and also hindered by globalization. As Aihwa Ong cogently demonstrates with her discussion of the "cultural logics of transnationality," seeking citizenship rights and documentation from the most developed Western nations is a strategy that the elite in many parts of the globe use to enhance their families' human and social capital.[3] For the elite in Asia (and Africa and Latin America), Western countries are deemed to be the best investment and most secure destinations. This group seeks educational opportunities as well as the citizenship rights inherent in the hegemonic Western passport. The recent European Union discussions pressuring Malta to require a year's residency before granting citizenship to those it lures with the prospect of European citizenship (in exchange for a €1.15 million investment in the country) highlights that, for the right price and in the right place, citizenship can be purchased.[4]

It should not be a surprise, then, that such flexible citizenship is sought not only by elites but also by poor refugees and migrants with no investment capital to offer. These coveted Western documents permit refugees to seek economic opportunities and physical and psychological security and provide the ability to lead the transnational lives necessary for families scattered around the globe. Of course, most refugees and migrants already have citizenship somewhere. But not all nations are created equal when it comes to crossing borders in a highly stratified nation-state system. This is clearly illustrated by the Somalis we have discussed, who understand very well that the world population can be divided into what Jennifer Hyndman called supracitizens and subcitizens.[5] Twenty-six of the thirty-three countries that the UAE exempts from its visa entry requirements are located in Europe and North America. Not a single country in Africa or Latin America appears in this list, and only a handful of Asian countries are included. Conversely, citizens of most Western European nations, along with citizens of Canada, the United States, and Australia, rank at the top of the worldwide travel index and can travel to more than 170 countries without visa requirements.[6]

Not surprisingly, Somalia, Afghanistan, and Iraq occupy the bottom of this list, with those carrying these countries' passports having the least access to visa-free travel around the globe.[7] These three Muslim countries are embroiled in conflict and remain the epicenter of the War on Terror. Despite, and in part because of, these stringent barriers to movement, refugees from these countries represent a large slice of the people around the globe who undertake dangerous migrations in the hope of making it into the developed world—their only option given their nationality and their exclusion from the market for flexible citizenship.

The comparative analysis in this book demonstrates the necessity of attending to nationality and its ability to facilitate or hinder mobility and transnational lives. Migrants and refugees from poorer regions of the world seeking to lead transnational lives face barriers that are distinct from the challenges of racialization that nonwhite elite migrants confront. These people of low socioeconomic position do not strive any less, or desire any less, to access the opportunities that citizenship from Western nations bestows on its carriers around the globe. The discussion of Somalis in the UAE, who see the economic opportunities that an American, Canadian, or Western European passport bestows on its carrier in terms of mobility, legal security, and psychosocial security—all of which are absent for those with Somali passports—highlights the significance of such citizenship. The protracted political crisis that made the Somali passport illegitimate leads Somali refugees all over Africa and the Middle East to aspire to free themselves from the stigma and immobility that Somali nationality entails.

But such freedom, as we have seen, is elusive. Flexible citizenship is open to a small number of elite migrants, as Ong argues, but it is *inflexible citizenship* that characterizes most of the world's population. Anthony Richmond argued in 1994 that the fortification of borders by the most developed nations of Europe, as well as by the United States, Canada, and Australia, to keep out those from least developed nations of the world represented "global apartheid" and a new world order. That tendency has only been further entrenched since 9/11, as the specter of terrorism guides our adamant embrace of security.[8]

Migration, as illustrated in this study, represents a window into one of the great paradoxes of globalization: it produces a world that is vastly interconnected, while at the same time creating barriers and restrictions that shut out large segments of the world's population.[9] Globalization and its contours are hence key to understanding migration today and the migrant's search for multiple forms of security. The importance of national borders is thus simultaneous with the increased imaginations of people in the farthest corners of the globe who seek to overcome those borders.

Each day, an infinitesimal proportion of these seekers is successful. For those people who do realize their migration dreams, however, new priorities, opportunities, and concerns arise in their new place of settlement. As we have seen throughout this book, the exigencies of new settlements call for a cultural "tool kit" both old and new. The comparative lens used in this book renders visible the different kinds, combinations, and levels of strategizing that migrants pursue, depending on the context of settlement and its own cultural, religious, political, and institutional arrangements.

For example, the UAE's labor regulations permitting only short work visas lead to an insecure and temporary legal status, putting migrants in that country in a stressful financial and legal position. This is true for the majority of the migrants to the UAE but more so for those from regions that remain lower in the stratification of global power. But unlike the difficulties of many migrants living and working in the Gulf region, the lack of rights and the limited physical mobility intrinsic to Somalis' legal status coexist with a strong sense of belonging and religious and ethnic affinity with the local population. By distinguishing themselves from other, mostly South Asian migrants (many of whom, ironically, are also Muslim), Somalis privilege their "special" status as Arabs, illustrating how *identity is situational* and is strategically managed even by the relatively powerless to fulfill particular needs. Here an identity that has become a barrier in international border crossings in this era of the War on Terror, where Muslims from conflict zones find increasing and stringent visa requirements, becomes an asset in bestowing on these migrants a unique emotional and spiritual well-being. Moreover, the Arab identity, which is normally weak in Somalia, takes greater importance among Somali migrants in the UAE in their search to find an affinity with the local Emirati citizens, despite the economic, political, and citizenship gaps between them. Thus what the UAE case shows is that migrants and refugees do not just draw from a fixed cultural tool kit but also modify and even create new additions to this repertoire as the context necessitates.

Interestingly, Somali refugees in South Africa also draw on their Islamic identity, but in a different way. Here racial affinity with South Africa's black majority is completely absent. Downplaying their "African-ness" in a place where black African natives occupy the lowest socioeconomic position within the wider society again is a strategy that fits the context. Somali newcomers assess their options, and the different ways they might racially position themselves, and then typically overplay their brotherhood with Indian Muslims. That anchor in Islam supersedes the racial and regional distinctions between the two groups. But the ability for Somalis to strategically distance themselves from South Africa's black majority is only possible because their strategy is supported by the successful Indian Muslim community, who has found in Somalis a source of cheap, trustworthy labor. By employing Somalis, by supplying them goods as hawkers and, eventually, as small store owners, these Indian Muslims are able to support fellow Muslims as they expand their own business interests.

It is also remarkable that Somali identity in South Africa is intrinsically tied to entrepreneurial skill. Somalis' economic success in South Africa is explained by a combination of their background (the informal economy is practically the only option in the conflict zones and refugee camps from which many came) and the conditions of reception in South Africa (the networks with Muslim Indian merchants as well as the vast informal black settlements and townships, nearly all economically marginal and underserved). But despite the socioeconomic opportunities possible for Somalis, the violence that all poor South Africans confront has devastating ramifications.

The Islamic umma affinity with Indians and the middleman minority niche that they have carved for themselves are not sufficient to surmount the omnipresent sense of physical insecurity that Somalis experience in South Africa. Such insecurity has an economic dimension in that looting always accompanies attacks against migrant-run shops.

What we witness in South Africa is thus a group that lifts itself from desperation into a strong merchant class by achieving economic security and legal refugee status. But Somalis' judgment of their migration experience here is ultimately defined by physical insecurity and the limited utility of South African travel documents for crossing international borders. This pervasive sense of insecurity is unique, in comparison to what Somalis in the UAE and United States experience; it defines Somali migrants' sense of belonging in South Africa and is the impetus for their continued pursuit of a new home.

Unlike the uncertainties around migration status that underpin Somalis' anxieties in the UAE and the physical insecurity of South Africa, those who have made it to the United States are seen as having hit the jackpot. These people have managed to enter the most coveted migration destination in the world. Most important, what makes the United States unique for Somali refugees is the ease with which they can obtain American citizenship, to which all refugees who come into the country are legally entitled once they fulfill the necessary residence requirements. As such, it is only this group (as well as those who made it to Canada and, to a lesser extent, certain Western European countries) that occupies the position equivalent to the earliest Somali Jannaalayaal who made it to the oil-rich Gulf region.

Yet, this book shows that the Somali experience in the United States is far from an earthly jannah. We have seen how the welfare provision rules that support poor families, often dominated by single mothers with children, shape the contact between new refugees and government institutions. This "privileging" of women with children dramatically shapes the Somali migration experience, leading to debates over women's empowerment and male emasculation.[10] Here we witness gender, migrant status, and class coming together to disrupt the basic dynamics of the Somali household, whose cultural and religious norms are challenged by the institutional arrangements that they enter. The standards of a new settlement thus reveal the constraints on the cultural tool kit that migrants and refugees bring with them.

The ongoing War on Terror, and the location of Somalia and Somalis as key actors in this war (both in the Horn of Africa and in the United States), also shapes Somalis' perception of their place in the United States. Low socioeconomic position, racial location, and religious alienation converge, causing many Somalis to idealize home and the idea of return. That idealization occurs even though the resources necessary for return and the political conditions in Somalia diminish the likelihood of actually acting on this desire. Thus, while refugees and migrants who occupy a marginal position within the larger American society dream of return as a way to solve their current problems, their ability to do so is itself constrained by their position within the power structures of the United States.

Despite the idealization of home, Somalis still recognize the importance of American citizenship and its inherent power around the world. Thus such citizenship is regarded as an asset even by those most disillusioned with migration to the United States, as they now are guaranteed mobility and have a country they can always fall back on if their plans for returning to the Horn or the Middle East fail. This makes U.S. migration distinctive in providing *somewhat* flexible citizenship, compared with those with Somali passports in the UAE, who risk being barred from reentry if they get out of that country, and those in South Africa, who are rarely able to translate their legal refugee papers into access to visas and international travel. Still, as mentioned earlier, the needs and hopes of a migrant are always multifaceted. Even though these Somalis have "hit the jackpot," they still balance their highly coveted U.S. citizenship with the need for the emotional, psychological, and religious stability necessary to lead fulfilled lives.

Compared to the UAE and South Africa, Somali settlement in the United States showcases how the welfare apparatus, as well as the absence of religious and ethnic groups with which Somalis can affiliate, produces a liminal refugee identity. The black–white racial binary that still pervades the United

States and the government's institutional efforts to aid refugees close off the strategies that Somalis utilize in other settings. The Arab and Islamic facets of identity as well as the middleman minority strategy aid settlement in the UAE and South Africa but have no currency for Somalis in the United States. Instead, Somalis maneuver structural barriers by working the margins of U.S. institutions, pursuing economic strategies that combine welfare and work, for example, or women claiming to be separated from their husbands to qualify for public assistance. With less success than in South Africa, we also witness how Somalis resist their identification as black in racial terms, thus overtly distinguishing themselves from black Americans, whom they see as marginalized and outside of the imagined American community. Even in their most coveted destination, then, Somalis encounter major barriers alongside the many benefits of life in the United States. As they seek to create a life for themselves, they must also work hard to define themselves against preconceived categories of race, religion, class, and gender. Prescribed cultural norms—everything from welfare stereotypes to the post-9/11 security apparatus—pigeonhole these Somalis into more familiar American categories: black, poor, welfare queen, Muslim. This U.S. experience further demonstrates how structure constrains and even transforms culture in the everyday, unsettled lives of migrants and refugees.

Regardless of where migrants and refugees end up, their lives remain linked to their kin and their country still in crisis. Individuals maintain transnational relationships, of all sorts, with those left behind. But just as important as the connections themselves are how those connections with home continue to shape migrants' lives in their new home. As we have seen, the often reified identities of nationality, race, class, and religious affiliation nearly always define migrants as other, as outside of the "imagined community" in the place of settlement. As much as migration is desired, pursued, and imagined, home is concurrently also imagined, reimagined, and idealized as a result of emotional dislocation in the new places of settlement.

In this imaginary, both divergences and common experiences emerge as we look across different countries. We see such divergence and convergence with Somalis in the United States. Ironically, the destination that is most desired and most popular with Somali migrants and refugees around the globe is also the place where Somalis are most likely to express iterations of the idea that "there is no place like home." The cultural and ethnic affinity with the nation and its citizens that Somalis in the UAE articulate, despite their lack of citizenship rights, prospects, and opportunities for mobility, stands in sharp contrast to the sense of dislocation and alienation felt by Somalis in the United States. Here we capture something amorphous but essential, rarely included in discussions of how migration is experienced. Refugees' intrinsic sense of alienation is also driven by their socioeconomic status and their location within the wider racial, social, and religious hierarchies prevailing in their new country. Of the three cases covered in this book, the United States emerged to have the most rigid and disabling constructions of these axes of power.

Despite the dislocation at the heart of the migrant experience, we have also seen the prestige attached to being a migrant in the eyes of those left behind. The act of migrating bestows on the migrant this prestige, the privilege of being a provider, a resource remitter. That privilege, however, is far from innocuous; it can also be a burden and can exacerbate the pressures migrants and refugees confront in their places of settlement. Migrants, then, even when they are refugees with limited human capital, carry heavy expectations of families, communities, and, in a sense, nations.

The source and the consequences of such burdens are rarely addressed by the literature on transnationalism, which remains mostly celebratory.[11] This enthusiasm is justified, of course, particularly given the wide-ranging evidence of the leverage that transnational communities have against leaders in their home countries.[12] Moreover, emphasis on the hybrid identities that emerge from this transnational belonging is warranted given how advancements in communication and transportation have facilitated linkages with those left behind. However, the celebratory tone surrounding transnational relations and the transnational condition itself fails to appreciate the diversity of the "transnational experience" and all that it "conceals," as scholars such as Rhacel Parrenas have cogently demonstrated.[13] This includes the burden of costly remittances, for example, which not only hinders the ability of migrants and refugees to make long-term investments in their children's futures but also creates emotional stresses that are as immense as they are invisible, at least to outsiders.

Emphasizing the positive outcomes of transnationalism is, of course, understandable; we cannot help but admire people who sacrifice so much to support their families. But consolidating linkages with home, and other locales where community and kin live, is a near-inevitable reaction of migrants' experiences of dislocation and alienation in their new settlement.[14] It is therefore paramount to pay more attention to how nationality, race, class, gender, religion, and geographical distance from the home country inform this transnational experience. Only then will we more fully grasp how living across borders constrains or liberates the migrant's ability to achieve economic, social, and emotional security in his multiple homes.

Although we cannot predict the future with any certainty, the current political impasse in Somalia suggests that Somali migration across the globe will continue. Increasingly fortified borders, which increasingly close out refugees and migrants from poorer regions of the world, will push more and more of these potential migrants toward the high seas, as we are witnessing with the crisis over movement across the Mediterranean toward Italy and Malta. The challenges Somali men and women face are structural and often beyond the power of the individual migrants and refugees. As much as these men and women struggle to manage their lives in the margins, they have little power to influence, for example, the UAE to grant citizenship rights to second-generation migrants or the South African government to combat corruption or provide better social services to the underserved black townships and informal settlements where most of the violence against migrants occurs. For those in the United States, the sense of dislocation expressed by first-generation migrants may already be shaping the second generation. There is a burgeoning movement of Somali-run charter schools, both in Minnesota and elsewhere, that segregate Somali children from mainstream traditional public schools. I believe this instinct of Somalis to educate their children separately is an outcome of this sense of alienation from mainstream institutions and society. I hope that future research will delve further into intergenerational similarities and differences in how Somalis locate themselves within the larger American mosaic.

In sum, the search by migrants and refugees for citizenship, security, and belonging brings to the fore the extraordinary complexity of migration, from the motivations for leaving home to the decisions about how and where to find a new home. Instead of only focusing on economic incorporation or taking a celebratory position on transnational lives and identities, the case studies presented in this book call for more attention to the role of the imaginary, to geopolitical forces, and to nationality as well as to the migrant's social, religious, racial, and gender positioning in the country of settlement. These multiple positionings ultimately shape how the cultural tool kit that migrants bring with them is reconstituted in light of the structural arrangements they encounter in their new settlements. It is in this meeting—between the individual and surrounding social structures—that all of our lives are given shape. The migrant experience, of course, necessitates an additional, and more complex, meeting, as the individual reckons with social structures across multiple borders. It is my hope that by immersing ourselves in the particulars of these transnational lives, we can gain a better understanding both of migrants and refugees themselves and of the shifting contours of our globalized yet highly bordered world.

NOTES

Introduction

1. To protect the identities of my informants, I use pseudonyms throughout this book.
2. Cawo M. Abdi, "Threatened Identities and Gendered Opportunities: Somali Migration to America," *Signs* 39, no. 21 (2014): 459–83.
3. Nancy L. Green, "The Comparative Method and Poststructural Structuralism: New Perspective for Migration Studies," *Journal of American Ethnic History* 12, no. 4 (1994): 3–22; Nancy Foner, *In a New Land: A Comparative View of Immigration* (New York: New York University Press, 2005); Foner, "Race and Color: Jamaican Migrants in London and New York City," *International Migration Review* 19, no. 4 (1985): 708–27; Roger Waldinger and Yenfen Tseng, "Divergent Diasporas: The Chinese Communities of New York and Los Angeles Compared," *Revue Europeanne des Migrations Internationales* 8, no. 3 (1992): 91–116; Donna R. Gabaccia, *Italy's Many Diasporas* (Seattle: University of Washington Press, 2000).
4. Patricia Boyle, K. Halfacree, and V. Robinson, *Exploring Contemporary Migration* (Harlow, UK: Longman, 1998).
5. Yen Le Espiritu, "Toward a Critical Refugee Study: The Vietnamese Refugee Subject in US Scholarship," *Journal of Vietnamese Studies* 1, nos. 1–2 (2006): 410. The United Nations's 1951 definition of *refugee* refers to a person who, "owing to well-founded fear of persecution for reasons of race, religion, nationality, membership of a particular social group or political opinion, is outside the country of his nationality and is unable or, owing to such fear, is unwilling to avail himself of the protection of

that country; or who, not having a nationality and being outside the country of his former habitual residence as a result of such events, is unable or, owing to such fear, is unwilling to return to it."

6. Douglas S. Massey, Joaquin Arango, Graeme Hugo, Ali Kouaouci, Adela Pellegrino, and J. Edward Taylor, "Theories of International Migration: A Review and Appraisal," *Population and Development Review* 19, no. 3 (1993): 448–49; Douglas S. Massey, Joaquin Arrango, Graeme Hugo, Adela Pellegrino, and J. Edward Taylor, *Worlds in Motion: Understanding International Migration at the End of the Millennium* (New York: Oxford University Press, 1998); Nancy Foner, Ruben G. Rumbaut, and Steven J. Gold, *Immigration Research for a New Century: Multidisciplinary Perspectives* (New York: Russell Sage Foundation, 2000); Peter Kivisto, "Theorizing Transnational Immigration: A Critical Review of Current Efforts," *Ethnic and Racial Studies* 24, no. 4 (2001): 549–77; Thomas Faist, "Transnationalization in International Migration: Implications for the Study of Citizenship and Culture," *Ethnic and Racial Studies* 23, no. 2 (2000): 189–222.

7. Caroline Brettell and James Frank Hollifield, eds., *Migration Theory: Talking across Disciplines* (New York: Routledge, 2008), 5; Ruben G. Rumbaut, Nancy Foner, and Seven Gold, "Introduction: Immigration and Immigration Research in the United States," *American Behavioral Scientist* 42, no. 9 (1999): 1258–63.

8. Nina Glick Schiller and Georges Eugene Fouron, *Georges Woke Up Laughing: Long-Distance Nationalism and the Search for Home* (Durham, N.C.: Duke University Press, 2001); Linda Basch, Nina Glick Schiller, and Christina Blanc-Szanton, *Nations Unbound: Transnational Projects, Postcolonial Predicaments, and Deterritorialized Nation-States* (Amsterdam: Gordon and Breach, 1994); Ruben G. Rumbaut, "Severed or Sustained Attachments? Language, Identity, and Imagined Communities in the Post-Immigrant Generation," in *The Changing Face of Home: The Transnational Lives of the Second Generation,* ed. Peggy Levitt and Mary C. Waters, 43–95 (New York: Russell Sage Foundation, 2002).

9. For examples of sociologists who employ a comparative perspective, please see Rogers Brubaker, *Immigration and the Politics of Citizenship in Europe and North America* (Washington, D.C.: German Marshall Fund of the United States, 1989); Caroline B. Brettell, "Is the Ethnic Community Inevitable? A Comparison of the Settlement Patterns of Portuguese Immigrants in Toronto and Paris," *Journal of Ethnic Studies* 9, no. 3 (1981): 1–17; Foner, *In a New Land*; Foner, "Race and Color."

10. Alejandro Portes and Robert L. Bach, *Latin Journey: Cuban and Mexican Immigrants in the United States* (Berkeley: University of California Press, 1985); Barbara S. Heisler, "The Sociology of Immigration," in Brettell and Hollifield, *Migration Theory,* 83–111.

11. Work that successfully bridges this divide includes Nazli Kibria, *Muslims in Motion: Islam and National Identity in the Bangladeshi Diaspora* (New Brunswick, N.J.: Rutgers University Press, 2011); Nazli Kibria, *Family Tightrope: The Changing Lives of Vietnamese Americans* (Princeton, N.J.: Princeton University Press, 1993); Rhacel Salazar Parrenas, ed., *Servants of Globalization: Women, Migration, and Domestic Work* (Stanford, Calif.: Stanford University Press, 2001); Parrenas, *Children of Global Migration: Transnational Families and Gendered Woes* (Stanford, Calif.: Stanford University Press, 2005); Peggy Levitt, *God Needs No Passport: Immigrants and the Changing Religious Landscape* (New York: New Press, 2007); Foner, *In a New Land*; Steven J. Gold, "Gender, Class, and Networks: Social Structure and Migration Patterns among Transnational Israelis," *Global Networks* 1, no. 1 (2001): 57–78.

12. Aneesh Aneesh, "Between Fantasy and Despair: The Transnational Condition and High-Tech Immigration," in *Immigrant Life in the US: Multi-Disciplinary Perspectives*, ed. Donna R. Gabaccia and Colin Wayne Leach, 51–64 (New York: Routledge, 2004).

13. Ibid., 62.

14. United Nations, "232 Million International Migrants Living Abroad Worldwide—New UN Global Migration Statistics Reveal," http://esa.un.org/.

15. Andrew Smith, "'If I Have No Money for Travel, I Have No Need': Migration and Imagination," *European Journal of Cultural Studies* 9, no. 1 (2006): 47–62.

16. Cindy Horst, "Buufis amongst Somalis in Dadaab: The Transnational and Historical Logics behind Resettlement Dreams," *Journal of Refugee Studies* 19, no. 2 (2006): 143–57; Cindy Horst, *Transnational Nomads: How Somalis Cope with Refugee Life in the Dadaab Camps of Kenya* (New York: Berghahn Books, 2007).

17. Kivisto, "Theorizing Transnational Immigration."

18. Peggy Levitt and Nadya B. Jaworsky, "Transnational Migration Studies: Past Developments and Future Trends," *Annual Review of Sociology* 33 (2007): 129–56.

19. Peggy Levitt, "Transnational Migration: Taking Stock and Future Directions," *Global Networks* 1, no. 3 (2001): 202–3.

20. Robin Cohen, *Global Diasporas: An Introduction* (Seattle: University of Washington Press, 1997), 21.

21. Franck Düvell and Bastian Vollmer, "Improving EU and US Immigration Systems' Capacity for Responding to Global Challenges: Learning from Experiences," background paper, European University Institute, 2011, http://www.eui.eu/; Michelle Mittelstadt, Burke Speaker, Doris Meissner, and Muzaffar Chishti, "Through the Prism of National Security: Major Immigration Policy and Program Changes in the Decade since 9/11," Migration Policy Institute, August 2011, http://www.migrationpolicy.org/.

22. Amnesty International, "Kenya: Somali Refugees Need Protection Not Abuse," December 8, 2010, http://www.amnesty.org/en/; Jane Mayer, "Outsourcing Torture:

The Secret History of America's 'Extraordinary Rendition' Program," *New Yorker*, February 14, 2005; Human Rights Watch, "People Fleeing Somalia War Secretly Detained: Kenya, US and Ethiopia Cooperate in Secret Detention and Renditions," March 30, 2007, http://www.hrw.org/news/.

23. Massey et al., "Theories of International Migration"; Vilna Francine Bashi, *Survival of the Knitted: Immigrant Social Networks in a Stratified World* (Stanford, Calif.: Stanford University Press, 2007), 16–25.

24. Thomas Faist, "The Crucial Meso-Level," in *International Migration: Immobility and Development*, ed. T. Hammar, G. Bronchmann, K. Tamas, and T. Faist, 187–218 (Oxford: Berg, 1997).

25. Ibid., 13.

26. Green, "Comparative Method and Poststructural Structuralism"; Foner, *In a New Land*; Kevin Kenny, "Diaspora and Comparison: The Global Irish as a Case Study," *Journal of American History* 90, no.1 (2003): 134–62.

27. Foner, *In a New Land*; Foner, "Race and Color."

28. Foner, *In a New Land*; Foner, "Race and Color"; Waldinger and Tseng, "Divergent Diasporas"; Caroline Brettell, "Is Ethnic Community Inevitable?," in *From Mogadishu to Dixon: The Somali Diaspora in a Global Context*, ed. Abdi M. Kusow and Stephanie R. Bjork (Trenton, N.J.: Red Sea Press, 2007), focuses on Somalis in different regions of the world, but this volume does not make any concerted effort to tease out the comparative elements in the different experiences in various settlements.

29. Ann Swidler, "Culture in Action: Symbols and Strategies," *American Sociological Review* 51, no. 2 (1986): 276.

30. Ibid., 280.

31. Ibid., 278.

32. Beth B. Hess and Myra Marx Ferree, eds., introduction to *Analyzing Gender: A Handbook of Social Science Research* (London: Sage, 1987), 17.

33. Green, "Comparative Method and Postructural Structuralism"; Foner, *In a New Land*; Foner, "Race and Color"; Gabaccia, *Italy's Many Diasporas*; Waldinger and Tseng, "Divergent Diasporas."

34. Erving Goffman, "On Fieldwork," transcr. and ed. Lyn H. Lofland, *Journal of Contemporary Ethnography* 18 (1989): 123–32; Christian Lüders, "Field Observation and Ethnography," in *Companion to Qualitative Research*, ed. Uwe Flick, Ernst Von Kardorff, and Ines Steinke, 222–30 (London: Sage, 2004).

35. For the case of one Emirati man who works on human rights issues, see Human Rights Watch, "UAE: Investigate Attacks on Rights Defender," October 3, 2012, http://www.hrw.org/news/; Human Rights Watch, "UAE: Unfair Mass Trial of 94 Dissidents: Investigate Allegations of Torture, Grant Public Access to Sessions," April 3, 2013, http://www.hrw.org/news/.

1. The Genesis of Contemporary Somali Migrations

1. This reference to *clannism* as a practice is used for rural dwellers who are thought to attach more importance to genealogy compared to urban dwellers, a common belief in the Somali community.

2. Ahmed I. Samatar, "Somalia: Stateless as Homelessness," in *The African State: Reconsiderations*, ed. Abdi Ismail Samatar and Ahmed I. Samatar (Portsmouth, N.H.: Heinemann, 2002), 240.

3. I use the "Horn" and "Horn of Africa" interchangeably to refer to the areas where Somalis are mostly concentrated (Somalia, Ethiopia, Kenya, and Djibouti). Though Kenya is often not included in this grouping, I think it is warranted to do so, not only because of the large Somali refugee population there since 1991 but also because of its own significant Somali ethnic population concentrated in the Northeastern Province.

4. Samatar, "Somalia."

5. For more discussion of Somali minority groups, please see Catherine Besteman, *Unraveling Somalia: Race, Violence, and the Legacy of Slavery* (Philadelphia: University of Pennsylvania Press, 1999); also see Catherine Besteman and Lee V. Cassanelli, *The Struggle for Land in Southern Somalia: The War behind the War* (London: Haan, 2000); Ali Jimale Ahmed, *The Invention of Somalia* (Lawrenceville, N.J.: Red Sea Press, 1995).

6. Louis FitzGibbons, *The Betrayal of Somalis* (London: Collings, 1982); Ahmed, *Invention of Somalia*. Somali population estimates are all approximations at best. The last and only population census in Somalia was in 1975, and many of the current estimates utilize those data to estimate current population numbers.

7. William I. Zartman, *Collapsed States: The Disintegration and Restoration of Legitimate Authority* (Boulder, Colo.: Lynne Rienner, 1995); Taisier M. Ali and Robert O. Matthews, eds., *Civil Wars in Africa: Roots and Resolution* (Montreal: McGill–Queens University Press, 1999).

8. FitzGibbons, *Betrayal of Somalis*; Terrence Lyons, "Crisis on Multiple Levels: Somalia and the Horn of Africa," in *The Somali Challenge: From Catastrophe to Renewal?*, ed. Ahmed I. Samatar, 189–207 (Boulder, Colo.: Lynne Rienner, 1994).

9. FitzGibbons, *Betrayal of Somalis*; Abdisalam M. Issa-Salwe, *The Collapse of the Somali State: The Impact of the Colonial Legacy* (London: Haan, 1996); Abdisalam M. Issa-Salwe, *The Cold War Fallout: Boundary Politics and Conflict in the Horn of Africa* (London: Haan, 2002).

10. In Abdi Ismail Samatar and Ahmed I. Samatar, "Somalis as Africa's First Democrats: Premier Abdirazak H. Hussein and President Aden A. Osman," *Bildhaan: An International Journal of Somali Studies* 2 (2002): 1–64.

11. Organization for African Unity, "OAU Charter," Article 3, signed in Addis Ababa, Ethiopia, May 25, 1963.

12. The question of Djibouti was less of a challenge for Somali nationalism following a referendum in this region in 1967, when over 60 percent of the population voted to remain under French rule. Lyons, "Crisis on Multiple Levels," 196–97.

13. Lyons, "Crisis on Multiple Levels," 195.

14. FitzGibbons, *Betrayal of Somalis*, 45.

15. Lyons, "Crisis on Multiple Levels"; Issa-Salwe, *Collapse of the Somali State*.

16. Issa-Salwe, *Collapse of the Somali State*.

17. Peter Woodward, *The Horn of Africa: State Politics and International Relations* (London: I. B. Taurus, 1996); Abdi Sheik-Abdi, "Ideology and Leadership in Somalia," *Journal of Modern African Studies* 19, no. 1 (1981): 163–72; Samatar and Samatar, "Somalis as Africa's First Democrats."

18. Sheik-Abdi, "Ideology and Leadership in Somalia"; FitzGibbons, *Betrayal of Somalis*.

19. Woodward, *Horn of Africa*, 67.

20. Sheik-Abdi, "Ideology and Leadership in Somalia," 165.

21. The regime introduced Somali orthography in 1972 and subsequently undertook a successful massive literacy campaign. Samatar, "Somalia," 230; Sheik-Abdi, "Ideology and Leadership in Somalia," 170–71.

22. Lyons, "Crisis on Multiple Levels"; Abdi I. Samatar and W. Machaka, "Conflict and Peace in the Horn of Africa: A Regional Approach," in *Quest for a Culture of Peace in the IGAD Region*, 26–55 (Nairobi: Heinrich Boll Foundation, 2006).

23. Woodward, *Horn of Africa*, 68–69.

24. FitzGibbons, *Betrayal of Somalis*; Woodward, *Horn of Africa*.

25. Hussein M. Adam, "Somali Civil Wars," in *Civil Wars in Africa: Roots and Resolution*, ed. Taisier M. Ali and Robert O. Matthews, 169–92 (Montreal: McGill–Queens University Press, 1999); Bereket Habte Selassie, *Conflict and Intervention in the Horn of Africa* (New York: Monthly Review Press, 1980); Colin Legum and Bill Lee, *Conflict in the Horn of Africa* (London: Rex Collings, 1977).

26. Ahmed I. Samatar, "The Curse of Allah: Civic Disembowelment and the Collapse of the State in Somalia," in *The Somali Challenge: From Catastrophe to Renewal*, ed. Ahmed I. Samatar, 95–146 (Boulder, Colo.: Lynne Rienner, 1994), 117.

27. FitzGibbons, *Betrayal of Somalis*; Woodward, *Horn of Africa*.

28. Gaim Kibreab, *African Refugees: Reflections on the African Refugee Problem* (Lawrenceville, N.J.: Africa World Press, 1985); Sidney Waldron and Naima A. Hasci, "Somali Refugees in the Horn of Africa: State of the Art Literature Review," *Studies on Emergencies and Disaster Relief*, no. 3 (1995): 1–87.

29. Legum and Lee, *Conflict in the Horn of Africa*; Basil Davidson, *The Black Man's Burden* (Oxford: James Currey, 1992); Colin Legum, *Africa since Independence* (Bloomington: Indiana University Press, 1999).

30. Woodward, *Horn of Africa*, 67; Adam, "Somali Civil Wars," 179.

31. Woodward, *Horn of Africa*; Samatar, *Somali Challenge*; Adam, "Somali Civil Wars."

32. Issa-Salwe, *Collapse of the Somali State*; Issa-Salwe, *Cold War Fallout*.

33. Adam, "Somali Civil Wars."

34. Samatar, "Curse of Allah," 126; *qat* or *khat* is the fresh leaves of the *Catha edulis* shrub, cultivated primarily in East Africa and the Arabian Peninsula. Men in Somalia, Ethiopia, Yemen, and Djibouti, among other places, chew the leaves as a stimulant. This is a drug that is used as an accepted recreational diversion by many men and a small number of women. The ritual of chewing takes many hours per day. The use of this drug in Somalia has risen exponentially since the civil war because of the absence of employment and the ample time available to men.

35. Ioan M. Lewis, *Blood and Bone: The Call of Kinship in Somali Society* (Lawrenceville, N.J.: Red Sea Press, 2004); Lewis, *A Pastoral Democracy: A Study of Pastoralism and Politics among the Northern Somali of the Horn of Africa* (London: Oxford University Press, 1961); Lewis, *Peoples of the Horn of Africa* (London: International African Institute, 1955); David Laitin and S. Samatar, *Somalia: Nation in Search of a State* (Boulder, Colo.: Westview Press, 1987). For more on clan as an essential force accounting for all understanding of Somali society, see Abdi Ismail Samatar, "Destruction of State and Society in Somalia: Beyond the Tribal Convention," *Journal of Modern African Studies* 30, no. 4 (1992): 624–41; Samatar, *The State and Rural Transformation in Northern Somalia, 1884–1986* (Madison: University of Wisconsin Press, 1989).

36. Besteman, *Unraveling Somalia*, 19–20.

37. Ibid.; Besteman and Cassanelli, *Struggle for Land in Southern Somalia*.

38. Transparency International, "Overview of Corruption and Anti-corruption in Somalia," July 13, 2012, http://www.transparency.org/.

39. UNHCR, "UNHCR Country Operations Profile: Yemen Working Environment, 2013," http://www.unhcr.org/.

40. Integrated Regional Information Networks, "Somalia: UNHCR Disturbed by Deaths of Smuggled Immigrants," 2005, http://www.irinnews.org/.

41. Barbara McMahon, "Asylum Seekers' Voyages of Hell," *The Observer*, July 17, 2005.

42. Besteman, *Unraveling Somalia*, 18.

43. UNHCR, "Review of UNHCR's Kenya–Somalia Cross-Border Operation," December 1994, http://www.unhcr.org/.

44. UNHCR, "Dadaab—World's Biggest Refugee Camp 20 Years Old," February 21, 2012, http://www.unhcr.org/. This figure includes some ten thousand third-generation refugees born in Dadaab to refugee parents who were also born there, according to this report.

45. The Kenyan parliament only enacted a Refugee Act bill in November 2006, a bill that had been frozen in parliament for more than fifteen years despite Kenya being a signatory to the 1951 UN Refugee Convention and the 1969 OAU Refugee Convention. Eva Ayiera, "Bold Advocacy Finally Strengthens Refugee Protection in Kenya," *Forced Migration Review* 28 (2007): 26–28. For more details on Kenya's new Department of Refugee Affairs, see http://www.refugees.go.ke/.

46. Awa M. Abdi, "Refugees, Gender-Based Violence, and Resistance: A Case Study of Somali Refugee Women in Kenya," in *Gender, Migration, and Citizenship: Making Local, National, and Transnational Connections,* ed. Evangelia Tastsoglou and Alexandria Dobrowolsky, 231–51 (Aldershot, U.K.: Ashgate, 2006); Awa M. Abdi, "In Limbo: Dependency, Insecurity, and Identity amongst Somali Refugees in Dadaab Camps," *Refuge: Canada's Journal on Refugees* 22, no. 2 (2005): 6–14; Cindy Horst, "Xawilaad: The Importance of Overseas Connections in the Livelihoods of Somali Refugees in the Dadaab Camps of Kenya," working paper TC-02-14, 2002, http://www.transcomm.ox.ac.

47. Medecins Sans Frontiers, "Leaders Must Not Fail Refugees in Dadaab, the World's Largest Camp," January 10, 2012, http://somalia.msf.org/.

48. UNHCR, "Finding Durable Solutions," Global Report, http://www.unhcr.org/.

49. Jeff Crisp, "A State of Insecurity: The Political Economy of Violence in Kenya's Refugee Camps," *African Affairs* 99 (2000): 601–32.

50. The Somali enclave of Eastleigh in Nairobi has a substantial number of Somalis who chose to settle in urban areas, though the Kenyan government does not officially endorse this.

51. Amnesty International, "Insecurity and Indignity: Women's Experiences in the Slums of Nairobi, Kenya," 2010, http://www.amnesty.org/en/; Robert Pollin and James Heintz, *Expanding Decent Employment in Kenya: The Role of Monetary Policy, Inflation Control, and the Exchange Rate,* Political Economy Research Institute report ipccountrystudy006 (Amherst: University of Massachusetts, 2007).

52. Human Rights Watch, "'Welcome to Kenya': Police Abuse of Somali Refugees," 2010, http://www.hrw.org/.

53. Ibid.; Amnesty International, "Insecurity and Indignity"; Abdi, "In Limbo"; Abdi, "Refugees, Gender-Based Violence, and Resistance"; Crisp, "A State of Insecurity."

54. Kevin Mwachiro, "Kenya Corruption Costs Government Dearly," December 3, 2010, http://www.bbc.co.uk/news/.

55. Mwangi Kibathi, "Immediate Reforms Needed to Change the Image of Kenya Police," *Transparency International Kenya*, December 19, 2011.
56. Ibid.
57. Samuel Siringi, "Public Servants Earn Pay Boost This Month," *Daily Nation*, July 3, 2012, http://www.nation.co.ke/.
58. Abdi, "In Limbo"; Abdi, "Refugees, Gender-Based Violence, and Resistance."
59. UNHCR, "New Procedures Set for Somali Refugees to Return Home Voluntarily from Kenya," November 11, 2013, http://www.unhcr.org/.
60. UNHCR, "Resettlement: A New Beginning in a Third Country," 2013, http://www.unhcr.org/.
61. UNHCR, "Frequently Asked Questions about Resettlement," April 1, 2012, http://www.unhcr.org/.
62. UNHCR, "Resettlement."
63. UNHCR, "US Resettlement Overview."
64. I came across this and other similar cases through requests to provide affidavits and expert witness for Somali asylum cases.
65. UNHCR, "US Resettlement Overview," 5.
66. This method of bringing in immediate family was possible until March 2008, when U.S. Immigration suspended the loophole and introduced a DNA testing requirement to proof blood relationships. For more on this, please see U.S. Department of State, *Fraud in the Refugee Family Reunification (Priority Three) Program* (Washington, D.C.: U.S. Department of State, Bureau of Population, Refugees, and Migration, 2008).
67. Pearl Stewart, "Who Is Kin? Family Definition and African American Families," *Journal of Human Behavior in the Social Environment* 15, nos. 2–3 (2007): 163–81; Robin L. Jarrett and Linda M. Burton, "Dynamic Dimensions of Family Structure in Low-Income African American Families: Emergent Themes in Qualitative Research," *Journal of Comparative Family Studies* 30, no. 2 (1999): 177–87.
68. The idea is that this sister in a sense is now the de facto mother for her siblings as her mother passed on. In Somalia and Kenya, she would have been the guardian and legally responsible for them.
69. Close to one-fourth of 640 million (150 million) adults polled by Gallup around the world chose the United States as the destination to which they would permanently move if given the choice. The United Kingdom came second, with 7 percent stating that they would permanently settle there. For more on this, see Jon Clifton, "150 Million Adults Worldwide Would Migrate to the U.S.," April 20, 2012, http://www.gallup.com/poll/.
70. Al Jazeera English, "Migrants Suffocate to Death in Tanzania," June 27, 2012, http://www.aljazeera.com/news/.

71. Jennifer Hyndman, *Managing Displacement: Refugees and the Politics of Humanitarianism* (Minneapolis: University of Minnesota Press, 2000). Also see Hyndman, "Supra-citizen and Sub-citizen: Subjects and the Border," *Tessera* 18 (1995): 78–89.

72. UNHCR, "Iraqis, Afghans, and Somalis Top List of Asylum Seekers in Industrialized World," press release, October 21, 2009, http://www.unhcr.org/.

2. United Arab Emirates

1. Michel Korinman and John Laughland, *The Long March to the West: Twenty-First Century Migration in Europe and the Greater Mediterranean Area* (London: Valentine Michel Academic, 2007); Ariane Chebel D'Appollonia and Simon Reich, eds., *Immigration, Integration, and Security: America and Europe in Comparative Perspective* (Pittsburgh, Pa.: University of Pittsburgh Press, 2008).

2. Benedict Anderson, *Imagined Communities: Reflections on the Origins and Spread of Nationalism* (London: Verso, 1991).

3. Human Rights Watch, *World Report 2011: United Arab Emirates* (New York: Human Rights Watch, 2011), http://www.hrw.org/.

4. Israel, Egypt, and Yemen are the only Middle Eastern nations that have signed the Refugee Convention. See UNHCR, "United Arab Emirates: 2013 UNHCR Regional Operations Profile—Middle East," 2013, http://www.unhcr.org/.

5. Frauke Heard-Bey, "The United Arab Emirates: Statehood and Nation-Building in a Traditional Society," *Middle East Journal* 59, no. 3 (2005): 361; Nasra M. Shah, "Irregular Migration and Some Negative Consequences for Development: Asia-GCC Context," discussion paper for the Civil Society Days of the Global Forum on Migration and Development, Manila, 2008, 5. For more on the existential crisis created by the skewed proportion of the foreign population to citizens, see Andrzej Kapiszweski, "De-Arabization in the Gulf: Foreign Labor and the Struggle for Local Culture," *Georgetown Journal of International Affairs* 8, no. 2 (2007): 81–88.

6. For in-depth analysis of the emergence of UAE sheikhdoms and their rise to dominance in this region, see Christopher M. Davidson, *Dubai: The Vulnerability of Success* (New York: Columbia University Press, 2008).

7. Heard-Bey, "United Arab Emirates," 360.

8. Rosemarie Said Zahlan, *The Making of the Modern Gulf States: Kuwait, Bahrain, Qatar, the United Arab Emirates, and Oman* (Berkshire, U.K.: Ithaca Press, 1998), 20.

9. Ibid.

10. Ibid., 14–15.

11. This guaranteed British hegemony in the oil concessions that followed oil discoveries in the region, with Bahrain, Kuwait, and later on Qatar and the UAE all bound

by treaties to privilege British oil firms over other competitors. See Zahlan, *Making of the Modern Gulf States*.

12. For more details on the British rule of this region as well as the discovery of oil in the region, see Zahlan, *Making of the Modern Gulf States*, 23–30. Also see Heard-Bey, "United Arab Emirates," 363–67, for discussion of the largesse of the richest and biggest power within this union, Abu Dhabi, in the affairs of the other states.

13. Heard-Bey, "United Arab Emirates," 360; Shuchita Kapur, "Abu Dhabi's Oil Reserves to Last Another 150 Years," *Emirates 24/7*, March 31, 2010, http://www.emirates247.com/.

14. Heard-Bey, "United Arab Emirates," 360.

15. Zahlan, *Making of the Modern Gulf States*, 161.

16. Heard-Bey, "United Arab Emirates," 361.

17. "Qatar, UAE among Richest Countries: Forbes," *Emirates 24/7*, February 26, 2012, http://www.emirates247.com/.

18. Kapiszewski, "De-Arabization in the Gulf," 86–87.

19. Ibid., 82; also see Andrzej Kapiszewski, "Population, Labor, and Education Dilemmas Facing the GCC States at the Turn of the Century," seminar presented at the Technological Education and National Development Conference, Abu Dhabi, April 9, 2000, http://crm.hct.ac.ae/.

20. Kapiszewski, "De-Arabization in the Gulf," 82.

21. UAE Interact, "UAE Population Put at 7.2 Million," March 4, 2012, http://www.uaeinteract.com/.

22. K. C. Zachariah, B. A. Prakash, and S. Irudaya Rajan "The Impact of Immigration Policy on Indian Contract Migrants: The Case of the United Arab Emirates," *International Migration* 41, no. 4 (2003): 163–65.

23. Christopher M. Davidson, "Dubai: Foreclosure of a Dream," *Middle East Report* 251 (2009): 8–13; Mohamed Shihab, "Economic Development in the UAE," in *United Arab Emirates: A New Perspective*, ed. Ibrahim al-Abed and Peter Hellyer, 249–59 (New York: Trident Press, 2001); Nick Hund, "From the Front Line: Dubai's Labor Trap," *Political Insight* 2 (2011): 24; Francesca Levy, "Why the Burj Khalifa Doesn't Matter," *Forbes*, April 1, 2010, http://www.forbes.com/.

24. Nasra M. Shah, *Restrictive Labor Immigration Policies in the Oil-Rich Gulf: Effectiveness and Implications for Sending Asian Countries* (Mexico City: United Nations Expert Group Meeting on Social and Economic Implications of Changing Population Age Structure, Population Division, Department of Economic and Social Affairs, United Nations Secretariat, 2006), http://www.un.org/esa/, 4–8; Anh Nga Longva, "Keeping Migrant Workers in Check: The Kafala System in the Gulf," *Middle East Report* 211 (1999): 20–21.

25. Kapiszewski, "De-Arabization in the Gulf," 83.
26. Ibid.
27. Ibid., 85.
28. Andrzej Kapiszewski, "Arab versus Asian Migrant Workers in the GCC Countries" (Beirut: United Nations Expert Group Meeting on International Migration and Development in the Arab Region, Population Division, Department of Economic and Social Affairs, United Nations Secretariat, 2006), http://www.un.org/esa/.
29. Sean Foley, *The Arab Gulf States: Beyond Oil and Islam* (Boulder, Colo.: Lynne Rienner, 2010); Nga Longva, "Keeping Migrant Workers in Check."
30. Abu Dhabi Government, "UAE Labor Law," 2012, http://www.abudhabi.ae/.
31. Kapiszewski, "Arab versus Asian Migrant Workers," 6–10; Foley, *Arab Gulf States*, 49.
32. Peter D. Little, *Somalia: Economy without State* (Bloomington: Indiana University Press, 2003).
33. For a description of Canada's Immigrant Investor Program, see "Investors," http://www.cic.gc.ca/.
34. "Green Card through Investment," http://www.uscis.gov/.
35. Aihwa Ong, "On the Edge of Empires: Flexible Citizenship among Chinese in Diaspora," *Positions* 1, no. 3 (1993): 745–78.
36. Michael Matly and Laura Dillon, *Dubai Strategy: Past, Present, Future* (Cambridge, Mass.: Harvard Business School, 2007), 1–20, http://www.cfci.org/.
37. See Nga Longva, "Keeping Migrant Workers in Check"; Kapiszewski, "Arab versus Asian Migrant Workers"; Foley, *Arab Gulf States*.
38. Davidson, "Dubai," 115.
39. See Nga Longva, "Keeping Migrant Workers in Check."
40. The Fédération Internationale de Football Association (FIFA) (in English, International Federation of Association Football).
41. Samir Salama, "Fraudsters Exploit Loopholes to Deal in Illegal Work Visas," *Gulf News*, November 11, 2003, http://gulfnews.com/news/.
42. The term of the residential visa has since been reduced from three years to two. UAE Interact, "UAE Residence Visa Validity Reduced to Two Years," December 9, 2010, http://www.uaeinteract.com/.
43. What Faysal refers to as *bajaa* is neither Somali nor Arabic but probably is *bachcha*, which means "child" in Hindi. This again illustrates the role of Hindi and Urdu as the dominant languages in this country.
44. Young men have to seek their own employment visa when they reach eighteen years of age, as they are no longer recognized as dependents under a family visa. This is not true for young women, who until marriage are considered as dependents of their father within this Muslim culture.

45. In an extreme case that was reported recently, a Somali elder who came to the UAE in the 1950s, Mohammed Jamua Yousuf, faced deportation after overstaying his visa, which expired in 1991. Yasin Kakande, "Oldest UAE Illegal's Dismay at Having to Leave His Home of 50 years," *The National,* January 14, 2013, http://www.thenational.ae/news/.

46. Alejandro Portes and Leif Jensen, "The Enclave and the Entrants: Patterns of Ethnic Enterprise in Miami before and after Mariel," *American Sociological Review* 54 (1989): 929.

47. Ibrahim Balkir, Fatma Hassan Ismail, and Sabri Al-Segini, "Determinants of Fund Allocations Out of Housing Programs in the UAE," *Journal of Economic and Administrative Sciences* 22, no. 1 (2006): 25–40. For more on this, see Karim Hadjri, "Dubai's New Urban Landscape: A Critical Look at Its Emerging Housing Forms," paper presented at the Thirty-Third IAHS World Congress on Housing, "Transforming Housing Environments through Design," Pretoria, South Africa, September 27–30, 2005, 1–11.

48. "Minimum Wages Hiked for Indian Workers in UAE," *The Economic Times,* March 16, 2011, http://articles.economictimes.indiatimes.com/.

49. Mulki Al-Sharmani, "Living Transnationally: Somali Diasporic Women in Cairo," *International Migration* 44, no. 1 (2006): 55–77.

50. Ahmed Mustafa Elhussein Mansour, "The Impact of Privatization on the United Arab Emirates (UAE) Federal Public Sector," *International Public Management Review* 9, no. 2 (2008): 66–89.

51. At the time of the interview (December 2011), the political conflict in Yemen that eventually led to the fall of the Saleh government had begun.

52. *Ubah* refers to different mothers (three in this case). This is very common in Somali families, and especially for older men, who often married up to four women either over time, with divorces along the way, or even four at a given time.

53. Ray Jureidini, *Migrant Workers and Xenophobia in the Middle East: Identities, Conflict, and Cohesion,* Programme Paper 2 (Beirut: United Nations Research Institute for Social Development, 2003), 4.

54. Kapiszewski, "De-Arabization in the Gulf," 87. For detailed discussion on the UAE's educational system and its challenges, see William E. Gardner, "Developing a Quality Teaching Force for the United Arab Emirates: Mission Improbable," *Journal of Education for Teaching: International Research and Pedagogy* 21, no. 3 (1995): 289–302. Also see Jureidini, *Migrant Workers and Xenophobia,* 8–9.

55. Apartments and houses are rented by the year, not by the month. The main renter has to pay this money up front, while those occupying beds or rooms only pay by the month.

56. See Abdi, "Threatened Identities and Gendered Opportunities," for shifting gender practices in Somalia and in the Somali diaspora.

57. Rima Sabban, *United Arab Emirates: Migrant Women in the United Arab Emirates: The Case of Female Domestic Workers*, GENPROM Working Paper 10, Series on Women and Migration (Geneva: International Labor Office, 2002), 1–62. Also see Ray Jureidini, "Trafficking and Contract Migrant Workers in the Middle East," *International Migration* 48, no. 4 (2010): 142–63.

58. Jureidini, *Migrant Workers and Xenophobia*, 6–8.

59. Ibid.

60. Parrenas, *Servants of Globalization*. Also see Rhacel Salazar Parrenas, "The Reproductive Labor of Migrant Workers," *Global Networks* 12, no. 2 (2012): 269–75.

61. Parrenas, *Servants of Globalization*; Parrenas, *Children of Global Migration*.

62. Kapiszewski, "De-Arabization in the Gulf," 86; "Anger at Saudi Beheading of Sri Lankan Maid," *Al Jazeera English*, January 10, 2013, http://www.aljazeera.com/news/.

63. Jureidini, *Migrant Workers and Xenophobia*; Sabban, *United Arab Emirates*.

64. Bassam Za'za, "Most Offenders of 2011 Were Drunk Drivers," *Gulf News*, January 18, 2012, http://gulfnews.com/news/.

65. Kibria, *Muslims in Motion*.

66. Jureidini, "Trafficking and Contract Migrant Workers in the Middle East."

67. As a Somali traveling with an American passport, I found that my dealings with security officers were actually more pleasant in Dubai than during my reentry to the United States, with no questions asked about the purpose of my trip or my intended length of stay and no fees collected or visa requirements imposed.

68. United Nations Office on Drugs and Crime, *Smuggling of Migrants by Sea*, issue paper (Vienna: United Nations Office on Drugs and Crime, 2011), 1–71, http://www.unodc.org/.

69. For recent mass deportations of Somalis from Saudi Arabia, see Human Rights Watch, "Saudi Arabia: 12,000 Somalis Expelled: Mass Deportation without Considering Refugee Claims," 2014, http://www.hrw.org/news/.

3. South Africa

1. Rieko Karatani, "How History Separated Refugee and Migrant Regimes: In Search of Their Institutional Origins," *International Journal of Refugee Law* 17, no. 2 (2005): 517–41.

2. Goolam Vahed and Shamil Jeppie, "Multiple Communities: Muslims in Post-Apartheid South Africa," in *State of the Nation, 2004–2005*, ed. Daniel John, Roger Southall, and Jessica Lutchman, 252–86 (Pretoria: Human Sciences Research Council Press, 2005).

3. See Steven J. Gold, *The Store in the Hood: A Century of Ethnic Business and Conflict* (New York: Rowman and Littlefield, 2010), for similar discussion on the U.S. context and conflicts arising between new ethnic groups and minority natives in poor urban and rural areas.

4. Bill Dixon and Elrena van der Spuy, eds., *Justice Gained? Crime and Control in South Africa's Transition* (Cape Town: University of Cape Town Press, 2004).

5. John Parkington and Martin Hall, "Patterning in Recent Radiocarbon Dates from Southern Africa as a Reflection of Prehistoric Settlement and Interaction," *Journal of African History* 28 (1987): 1–25; Paul Mellars, "Why Did Modern Human Populations Disperse from Africa ca. 60,000 Years Ago? A New Model," *PNAS* 103, no. 25 (2006): 9381–86.

6. Paul Maylam, "Explaining the Apartheid City: 20 Years of South African Historiography," *Journal of Southern African Studies* 21, no. 1 (1995): 35.

7. See Charles H. Feinstein, *An Economic History of South Africa: Conquest, Discrimination, and Development* (New York: Cambridge University Press, 2005), 59, for a discussion of the overt policies to introduce European goods to the blacks to create a market for white businesses as well as the increasing number of black clients willing to spend their earnings with the white-owned traders.

8. Sampie Terreblanche, *A History of Inequality in South Africa 1652–2002* (Pietermaritzburg, South Africa: University of Natal Press, 2002); see also Feinstein, *An Economic History of South Africa*; Bernard Magubane Makhosezwe, *The Political Economy of Race and Class in South Africa* (New York: Monthly Review Press, 1979).

9. Interviewees as well as South Africans use "township" and "location" interchangeably when referring to these black residential areas. The apartheid policies of separation produced these peripheral settlements around the main white towns and cities.

10. P. B. Rich, "Ministering to the White Man's Needs: The Development of Urban Segregation in South Africa, 1913–1923," *African Studies* 37, no. 2 (1978): 177–91.

11. Statistics South Africa, "General Household Survey 2008," Statistical Release P0318, September 2009, cited in Hein Marias, *South Africa Pushed to the Limit: The Political Economy of Change* (London: Zed Books, 2011), 213.

12. Marais, *South Africa Pushed to the Limit*, 212–13.

13. Brij Maharaj, "Apartheid, Urban Segregation, and the Local State: Durban and the Group Areas Act in South Africa," *Urban Geography* 18, no. 2 (1997): 135–54; for more on this, see Goolam Vahed, "Indians, Islam, and the Meaning of South African Citizenship: A Question of Identities," *Transformations* 43 (2000): 30; see Makhosezwe, *Political Economy of Race and Class in South Africa*, 77–79, for the Chinese Labor Ordinance banning the import of more Chinese labor and providing for the repatriation of all earlier arrivals, with few exceptions.

14. UNHCR, "Country Operations Profile: South Africa," 2012, http://www.unhcr.org/; also see Parliamentary Monitoring Group, "State of Ports of Entry and Refugee Reception Offices," May 22, 2012, http://www.pmg.org.za/.

15. Tal Hanna Schreier, "An Evaluation of South Africa's Application of the OAU Refugee Definition," *Refuge* 25, no. 2 (2008): 54–57.

16. Department of Home Affairs, "Refugee Status and Asylum," http://www.home-affairs.gov.za/.

17. The *khamis*, or *qamis*, is a long robe often worn by Muslims in the Middle East and South Asia. Though not common in Somalia, some in the diaspora have now adopted wearing this robe for the Friday prayers. The *taqiyah* is a skullcap, often white, and, like the *khamis*, is more commonly worn in South Asia and the Middle East but is also found throughout the Muslim world.

18. Mayfair was in fact designated a white residential area during apartheid but was taken over by Indians shortly after the fall of the apartheid regime and now is home to Indians as well as migrants from Pakistan, Bangladesh, and the rest of Africa.

19. Hasan Hanafi, "Alternative Conceptions of Civil Society: A Reflective Islamic Approach," in *Alternative Conceptions of Civil Society*, ed. Simone Chambers and Will Kymlicka, 171–89 (Princeton, N.J.: Princeton University Press, 2002), 177.

20. Though little is known about them, dozens of Somali men came to the Cape area in the 1940s as seamen with the British. They settled and intermarried within the Cape Malay and Indian communities.

21. Somali women's presence in mosques was not encouraged and still remains rare. Except for the Muslim holidays, Somali women mostly pray at home. This is both cultural and a result of a common belief in Somali religious teachings that women are religiously encouraged to spend their time at home. But another practical reason within the Somali context was the limited mosque spaces available, with most mosques not having space allocated to women. Thus economic as well as patriarchal rationales often framed as religious teachings produced a culture where Somali women are still rarely present in mosques. See Vahed, "Indians, Islam, and the Meaning of South African Citizenship," 33–34, on the experience of Indian Muslims in South Africa.

22. David Neves, Michael Samson, Ingrid van Niekerk, Sandile Hlatshwayo, and Andries du Toit, *The Use and Effectiveness of Social Grants in South Africa* (Cape Town: Institute of Poverty, Land, and Agrarian Studies, University of the Western Cape, 2009), 11–12.

23. Nicoli Nattrass and Jeremy Seekings, "'Two Nations'? Race and Economic Inequality in South Africa Today," *Daedalus* 130, no. 1 (2001): 57.

24. Neves et al., "Use and Effectiveness of Social Grants in South Africa," 14–15.

25. Ibid., 46.

26. Charles Meth and Rosa Dias, "Increase in Poverty in South Africa, 1999–2002," *Development South Africa* 21, no. 1 (2004): 60–61.

27. Robert Mattes, "South Africa: Democracy without the People?," *Journal of Democracy* 13, no. 1 (2002): 24.

28. For more discussion of race in Somalia, see Besteman, *Unraveling Somalia*; Abdi M. Kusow, "Migration and Racial Formations among Somali Immigrants in North America," *Journal of Ethnic and Migration Studies* 32, no. 3 (2006): 533–51.

29. Marais, *South Africa Pushed to the Limit*.

30. Charles Meth, "Income Poverty in 2004: A Second Engagement with the Recent van der Berg et al. Figures," Working Paper 47, School for Development Studies, University of KwaZulu-Natal, September 2006, cited in Marais, *South Africa Pushed to the Limit*, 203.

31. Social Housing Foundation, "Shack Rentals in South Africa," December 2008.

32. Christian Rogerson, "The Underdevelopment of the Informal Sector: Street Hawking in Johannesburg, South Africa," *Urban Geography* 9, no. 6 (1988): 554–55.

33. For a thorough overview of this underdevelopment, see Rogerson, "Underdevelopment of the Informal Sector."

34. Nsolo J. Mijere, "Urbanization and the Informal Sector in the Former South African Ethnic Homelands: A Study of Parallel Trading in Transkei," *African Population Studies* 12, no. 1 (1997): 1–6.

35. Christian Rogerson, "Urban Poverty and the Informal Economy in South Africa's Economic Heartland," *Environment and Urbanization* 8 (1996): 172.

36. Keith Buchanan and N. Hurwitz, "The Asiatic Immigrant Community in the Union of South Africa," *Geographical Review* 39, no. 3 (1949): 440–49; Goolam Vahed, "Control and Repression: The Plight of Indian Hawkers and Flower Sellers in Durban, 1910–1948," *International Journal of African Historical Studies* 32, no. 1 (1999): 19–48.

37. See Barak D. Richman, "How Community Institutions Create Economic Advantage: Jewish Diamond Merchants in New York," *American Law and Economics Association Annual Meetings* (2005): 6–9, for a detailed discussion of how domination or concentration of an ethnic group requires a combination of different theories on history, path dependency, human capital, religious networks, and ethnic cartels.

38. Pyong Gap Min, "From White Collar Occupations to Small Business: Korean Immigrants' Occupational Adjustment," *Sociological Quarterly* 25, no. 3 (1984): 333–52.

39. Ulrich Jurgens and Ronnie Donaldson, "A Review of Literature on Transformation Processes in South African Townships," *Urban Forum* 23, no. 2 (2012): 156. Also see Maylam, "Explaining the Apartheid City," 31–33, for a detailed discussion of how African enterprise was repressed to service white monopolies and fill state coffers.

40. Edna Bonacich, "A Theory of Middleman Minorities," *American Sociological Review* 38, no. 5 (1973): 583–94. Also see Gold, *Store in the Hood*, for more in-depth historical and empirical discussion on this subject.

41. See Vahed, "Plight of Indian Hawkers and Flower Sellers," for more discussion of the closer ties and the "status gap" between Africans and Indians in Durban.

42. Vahed, "Indians, Islam, and the Meaning of South African Citizenship," 31.

43. The exchange rate of the South African rand to the U.S. dollar fluctuated from around R8 to the dollar to R12 to the dollar between January and December 2001.

44. Gold, *Store in the Hood*; Jeremy Hein, *From Vietnam, Laos, and Cambodia: A Refugee Experience in the United States* (New York: Twayne, 1995); Bonacich, "A Theory of Middleman Minorities," 584–85; Evan Light and Steven J. Gold, *Ethnic Economies* (San Diego, Calif.: Academic Press, 2000); Jennifer Lee, "Retail Niche Domination among African American, Jewish, and Korean Entrepreneurs: Competition, Coethnic Advantage and Disadvantage," *American Behavioral Scientist* 42, no. 9 (1999): 1398–1416.

45. *Haji* is a title given to a Muslim who performed the pilgrimage to Mecca. The title is put in front of the name of such a person, to acknowledge this special position that only a small number of the global Muslim population can afford to undertake.

46. "Location" is interchangeable for "township" in South Africa.

47. Rogerson, "Urban Poverty and the Informal Economy," 173.

48. Goolam Vahed and Ashwin Desai, "Identity and Belonging in Post-Apartheid South Africa: The Case of Indian South Africans," *Journal of Social Science* 25, nos. 1–3 (2010): 3.

49. Guy Lamb, "'Under the Gun': An Assessment of Firearm Crime and Violence in South Africa," Institute for Security Studies Report compiled for the Office of the President, Pretoria, South Africa, 2008, 1; also see Martin Schönteich and Antoinette Louw, "Crime in South Africa: A Country and Cities Profile," Occasional Paper 49, Crime and Justice Programme, Institute for Security Studies, 2001, 7–9, http://www.issafrica.org/.

50. Lamb, "Under the Gun."

51. Gold, *Store in the Hood*; Lee, "Retail Niche Domination"; Jennifer Lee, "From Civil Relations to Racial Conflict: Merchant–Customer Interactions in Urban America," *American Sociological Review* 67, no. 1 (2002): 77–98.

52. Naeemah Abrahams, Rachel Jewkes, and Shanaaz Mathews, "Guns and Gender-Based Violence in South Africa," *South Africa Medical Journal* 100 (2010): 589; Medical Research Council, "Preventing Rape and Sexual Violence in South Africa: Call for Leadership in a New Agenda for Action," Policy Brief, November 1–2, http://www.mrc.ac.za/.

53. Mail and Guardian, "MRC: Quarter of Men in South Africa Admit Rape," June 18, 2009, http://mg.co.za/.

54. Shaun Gillham, "Somalis Outraged after Pregnant Woman Strangled," *The Herald,* September 17, 2012, http://www.peherald.com/.

55. Lidwien Kapteijns, "Gender Relations and the Transformation of the Northern Somali Pastoral Tradition," *International Journal of African Historical Studies* 28, no. 2 (1995): 241–59.

56. Parrenas, *Children of Global Migration;* Pierrette Hondagneu-Sotelo, *Gendered Transitions: Mexican Experiences of Immigration* (Berkeley: University of California Press, 1994); Pierrette Hondagneu-Sotelo and Ernestine Avila, "'I'm Here, but I'm There': The Meanings of Latina Transnational Motherhood," *Gender and Society* 11, no. 5 (1997): 548–71.

57. Innovative Medicines South Africa, "Income and Social Solidarity in South Africa," National Health Insurance Policy Brief 25, 2012, 3, http://www.imsa.org.za/.

58. Statistics South Africa, "Income and Expenditure of Households: 2005/2006: Analysis of Results," Report 01-00-01, 6.

59. Ibid.

60. Joubert Pearlie, "Wiped Out in SA," *Mail and Guardian,* October 5, 2008.

61. *Mail and Guardian,* "Mining Unrest 'Not a Symptom of Inequality,'" September 27, 2012, http://mg.co.za/; British Broadcasting Channel, "South Africa's Lonmin Marikana Clashes Killed 34," August 17, 2012; *Al Jazeera English,* "South Africa's Marikana Miners Defy Deadline," September 11, 2012.

62. News 24, "Strikers Shot at Cops, Inquiry Hears," November 9, 2012; David Smith, "South African Police 'Shot Miners to Protect Themselves,'" *The Guardian,* August 17, 2012. To clarify the terminology, panga (machetes) are cleaverlike tools used for agricultural purposes but that can also be used as weapons in times of conflict. A knobkerrie is a walking stick with a knob at the top that again can serve as a weapon in times of conflict. See Sarah Evans, "Farlam Commission: Police May Face Perjury Charges," *Mail and Guardian,* September 27, 2013, http://mg.co.za/.

63. *Mail and Guardian,* "Strikers Return to Work at Three Gold Field Shafts," October 17, 2012; *Mail and Guardian,* "Leaderless Farm Strike Is 'Organic,'" October 16, 2012.

64. For more on the protests over public services, see *Mail and Guardian,* "SA Hit by Service Delivery Protests," July 22, 2009, http://mg.co.za/.

65. Graeme Hosken and Amukeani Chauke, "Miners Turn Anger onto Foreign Traders," *Sowetan,* October 4, 2012, http://www.sowetanlive.co.za/news/.

66. Schönteich and Louw, "Crime in South Africa," 5.

67. *Mail and Guardian*, "A Place of Violence, Where Necklacing Is the Only Choice," July 27, 2011, http://mg.co.za/. Also see IOL News, "Vigilantism Claims 7 More Lives," June 28, 2011, http://www.iol.co.za/news/.

68. "A Place of Violence"; also see Bill Dixon and Lisa-Marie Johns, "Gangs, PAGAD & the State: Vigilantism and Revenge Violence in the Western Cape," Center for the Study of Violence and Reconciliation, Violence and Transition Series, 2 (2001), 1–71, for more discussion of popular activism against gangs and drugs in the Western Cape as it relates to People against Gangsterism and Drugs (PAGAD).

69. Lee, "From Civil Relations to Racial Conflict," 78. Also see Lee, "Retail Niche Domination among African American, Jewish, and Korean Entrepreneurs," for more discussion on this topic.

70. Cawo Mohamed Abdi, "Moving beyond Xenophobia: Structural Violence, Conflict, and Encounters with the 'Other' Africans," *Development Southern Africa* 28, no. 5 (2011): 691–704.

71. *Mail and Guardian*, "Toll from Xenophobic Attacks Rises," May 31, 2008, http://mg.co.za/.

72. Ibid.

73. Alan Morris, "'Our Fellow Africans Make Our Lives Hell': The Lives of Congolese and Nigerians Living in Johannesburg," *Ethnic and Racial Studies* 21, no. 6 (1998): 1116–36; Michael Neocosmos, "The Politics of Fear and the Fear of Politics (Essay on the Pogroms)," *Abahlahli base Mjondolo*, June 5, 2008, http://www.abahlali.org/; Marion Ryan Sinclair, "'I Know a Place That Is Softer Than This . . .'—Emerging Migrant Communities in South Africa," *International Migration* 37, no. 2 (1999): 465–83.

74. Peter Luhanga, "Meeting on Somali Spaza Tensions," *New Age*, March 9, 2012, http://www.thenewage.co.za/.

75. Andrew Faull, "Corruption and the South African Police Service: A Review and Its Implications," *Institute for Security Studies Papers* 150 (2007): 1–20; Gareth Newham, "Tackling Police Corruption in South Africa," *Africa do Sul: Centre for the Study of Violence and Reconciliation* (2002): 1–19.

76. Halal food is prepared according to Islamic law; *haram* denotes impermissible acts, in this case, food that is not fit for Muslim consumption.

77. Integrated Regional Information Networks, "REFUGEES: Resettlement Still a Last Resort," August 1, 2012, http://www.irinnews.org/.

78. Ibid.

79. UNHCR, "Frequently Asked Questions about Resettlement," 2012.

80. UNHCR, "Country Operations Profile"; also see Parliamentary Monitoring Group, "State of Ports of Entry and Refugee Reception Offices."

81. *Mail and Guardian*, "US Slams 'Corrupt' SA Home Affairs Department," May 7, 2009, http://mg.co.za/.

82. Harris Selod and Yves Zenou, "Private versus Public Schools in Post-Apartheid South African Cities: Theory and Policy Implications," *Journal of Development Economics* 71, no. 2 (2003): 351–94; The Economist, "South Africa's Education System: No One Gets Prizes," January 14, 2010, http://www.economist.com/.

83. Parrenas, *Children of Global Migration*; Hondagneu-Sotelo and Avila, "I'm Here, but I'm There."

4. United States

1. Mahamud Abdulahi Sangub, "Qabyo I."
2. Lazarus, "New Colossus," 1983.
3. Paul Spickard, *Almost All Aliens: Immigration, Race, Colonialism in American History and Identity* (New York: Routledge, 2009). This remains the most thorough work to go as far back as the founding of the United States and closes with the current policies, groups, and relations in America at the dawn of the twenty-first century.
4. Ibid.; Alejandro Portes and Ruben G. Rumbaut, *Immigrant America: A Portrait* (Berkeley: University of California Press, 2006).
5. Migration Policy Institute, "MPI Data Hub," 2012, http://www.migrationinformation.org/.
6. John A. Arthur, *Invisible Sojourners: African Immigrant Diaspora in the United States* (Westport, Conn.: Praeger, 2000), 154.
7. Ibid.
8. Immigration Policy Center, "African Immigrants in America: A Demographic Overview," June 28, 2012, http://www.immigrationpolicy.org/.
9. Mary Mederios Kent, *Immigration and America's Black Population* (Washington, D.C.: Population Reference Bureau, 2007).
10. The Economist, "Minnesota's Job Market: Land of 10,000 Opportunities," May 27, 1999, http://www.economist.com/.
11. Barbara Roningen, "Minnesota's African Population," paper presented at the Africans in the Diaspora Conference, University of Minnesota, Minneapolis, June 18, 2004.
12. U.S. Census Bureau, American Community Survey, "2010–12 American Community Survey 3-Year Estimates," Table S0201, generated by Cawo M. Abdi using American FactFinder, December 30, 2013.
13. Office of Refugee Resettlement, "Refugee Arrival Data," July 17, 2012, http://www.acf.hhs.gov/; U.S. Immigration and Naturalization Service, *Statistical Yearbook of the Immigration and Naturalization Service, 2000* (Washington, D.C.: U.S. Government Printing Office, 2002), 95; U.S. Department of Homeland Security, *Yearbook of Immigration Statistics: 2011* (Washington, D.C.: U.S. Department of Homeland Security, Office of Immigration Statistics, 2012), 40.

14. U.S. Immigration and Naturalization Service, *Statistical Yearbook*, 38.

15. Andorra Bruno, "United States Refugee Resettlement Assistance," CRS Report for Congress, 2004, 6–7; Aristide R. Zolberg, Astri Suhrke, and Sergio Aguayo, *Escape from Violence: Conflict and the Refugee Crisis in the Developing World* (New York: Oxford University Press, 1989).

16. Bruno, "United States Refugee Resettlement Assistance," 5.

17. For a thorough discussion of the vital role these remittances play in the lives of Somalis still in the Horn, please see Anna Lindley, *The Early Morning Phone Call: Somali Refugees' Remittances* (New York: Berghahn Books, 2010).

18. Marta Tienda and Karen Booth, "Gender, Migration, and Social Change," *International Sociology* 6, no. 1 (1991): 51; Ousmane Oumar Kane, *The Homeland Is the Arena: Transnationalism and the Integration of Senegalese Immigrants in America* (New York: Oxford University Press, 2011).

19. Kibria, *Family Tightrope*; Patricia R. Pessar, "Engendering Migration Studies: The Case of New Immigrants in the United States," *American Behavioral Science* 42, no. 4 (1999): 577–600; Hondagneu-Sotelo, *Gendered Transitions*; Parrenas, *Children of Global Migration*.

20. Kathryn J. Edin and Laura Lein, "Work, Welfare, and Single Mothers' Economic Survival Strategies," *American Sociological Review* 61 (1996): 254–66; Frances Fox Piven, "Welfare and Work," *Social Justice* 25, no. 1 (1998): 67–78; Gary T. Burtless, "Welfare Recipients' Job Skills and Employment Prospects," *The Future of Children* 7, no. 1 (1997): 39–51.

21. Minnesota Department of Human Services, "Racial/Ethnic and Immigrant Groups Participating in the Minnesota Family Investment Program and the Diversionary Work Program," MDHS REIS 16, December 2010.

22. Doris Ng, "Welfare Reform in Santa Clara County: The Experience of Mexican and Vietnamese Immigrant Women," in *Immigrants, Welfare Reform, and the Poverty of Policy*, ed. Philip Kretsedemas and A. Aparicio, 159–83 (Westport, Conn.: Praeger, 2004); Bob Paral, "Disparate Welfare Needs and Impacts of Welfare Reform among Illinois Immigrants," in ibid., 89–105.

23. Minnesota Department of Human Services, "At the Limit: December 2010 Minnesota Family Investment Program (MFIP) Cases That Reached the 60-Month Time Limit," DHS-5092F-ENG 12-11, 2011.

24. Piven, "Welfare and Work."

25. Ibid.

26. Awa (Cawo) M. Abdi, "Convergence of Civil War and Prominence of the Religious Right: Re-imagining Somali Women," *Signs* 33, no. 1 (2005): 183–207; Abdi, "Refugees, Gender-Based Violence, and Resistance."

27. Abdi, "Convergence of Civil War"; Abdi, "Refugees, Gender-Based Violence, and Resistance."
28. The U.S. Census calculates this based on "a set of money income thresholds that vary with family size and composition" and compares that to family income. For more, see U.S. Census Bureau, "Poverty in the United States: 2002," http://www.census.gov/.
29. Abdi, "Threatened Identities and Gendered Opportunities."
30. Minnesota Department of Human Services, "Characteristics of December 2003 Minnesota Family Investment Program Cases and Eligible Adults by Racial/Ethnic Groups and Subgroups," DHS-4262I-ENG 10-04, 2004, 8–14.
31. Minnesota Department of Human Services, "Racial/Ethnic and Immigrant Groups," 38.
32. These are random names Abshir used for illustrative purposes.
33. Rima Berns McGown, *Muslims in the Diaspora: The Somali Communities of London and Toronto* (Toronto: University of Toronto Press, 1999); Nauja Kleist, "Negotiating Respectable Masculinity: Gender and Recognition in the Somali Diaspora," *African Diaspora* 3, no. 2 (2010): 185–206.
34. Robert F. Schoeni, "Labor Market Outcomes of Immigrant Women in the United States: 1970–1990," *International Migration Review* 32, no. 1 (1998): 57–77; Candace Nelson and Marta Tienda, "The Structuring of Hispanic Ethnicity: Historical and Contemporary Perspectives," *Ethnic and Racial Studies* 8, no. 1 (1985): 49–74; Alejandro Portes and J. Borocz, "Contemporary Immigration: Theoretical Perspectives on Its Determinants and Modes of Incorporation," *International Migration Review* 23, no. 3 (1989): 606–30; Portes and Rumbaut, *Immigrant America*; Robert L. Bach and R. Caroll-Sequin, "Labor Force Participation, Household Composition, and Sponsorship amongst Southeast Asian Refugees," *International Migration Review* 20, no. 2 (1986): 381–404; William A. V. Clark, *Immigrants and the American Dream: Remaking the Middle Class* (New York: Guilford Press, 2003); Gary D. Sandefur and Steven T. Cook, "Duration of Public Assistance Receipt: Is Welfare a Trap?," Discussion Paper 1129-97 (Madison: University of Wisconsin, Institute for Research on Poverty, 1997).
35. Schoeni, "Labor Market Outcomes"; Portes and Rumbaut, *Immigrant America*.
36. Portes and Rumbaut, *Immigrant America*; Mary C. Waters and Karl Eschbach, "Immigration and Ethnic and Racial Inequality in the United States," *Annual Review of Sociology* 21 (1995): 419–46.
37. Waters and Eschbach, "Immigration and Ethnic and Racial Inequality in the United States."
38. Alejandro Portes and John Walton, *Labor, Class, and the International System* (New York: Academic Press, 1981), cited in Portes and Borocz, "Contemporary Immigration," 621.

39. William Julius Wilson, *Jobless Ghettoes: The Disappearance of Work and Its Effect on Urban Life* (New York: Knopf, 1991); Roger Waldinger and Jennifer Lee, "New Immigrants in Urban America," in *Strangers at the Gates*, ed. Roger Waldinger, 30–79 (Berkeley: University of California Press, 2001); Portes and Rumbaut, *Immigrant America*; Clark, *Immigrants and the American Dream*; Paral, "Disparate Welfare Needs."

40. Rebecca Blank and Heidi Shierholz, "How Are Low-Skilled Women Doing in the Labor Market?," Policy Brief 6 (Ann Arbor, Mich.: National Poverty Center, University of Michigan, 2006), http://www.npc.umich.edu/publications/.

41. Clark, *Immigrants and the American Dream*, 196.

42. Ibid., 20.

43. Ibid.; Portes and Rumbaut, "Immigrant America."

44. Parrenas, "Reproductive Labor of Migrant Workers"; also see Mary Zimmerman and Shirley A. Hill, "Health Care as a Gendered System" in *Handbook of the Sociology of Gender*, ed. Janet Saltzman Chafetz, 483–518 (New York: Springer, 2006).

45. Abdi, "Convergence of Civil War."

46. Pessar, "Engendering Migration Studies," 584; Ng, "Welfare Reform in Santa Clara County"; Burtless, "Welfare Recipients' Job Skills and Employment Prospects"; Piven, "Welfare and Work"; Sandefur and Cook, "Duration of Public Assistance Receipt."

47. Ng, "Welfare Reform in Santa Clara County."

48. Portes and Rumbaut, *Immigrant America*, 87.

49. My own mother, who did not belong to these minority clans, raised eight children selling meat in an open market in central Somalia.

50. U.S. Census Bureau, 2010–2013 American Community Survey.

51. Minnesota Public Radio, "Renewed Focus on Somali Community," September 27, 2013, http://minnesota.publicradio.org/; Public Radio International, "An Unwelcome Spotlight Falls on Minnesota's Somali Community Because of Nairobi Attack," *The World*, September 24, 2013, http://pri.org/.

52. Jessica Stern, "We Need to Worry about Somali Terrorists in the U.S.," *Time*, September 26, 2013, http://ideas.time.com/.

53. Andrea Elliott, "A Call to Jihad, Answered in America," *New York Times*, July 11, 2009, http://www.nytimes.com/.

54. Nadine Naber, "Ambiguous Insiders: An Investigation of Arab American Invisibility," *Ethnic and Racial Studies* 23, no. 1 (2000): 37–61.

55. Bach and Caroll-Sequin, "Labor Force Participation."

56. Eric Tang, "Collateral Damage: Southeast Asian Poverty in the United States," *Social Text* 62, no. 18 (2000): 55.

57. Abdi, "Threatened Identities and Gendered Opportunities."

58. Lidwien Kapteijns, *Women and the Crisis of Communal Identity: The Cultural Construction of Gender in Somali History* (Boston: African Studies Center, Boston University, 1993).

59. Portes and Rumbaut, *Immigrant America*; George J. Porjas, "The Self-Employment Experience of Immigrants," *Journal of Human Resources* 21, no. 4 (1986): 485–506.

60. Hussein Samatar, "Experiences of Somali Entrepreneurs in the Twin Cities," *Bildhaan: An International Journal of Somali Studies* 2 (2004): 78–91.

61. This estimate was based on a physical count I did of the main malls in the Twin Cities. Clothing stores often have only one person managing and running them. Hussein Samatar, "Experiences of Somali Entrepreneurs in the Twin Cities," 78, provided an estimate of 550 businesses around the Twin Cities from a survey conducted in 2004. My estimate is much lower, though some of the discrepancy might be due to high failure rates of small businesses. Also see the Somali Chamber of Commerce website for more information on this: http://www.soamcc.org/.

62. This is just an estimate, as the numbers of this population we get from the census and from the Somali community organizations vary so widely.

63. Samatar, "Experiences of Somali Entrepreneurs in the Twin Cities."

64. Sudhir Alladi Venkatesh, *Off the Books* (Cambridge, Mass.: Harvard University Press, 2006).

65. U.S. Census Bureau, "Poverty in the United States: 2002," http://www.census.gov/prod/2003pubs/p60-222.pdf.

66. U.S. Census Bureau, 2010–2013 American Community Survey; U.S. Census Bureau, "Census Bureau Data Show Characteristics of the U.S. Foreign-Born Population," American Community Survey, February 19, 2009, http://www.census.gov/newsroom. Somalis in the United Kingdom are also found to be faring much worse than all other groups. For more on this, please see *The Economist*, "Britain's Somalis: The Road Is Long," August 17, 2013, http://www.economist.com/. Also see Information Centre about Asylum and Refugees, "ICAR Briefing: The Somali Refugee Community in the UK," 2007, http://www.icar.org.uk/; A. Curry-Stevens and Coalition of Communities of Color, *The African Immigrant and Refugee Community in Multnomah County: An Unsettling Profile* (Portland, Oreg.: Portland State University, 2013).

67. Minnesota Department of Human Services, "Racial/Ethnic and Immigrant Groups," 46.

68. Ibid.

69. Minnesota Department of Human Services, "Welfare in Minnesota: Facts and Figures," 2005, http://www.dhs.state.mn.us/.

70. Clark, *Immigrants and the American Dream*; Ng, "Welfare Reform in Santa Clara County."

71. Holly Zachariah, "Police Use Pepper Spray to Handle Unruly Crowd," *Columbus Dispatch,* December 9, 2012, http://www.dispatch.com/.

72. Jemima Pierre, "Black Immigrants in the United States and the 'Cultural Narratives' of Ethnicity," *Identities: Global Studies in Culture and Power* 11, no. 2 (2004): 141–70.

73. For more on this, see Kristine J. Ajrouch and Abdi M. Kusow, "Racial and Religious Contexts: Situational Identities among Lebanese and Somali Muslim Immigrants," *Ethnic and Racial Studies* 30, no. 1 (2007): 72–94.

74. Allie Shah, "Minneapolis South High Clash Exposes Somali- and African-American Student Rift," *Star Tribune,* February 23, 2013, http://www.startribune.com/; Matthew Marx, "Lunchroom Fight: Police Stop Brawl at Mifflin between Black, Somali Teens," *Columbus Dispatch,* February 24, 2005.

75. Sarah J. Mahler, "Theoretical and Empirical Contributions towards a Research Agenda for Transnationalism," in *Transnationalism from Below,* ed. Michael Peter Smith and Luis Eduardo Guarnizo, 64–100 (New Brunswick, N.J.: Transaction, 2003); Nadje Al-Ali and Khalid Koser, eds., *New Approaches to Migration? Transnational Communities and the Transformation of Home* (London: Routledge 2002); Nadje Al-Ali, R. Black, and K. Koser, "Refugees and Transnationalism: The Experience of Bosnians and Eritreans in Europe," *Journal of Ethnic and Migration Studies* 27, no. 4 (2001): 615–34.

76. Al-Ali et al., "Refugees and Transnationalism"; Al-Ali and Khoser, *New Approaches to Migration?*; Mahler, "Theoretical and Empirical Contributions "; Sergio Diaz-Briquets and Jorge Perez-Lopez, "Refugee Remittances: Conceptual Issues and the Cuban and Nicaraguan Experiences," *International Migration Review* 31, no. 2 (1997): 411–47; Hondagneu-Sotelo, *Gendered Transitions.*

77. Laura Hammond, Mustafa Awad, Ali Ibrahim Dagane, Peter Hansen, Cindy Horst, Ken Menkhaus, and Lynette Obare, *Cash and Compassion: The Role of the Somali Disapora in Relief, Development and Peace-building* (Nairobi: United Nations Development Programme Somalia, 2011); Lindley, *Early Morning Phone Call.*

78. For more discussion on these tensions, see Parrenas, *Servants of Globalization*; Parrenas, *Children of Global Migration*; Gerald Sider, "The Contradictions of Transnational Migration: A Discussion," in *Towards a Transnational Perspective on Migration: Race, Class, Ethnicity, and Nationalism Reconsidered,* ed. Nina Glick-Schiller, Linda Basch, and Christina Blanc-Szanton, 231–40 (New York: New York Academy of Sciences, 1992); Luis Eduardo Guarzino and Michael Peter Smith, "The Locations of Transnationalism," in Smith and Guarnizo, *Transnationalism from Below,* 3–34.

79. Abdi, "Threatened Identities and Gendered Opportunities."

80. Guarnizo and Smith, "Locations of Transnationalism."

81. Basch et al., *Nations Unbound*, 279.

82. Oscar Handlin, *The Uprooted: The Epic Story of the Great Migration That Made the American People* (Boston: Little, Brown, 1973); Philip Lewis, *Islamic Britain: Religion, Politics, and Identity among British Muslims* (London: I. B. Tauris, 1994).

83. Min Zhou, "Segmented Assimilation: Issues, Controversies, and Recent Research on the New Second Generation," *International Migration Review* 31 (1997): 975–1008.

84. For more discussion of Somali women's perceived transgressions, see Abdi, "Threatened Identities and Gendered Opportunities."

85. Luin Goldring, "The Power of Status in Transnational Social Fields," in Smith and Guarnizo, *Transnationalism from Below*, 165–95; Takyiwaa Manuh, "'Efie' or the Meaning of 'Home' among Female and Male Ghanian Migrants in Toronto, Canada and Returned Migrants to Ghana," in *New African Diasporas*, ed. Khalid Koser (London: Routledge, 2003), 140–59.

86. I spent just more than three months in Dadaab camps in 2001 for my MA fieldwork. For more on this, please see Abdi, "Convergence of Civil War and the Prominence of the Religious Right"; Abdi, "Refugees, Gender-Based Violence, and Resistance."

87. Peggy Levitt, "Social Remittances: Migration Driven Local-Level Forms of Cultural Diffusion," *International Migration Review* 32, no. 4 (1998): 926–48; Peggy Levitt and Deepak Lamba-Nieves, "Social Remittances Revisited," *Journal of Ethnic and Migration Studies* 37, no. 1 (2011): 1–22.

88. Goldring, "Power of Status," 189.

89. Patricia Jeffery, *Migrants and Refugees: Muslim and Christian Pakistani Families in Bristol* (London: Cambridge University Press, 1976), 144–45.

90. I met Asha in Nairobi in May 2013 and followed this case from 2004, when I first interviewed her for my PhD work, to the completion the final stages of this book project.

91. Basch et al., *Nations Unbound*, 9; also see Mary Waters, "Ethnic and Racial Identities of Second Generation Black Immigrants in New York City," *International Migration Review* 28 (1994): 795–820.

92. Waters, "Ethnic and Racial Identities."

93. Pierre, "Black Immigrants in the United States," 162.

94. Kibria, *Family Tightrope*.

95. Until the recent conflict, Syria was a very popular destination for Somalis from Europe, Australia, and North America as well as middle-class and upper-middle-class Somalis in Kenya and Somalia. It provided good public education that was free for Somalis, who are part of the Arab League, and was also affordable for these families.

96. Returning girls to Somalia rarely involves female circumcision, which was often done to Somali girls at a very young age. In fact, my long-term fieldwork with Somalis in North America convinces me that this practice is rare within the diaspora, as religious education has increased and parents' interaction with other Muslim communities who have never known this practice has raised awareness. Also the cost of traveling to have young girls circumcised is itself prohibitive and may also contribute to the decrease in the practice, though it is reported that this does happen.

97. Hondagneu-Sotelo, *Gendered Transitions.*

98. Kelly Fernandez, M. Patricia, and Anna M. Garcia, "Power Surrendered, Power Restored: The Politics of Work and Family among Hispanic Garment Workers in California and Florida," in *Women, Politics, and Change,* ed. Louse A. Tilly and Patricia Gurin, 130–49 (New York: Russell Sage Foundation, 1990).

99. Guarzino and Smith, "Locations of Transnationalism," 23.

Conclusion

1. Kenny, "Diaspora and Comparison," 162.

2. Pierrette Hondagneu-Sotelo, "Families on the Frontier: From Braceros in the Fields to Braceras in the Home," in *The New Immigration: An Interdisciplinary Reader,* ed. Marcelo M. Suárez-Orozco, Carola Suárez-Orozco, and Desirée Qin-Hilliard, 167–77 (New York: Psychology Press, 2005).

3. Aihwa Ong, "On the Edge of Empires: Flexible Citizenship among Chinese in Diaspora," *positions* 1, no. 3 (1993): 745–78; Ong, *Flexible Citizenship: The Cultural Logics of Transnationality* (Durham, N.C.: Duke University Press, 1999).

4. Peter Laurence, "EU Questions Malta on Passport Sale for Rich Foreigners," BBC, January 23, 2014.

5. Hyndman, "Supra-citizen and Sub-citizen." Hyndman in fact is writing about Somali refugees in Kenyan camps, and different groups in it (refugee men and women, international NGO workers, Kenyan workers, etc.) are stratified and have unequal voices. But this concept can be used for those whose citizenship hinders border crossings around the world vis-à-vis those who can move without any visas around the globe.

6. These figures correspond to 2013. See Awad Mustafa, "UAE Ranks Second in Arab Countries for Visa-Free Travel," *The National,* October 2, 2013.

7. Henley and Partners Visa Restriction Index, https://www.henleyglobal.com/visa-restrictions/.

8. Anthony Richmond, *Global Apartheid: Refugees, Racism, and the New World Order* (Toronto: Oxford University Press, 1994).

9. United Nations Department of Economic and Social Affairs, Population Division, "232 Million International Migrants Living Abroad Worldwide—New UN Global Migration Statistics Reveal," http://esa.un.org/unmigration/wallchart2013.htm.

10. Cawo Mohamed Abdi, "Threatened Identities and Gendered Opportunities: Somali Migration to America," *Signs* 39, no. 2 (2014): 459–83.

11. Carole Nagengast and Michael Kearney, "Mixtec Ethnicity: Social Identity, Political Consciousness, and Political Activism," *Latin American Research Review* 25, no. 2 (1990): 61–91.

12. Glick-Schiller et al., *Towards a Transnational Perspective on Migration*; Linda Basch, Nina Glick-Schiller, and Cristina Szanton Blanc, *Nations Unbound* (Langhorne, Pa.: Gordon and Breach, 1993), 2–4; Peggy Levitt, "Transnational Migration: Taking Stock and Future Directions," *Global Networks* 1, no. 3 (2001): 195–216.

13. Sider, "Contradictions of Transnational Migration"; Parrenas, *Servants of Globalization*; Parrenas, *Children of Global Migration*.

14. Alejandro Portes, Luis E. Guarnizo, and Patricia Landolt, "The Study of Transnationalism: Pitfalls and Promise of an Emergent Research Field," *Ethnic and Racial Studies* 22, no. 2 (1999): 217–37; Luis Eduardo Guarnizo, "The Rise of Transnational Social Formations: Mexican and Dominican State Responses to Transnational Migration," *Political Power and Social Theory* 12 (1998): 45–94.

INDEX

Abu Dhabi, 62, 63–64, 74, 85
action. *See* agency
Africa, 233, 258n18; independence movements in, 35–37; postcolonial state-building projects, 32, 33–34; return to, 6, 8, 221–22; women's idealization of life in, 223, 224–25, 229. *See also* Kenya; South Africa; South Africa, Somalis in
agency: in migration, 9–12, 16–17, 58
Ahmed, Abdiweli Sheikh, 42
Aideed, Farah, 40
Aid to Families with Dependent Children (AFDC, U.S.): replacement programs for, 176, 177
alcohol consumption: Somali lack of exposure to, 98–99
alienation/isolation: of Somalis in the United States, 6–7, 178–79, 206, 228–29, 240–41
Anderson, Benedict, 59
Aneesh, Aneesh, 11
anthropologists: migration studies by, 10–11

apartheid, 131, 235; legacy of, 18, 111–14, 119, 157–58, 159. *See also* blacks, South African: apartheid's effects on; South Africa: postapartheid conditions
Arabian Gulf/Peninsula, 2–3, 19, 43, 87–92, 130. *See also* Gulf States; oil boom; United Arab Emirates; *and individual Gulf countries*
Arab League/Arabs: Somalis' identification with, 82, 91, 101, 121, 143, 200, 236, 239
Asians, 123, 186, 233; as labor migrants in UAE, 67–68, 78, 92, 96, 101. *See also* South Asians
assimilation, 66, 218–19. *See also* integration, Somali
asylum seeking, 20–21, 86, 213; in South Africa, 4, 114, 115, 162–63; in United States, 50, 52–53, 173, 174. *See also* refugees; refugees, Somali
Australia: fortification of borders by, 235; resettling refugees in, 49; Somali migration to, 106, 163–64, 178

Bahrain, 63, 64, 252–53n11
Bangladesh: migrants from, 101, 133, 258n18
Bantus: Somali (Jareer), 41, 51, 121, 143, 210; South African, 112. *See also* Gosha people
belonging, Somali sense of: in Arabian Gulf/Peninsula, 2–3; migration experience dependent on, 9, 10–11; in South Africa, 116–21, 167, 229, 237; transnational, 240–42; in UAE, 59–60, 81–82, 84, 101–9, 143, 229, 236. *See also* communities, Somali; families; kinship; umma (community of believers)
Berlin Conference (1896), 33–34, 38
Besteman, Catherine, 41
Bhutan: resettling from, 49
blacks, South African: apartheid's effects on, 18, 111–12, 113–14, 119, 157–58, 159; income levels, 140, 153, 154; marginalization of, 132, 156–57, 158; middle-class, 140; poor, 5–6, 151, 154; Somalis' distancing from, 6, 116, 121, 133–34, 142–47, 158–60, 167, 211–12, 236, 239; unemployment among, 126, 140, 151; as unskilled laborers, 125, 129, 132; violence against, 112, 143–47, 155–67, 237
blacks, U.S.: racialization of, 200, 210–11; Somalis' distancing from, 210–12, 226, 239; subsidized housing for, 207, 210–11
boat people, Somali, 43
Bonacich, Edna, 135
borders: colonial, 33–35, 42; contingencies required to cross, 11–12, 270n5; differences in class affecting crossing of, 79, 82; movement across, 8, 17, 55, 59, 111, 117; seeking security by crossing, 231, 232; smuggling refugees across, 55, 56, 117–18; Somalian colonial, 33–35, 42; Western travel documents facilitate crossing, 85–86. *See also* September 11, 2001, terrorist attacks: border security following
Brettell, Caroline, 10
British Somaliland, 33, 34, 42
businesses, Somali, in South Africa: cash-and-carry trade, 127–28; entrepreneurs, 112, 142; security threats to, 143–47, 149, 155, 156; shopping malls, 201; stores and spaza shops, 131–55, 160, 203, 236–37; women-owned, 147–55. *See also* employment, Somali, in South Africa
businesses, Somali, in UAE: entrepreneurs, 2, 74, 76, 78, 83–87, 93, 105; import-export, 1–2, 70, 79–80, 137, 170–71, 187. *See also* employment, Somali, in UAE
businesses, Somali, in United States, 201–7, 267n61. *See also* employment, Somali, in United States

camps. *See* Dadaab refugee camps; detention centers; refugee camps
Canada: citizenship in, 52, 72, 234–35; fortification of borders by, 235
Canada, Somalis in: migration to United States through, 173; as new earthly jannah, 3, 106, 237; resettling refugees in, 49, 166; smuggling Somalis into, 163–64; welfare programs for, 178, 185–86
capital, human and social: migrants', 8, 10, 14, 219; obstacles to development of, 5, 190–91, 193; of returnees, 221

INDEX

CARE: refugee camp management by, 44
chain migration, Somali, 49; to South Africa, 56, 136; to UAE, 73, 76, 83; to United States, 172–73, 194–95, 211. *See also* family reunification; migration, Somali; step-migration, Somali
charity: in Abu Dhabi, 118–21; in Canada, 167; in UAE, 95, 101; in United States, 176, 183, 216. *See also* Muslims: charity shown by
children and youth, Somali: challenge of disciplining in United States, 225, 226, 227; dreams of return, 222–23; gang involvement, 216–17; segmented assimilation of, 218–19
China: labor migrants from, 114, 257n13; medical schools in, 88, 108; trading with, 71, 74, 85, 105
citizenship: British, 86; Canadian, 57, 72, 234–35; flexible, 27, 60, 107, 218, 233–35, 238; inflexible, 25, 60, 163, 235; South African, 60, 114, 162; South Asian, 68; status of, 2, 3, 4, 5, 8, 29; UAE, 59, 60, 77–78, 103–4, 107, 240, 241–42. *See also* passports; Somalia, political turmoil in: citizens' uncertain legal status in; visas
citizenship, U.S.: advantages of, 57, 238, 251n69; available to migrants and refugees, 7, 60, 237; mobility associated with, 106, 234–35; respect associated with, 6, 28, 222. *See also* United States: passports
citizenship, Western: advantages of, 83, 107–8, 167, 233–34; goal of attaining, 3, 6, 26, 104–9, 112, 165; mobility associated with, 105–6, 218, 219, 234–35, 270n5

civil rights: basic, 8, 19, 232; South African situation, 119, 159, 161; UAE situation, 66, 68, 81, 96; U.S. movement for, 172. *See also* citizenship; citizenship, U.S.; citizenship, Western
clans, 247n1; chiefs of, 6; conflict between, 40–41, 42; identity in, 24–25, 33, 41; minority, 195, 266n49; rebel movements based in, 39–41
class: and attaining Western citizenship, 106–7; border crossings affected by, 79, 82; clans shaped by, 41; and poverty in the United States, 187, 209–10; in Somalia, 55, 70, 193–94; among Somali migrants in UAE, 72, 82, 84, 88; in South Africa, 125–26, 135
clothing, Somali: men's, 258n17; women's, 21–22, 188–89, 192
Cohen, Robin, 13
Columbus, Ohio, Somalis in: businesses owned by, 203; employment for women, 187; shopping malls for, 19–20, 201; subsidized housing for, 207, 209, 211. *See also* Ohio, Somalis in
communities, Somali, 57–58, 83–84, 138, 176, 194–95; networks of, 11, 104, 158, 195, 213. *See also* enclaves, Somali; networks; umma (community of believers)
coping mechanisms. *See* survival, refugees'
corruption: in Ethiopia, 79, 163; in Kenya, 46–48, 57, 163; in Somalia, 37, 41–42, 163; in South Africa, 159, 162–63, 241
Cuba, 38, 173
culture, 163, 229, 239; action's link to, 16–17; global circulation of, 12, 15;

migrants' outlook on, 10, 14; nomadic, 96–97; South African, 126, 134; U.S., 178–79; U.S.–Somali dissonance, 218–20, 222–23. *See also* tool kit, cultural

Dadaab refugee camps (Kenya), 21–22, 44–45, 47, 49, 181, 250n44. *See also* refugee camps: in Kenya
deportation, 107, 109, 254n45
detention centers, 52
Dhagahley refugee camp, 44, 108, 164
diaspora, Somali: emergence of, 31, 42–58, 69; legacy of, 111, 231; map of, 50; men in, 138, 220; Somali-owned businesses in, 70, 201, 203; transnationalism linked to, 13, 18, 213–18; women in, 179. *See also* migration, Somali; returnees, Somali
discrimination. *See* racism
displacement, Somali. *See* diaspora, Somali; Somalia, political turmoil in
divorce, 7, 83, 97, 166, 221, 223, 254n52. *See also* marriage(s)
Djibouti, 2, 33, 34, 35, 79, 248n12
domestic work/workers. *See* employment, Somali, in South Africa: domestic workers; employment, Somali, in UAE: domestic workers; race: and domestic work; women, Somali: domestic workers
dress practices, Somali. *See* clothing, Somali
Dubai, 74, 256n67; as de facto Somali port, 71, 75; Deira Gold Souk, 20, 60–61, 93–94; global cities of, 62, 103; housing prices in, 66, 84–85; quality of life in, 83–84; UAE dominated by, 63–64

East African Bribery Index, 46. *See also* corruption
economy: global, 96, 109; Somali, 1, 71, 193; U.S., 170, 186, 187, 200; Western, 85–86
economy, South African, 228, 260n43; cash-and-carry businesses, 127–28; diverse sectors, 122; exchange rate, 260n43; formal sector of, 126, 132; informal sector of, 126–27, 129–31, 131–55, 187, 193, 236–37; integration of Somali newcomers into, 127, 138, 192; median income, 153–54; postapartheid, 5–6, 126; poverty in, 5–7, 119, 125, 151, 156, 157; white, 113, 257n7. *See also* businesses, Somali, in South Africa; employment, Somali, in South Africa
economy, UAE, 62, 69; informal sector of, 71, 187, 193; opportunities for Somalis in, 82–101. *See also* businesses, Somali, in UAE; employment, Somali, in UAE
Edin, Kathryn J., 179
education: cultural, 227; Somali women's lack of, 179, 187, 189–90; in South Africa, 166; in Syria, 269n95; in UAE, 82, 84, 87, 88, 90, 93; in United States, 186, 192–93, 194, 222, 241; Western, 72
Egal, Mohamed Ibrahim, 37
Egypt: settling Somali families in, 87
employment, Somali, in South Africa: domestic workers, 150–51, 160; factory workers, 113, 123, 124; peddling and hawking, 122–31, 134, 148–50, 193, 236; self-employment, 206; women's, 166–67, 187, 193; working for Indian Muslims, 123, 124, 125, 126, 127, 129, 131,

INDEX

134, 236. *See also* businesses, Somali, in South Africa

employment, Somali, in UAE: domestic workers, 80–81, 92, 95, 96–101, 151; education-related, 93, 100; health care, 91; law enforcement, 91, 102; public-sector, 65, 84, 88, 89–91; racial hierarchy in, 103; self-employment, 206; taxi driving, 95, 101; visa renewal based on, 76, 88, 90, 102, 254n44; with Western passports, 87; women's, 92–94, 95, 96–101, 187, 193. *See also* businesses, Somali, in UAE

employment, Somali, in United States, 186–207; entry preference given for, 175; factory workers, 186, 187, 188–89, 192, 195, 197; men's, 193–201; self-employment, 201–7, 267n61; women's, 179, 187–93, 198, 201

enclaves, Somali, 11, 83; in Dubai, 20, 60–61, 93–94; in Kenya, 46–47, 228, 250n50; in South Africa, 20, 116, 120–21, 125, 138, 145, 149, 154, 161, 258n18; in UAE, 27, 83, 91, 102–3. *See also* Columbus, Ohio, Somalis in; communities, Somali; Minneapolis, Minnesota, Somalis in England. *See* Great Britain

entrepreneurs, Somali: migrant, 10, 14, 60; in South Africa, 112, 142; transnational, 70, 71–72; in UAE, 74, 76, 78, 83–87, 92, 93, 105; women, 128. *See also* businesses, Somali, in South Africa; businesses, Somali, in UAE; businesses, Somali, in United States

Esperitu, Yen, 9

Ethiopia: passport from, 79; rebel movements from Somalia operating in, 39–40; Somali migrants/refugees from, 43, 133; wars with Somalia, 37, 38–39; Western Somaliland as colony of, 33–34, 35, 36, 37

ethnic enclaves. *See* enclaves, Somali

Europe: colonial policies of, 33–35, 35–36, 37, 38, 113; fortification of borders by, 235. *See also* passports, European

Europe, Somalis in: migration by, 3, 5, 14, 43, 163–64, 173; as new earthly jannah, 106, 237; welfare programs for, 8, 178

exploitation, sexual. *See* violence: sexual-based gender violence

families: changing gender roles in United States, 179, 180–86; definitions of, 53–54, 192, 251n68; diasporic dispersal of, 213–18, 228; husband's role in, 4–5, 95, 215, 220–21, 222, 225, 228; networks of, 83–84, 87, 88, 90–91, 174, 194–95; women's roles in, 94, 100–101. *See also* welfare programs, U.S.: women with children given priority

family reunification: in South Africa, 162, 166; in United States, 49, 50–54, 169–70, 173, 232, 251n66; in Western countries, 56–57, 165. *See also* chain migration, Somali

Ferree, Myra Marx, 17

fiefdoms, Somali, 40–42, 42–43. *See also* warlords, Somali

Foner, Nancy, 15

food stamps, 176, 183, 196, 197, 215. *See also* welfare programs, U.S.

French Somaliland, 33

gender norms, Somali: migration experiences and, 147–48, 166; motivations

for return, 218–29, 221–22; in South Africa, 112; in UAE, 94; in United States, 7, 170–71, 180–86, 193, 198, 201, 226, 237–38. *See also* men, Somali; violence: sexual-based gender violence; women, Somali
globalization, 3, 8, 20, 66, 96, 233, 235
Gosha people, 44. *See also* Bantus
Great Britain: hegemony in oil concessions, 252–53n11; Somalis in, 185–86, 251n69, 267n66; UAE's interactions with, 62–63, 70
Green, Nancy, 14–15
Gulf Cooperation Council (GCC), 64–65, 66–69
Gulf States: Asianization of, 67–68; oil wealth in, 62–66, 69; Somalis in, 69, 108–9, 237. *See also* Arabian Gulf/Peninsula; oil boom; *and individual Gulf countries*

Hagadera refugee camp, 44
haji: use of term, 260n45
Hawaalado (remittance companies), 201. *See also* remittances
Hawiye clan, 40
hawkers. *See* employment, Somali, in South Africa: peddling and hawking
health care: in UAE, 75, 82, 84, 91; in United States, 177, 178, 181, 182, 184, 188, 197
Heard-Bey, Frauke, 63–64
Hess, Beth B., 17
Hispanics: poverty rate in United States, 207
Hmong refugees: in United States, 174, 177, 179, 206, 207. *See also* Vietnamese migrants

Hollifield, James Frank, 10
home: definitions of, 13, 229; search for, 231. *See also* returnees, Somali
Horn of Africa: migrants/refugees from Somalia in, 39, 51, 78, 80, 247n3; postcolonial European division of, 33–34; return from United States to, 218, 224, 225, 228, 229; Somalian reunification attempts in, 35–37; U.S. role in, 38. *See also individual Horn countries*
housing. *See* South Africa, Somalis in, housing for; United Arab Emirates (UAE), Somalis in: housing for; United States, Somalis in: subsidized housing for
human rights: abuses of, in Gulf region, 19; South African situation, 161; UAE situation, 66, 96. *See also* civil rights
Hussein, Abdirisak Hagi, 35
Hyndman, Jennifer, 234, 270n5

identity: clan, 24–25, 33, 41; cultural, 229; hybrid, 240–41; in migration experience, 10–11, 14, 17, 41, 221; racial, 167; religious, 167, 189, 222, 229; situational nature of, 112, 236; Somali, 69, 112; transnational, 242. *See also* Arab League/Arabs: Somalis' identification with; blacks, South African: Somalis' distancing from; gender norms, Somali; Muslims: Somalis' identification with; South Africa, Somalis in: affinity with Indian Muslims
Ifo refugee camp, 44
imagination. *See* migration: imagined; migration, Somali: imagined

INDEX

Immigration Act of 1924 (U.S.), 172
Immigration Act of 1965 (U.S.), 172–73
immigration policies, 17–18, 20, 59; South African, 18, 114–15, 125, 163; UAE, 65–68, 69, 72; U.S., 18, 52–54, 72, 171–75, 187, 251n66
India: labor migrants from, 11, 15, 68, 76–77, 101, 114, 258n18; Somali businesses in, 71, 79, 85; UAE trade with, 62–63, 71, 74, 101, 105. *See also* employment, Somali, in South Africa: working for Indian Muslims; Muslims: Indian; South Africa, Somalis in: affinity with Indian Muslims
informal settlements: Kenyan, 46; South African, 112–13, 121, 133, 157, 241. *See also* townships, South African
insecurities, Somali: in Kenyan refugee camps, 46; in South Africa, 5–6, 112, 143–47, 148, 149, 155–67, 180, 237; among UAE labor migrants, 66, 67–68; over uncertain legal status, 60, 104, 107, 108–9. *See also* security: migrants' search for; Somalia, political turmoil in; violence
integration, Somali: of migrants/refugees into host country, 10–11, 45, 46–48, 66; in South Africa, 127, 138, 192; in the United States, 188–91, 216–19, 223
Iraq, 49, 67, 234
Islam: food restrictions in, 161, 206, 262n76; husband's responsibilities in, 4–5, 151, 183–84, 185, 215; prejudice against, 199–200; prohibition against charging/paying interest, 203. *See also* Muslims
Italian Somaliland, 33, 34

Jannaalayaal: dreams of becoming, 2–3, 43, 70, 83, 87–92
jannah: migration as new earthly Eden, 2–3, 6, 12, 87–92, 106, 125, 178, 237
Jareer people. *See* Bantus
Jaworsky, Nadya B., 13
Jeffrey, Patricia, 222
Jensen, Leif, 83
jilbaab, 188, 192. *See also* clothing, Somali

kafeel system (UAE), 67–68, 72–78. *See also* visas, UAE: sponsorship for
Kapiszewski, Andrzej, 65, 67
Kenny, Kevin, 231
Kenya: buying forged passports in, 78–79; corruption in, 46–48, 57, 163; Nairobi Somali enclave, 46–47, 228, 250n50; Northeastern Province, 33–34, 35–36, 37, 247n3; as off-port economic center of Somalia, 1; Somali migration to South Africa from, 114; Somali migration to United States from, 50–56; Somali refugee camps, 2, 9, 12, 43–49, 194, 231–32, 270n5; Somali refugees in, 32, 33, 43–49, 111; Somali women–owned stores in, 203; Tripartite Agreement on Somali refugees, 48; UNHCR oversight of Somali refugees, 44, 45–49, 115, 121, 175; as War on Terror partner with United States, 13–14. *See also* Dadaab refugee camps; Westgate Mall attack
Kibria, Nazli, 102, 226
kinship: absence of, in United States, 224–25; cross-clan, 25; networks of, 55, 138, 146, 174; transnational ties of, 87, 212, 213–18, 239. *See also* communities, Somali; families

INDEX

Kivisto, Peter, 12
knobkerries, 155, 261n62
Kuwait, 64, 252–53n11

labor migrants: Chinese, 114, 257n13; Indian, 11, 15, 68, 76–77, 101, 114, 258n18; in South Africa, 114, 129, 131. *See also* United Arab Emirates: labor migrants in; United Arab Emirates, Somalis in: as labor migrants
language(s), 85, 130; Somalis' limited skills, 100, 141–42, 179, 187, 191, 192; in UAE, 62, 70, 91, 254n43
Latin America: migrants from, 227, 233; smuggling refugees to United States through, 54
law enforcement: Kenya, 46–48, 57; South Africa, 131, 143, 155; UAE, 46–48, 91, 102
Lee, Jennifer, 157
Lesotho: labor migrants from, 114
Levitt, Peggy, 13
Little, Peter: *Somalia: Economy without State*, 71

Mahdi, Ali, 40
maids. *See* employment, Somali, in South Africa: domestic workers; employment, Somali, in UAE: domestic workers; race: and domestic work; women, Somali: domestic workers
Malawi: migrants and refugees from, 55, 56, 118, 119–20, 126, 151, 154, 160
Malta, 43, 93, 164, 233, 241
marginalization: of blacks in South Africa, 132, 156–57, 158; socioeconomic, of Somalis, 8, 32, 44, 201, 220, 223, 228; of Somalis, in United States, 201, 207, 211, 228–29, 239; of U.S. welfare recipients, 190–91
Marikana miners, 155
marriage(s), 41, 254n52; Jannaalayaal migrants as ideal candidates, 88, 89, 220–21; obtaining citizenship/visas through, 78, 79. *See also* divorce
Maryam, Mengistu Haile, 38
Médecins Sans Frontières: refugee camp management by, 44, 45
men, Somali: changing gender roles in United States, 6, 170, 180–86; in diaspora, 138, 220; dreams of return, 219–23; employment experiences, 193–201; in South Africa, 112; in UAE, 94–95; in United States, 201–7. *See also* Islam: husband's responsibilities
Mexico: migrants from, 195, 227; migration through, 52, 164
Middle East, 38, 62; cost of living in, 225, 228; dream of returning to, 6, 8, 221–22, 223, 229; Somalis migrating to, 4, 5, 14, 31, 43, 87. *See also* oil boom; *and individual Middle East countries*
migrants: as agents, 9–12, 16–17, 58; conflicts between minority groups and, 156–58; human and social capital of, 8, 10, 14, 219; movement across multiple borders by, 17, 111; nonwhite elite, 234–35. *See also* labor migrants; refugee–migrant binary; refugees
migrants, Somali: dream of becoming Jannaalayaal, 2, 43, 70, 83, 87–92; otherness of, 23, 24, 130, 156, 200, 239; transnational lives of, 12, 234, 242. *See also* refugees, Somali; returnees, Somali; settlement process, Somali

INDEX

migration, 9–18; agency in, 9–12, 16–17, 58; alienation in, 240–41; anthropological vs. sociological studies of, 10–11; author's personal experiences with, 20–21, 22; comparisons of, 14–18, 20, 246n28; complexity of, 241–42; contemporary, 8, 231; convergent model of, 15; divergent model of, 15–16; globalization's challenges to, 8, 235; identity formation and, 10–11, 14, 17, 41, 221; imagined, 2–3, 8, 11–12, 13, 57; linear model of, 14; migrants' evaluations of, 8–9; motivations for, 9–14; socioeconomic advantages of, 107–8; transnational character of, 18, 170–71, 221, 228–29, 241–42

migration, Somali: to Arabian Peninsula during oil boom (1970s), 2–3, 18, 69, 70, 217–18; to Australia, 106, 163–64, 178; dreams of, 60, 112, 161–67, 195, 218, 235; ethnographic study of, 18–25; forces shaping, 59; imagined, 130–31, 227–28, 233, 239; post-1991 civil war, 3, 32–33, 42–58, 69, 217–18; to South Africa, 9, 15–16, 49–58, 115, 136, 232, 238. *See also* chain migration, Somali; diaspora, Somali; jannah; oil boom: Somali migration during; stepmigration, Somali; West, the, Somalis in: desire to migrate to

Minneapolis, Minnesota, Somalis in, 6–7, 19–20; businesses owned by, 203, 206; employment for women, 187; shopping malls for, 201, 202, 204, 205, 214, 267n61; subsidized housing for, 207, 208

Minnesota, Somalis in: businesses owned by, 201–7; employment for, 187, 192–93, 194, 198; expectations of, 225; population figures, 173–74, 197, 206; upper-middle-class, 193–94

Minnesota Family Investment Program (MFIP), 177, 179, 180

minorities: conflicts between migrants and, 156–58; failure to secure living wage jobs, 179–80; immigrant, 15; as labor migrants, 65, 66, 67; marginalization of, 41, 44; in Somalia, 33; in South Africa, 119, 121, 123, 157, 159, 167; in UAE, 18, 27, 65, 83, 84; in United States, 54, 179, 186–87, 197, 200, 206, 211, 226. *See also* Bantus; South Africa, Somalis in: as middleman minority

mobility, Somali: associated with Western passports, 105–6, 218, 219, 234–35, 270n5; constraints on, 13, 79, 85–86, 95, 112, 216–17, 236; socioeconomic, 131, 189–90, 223–29

Mogadishu, Somalia. *See* Somalia: Mogadishu

Mohamud, Hassan Sheikh, 42

mosques. *See* Muslims: mosque's significance to

Mozambique: labor migrants in, 114, 133; Somali migration through, 51, 55, 56, 118

Muslims: African, 112; Arab, 143; charity shown by, 95, 97, 118–22, 122–23, 139, 160–61, 170, 196; Indian, 131, 134, 142; Malay, 148; men's status in, 6, 95, 215, 220–21, 222, 225, 228; mosque's significance to, 116–18, 119–20, 123, 258n21; Somalis' identification with, 33, 59–60, 82, 239; South Asian, 68, 102; U.S. undermining identity of, 227, 228–29; War on Terror's impact on,

103–4, 236. *See also* employment, Somali, in South Africa: working for Indian Muslims; Islam; South Africa, Somalis in: affinity with Indian Muslims; umma (community of believers)
Myanmar: Somalis' resettling from, 49

Nairobi, Kenya. *See* Kenya
nationalism, Somali, 35–37, 38, 248n12
nation-states, 8, 20, 25, 27, 35. *See also* state-building
naturalization. *See* citizenship
nepotism, Somali, 37, 39, 41
networks: communication, 3, 5; community, 11, 104, 158, 195, 213; economic, 73; family and ethnic, 82–84, 87, 88, 90–91, 174; kinship, 55, 138, 146, 174; Muslim, 122–31, 237; religious, 111–12, 211; smuggling, 54–56, 79, 96–97; in South Africa, 5, 203, 237; transnational, 13–14, 165; in UAE, 3, 80, 95. *See also* communities, Somali; umma (community of believers)
nomads, Somali, 35, 41, 96–97, 139–40, 178
North America, Somalis in. *See* Canada, Somalis in; United States, Somalis in
Northern Frontier District (NFD), 33, 35, 44. *See also* Kenya: Northeastern Province

Ogaden region. *See* Western Somaliland
Ohio, Somalis in: businesses, 201, 206; employment, 192–93, 194, 198–99; expectations of life, 179, 225; population figures, 173, 174. *See also* Columbus, Ohio, Somalis in

oil boom (1970s), 62–66, 68–69, 178, 220, 252–53n11; Somali migration during, 2–3, 18, 31, 43, 69–70, 87–92, 103, 130, 217–18
Oman, 63, 64, 65, 69
Ong, Aihwa, 72, 233, 235
Organization of African Unity (OAU), 36; Refugee Convention of 1969, 250n45
orthography, Somali, 248n21
Osman, Aden Abdullah, 35
otherness of Somali migrants, 23, 24, 130, 156, 200, 239

Pakistan: labor migrants from, 68, 71, 76–77, 101, 258n18
pangas (machetes), 155, 261n62
Parrenas, Rhacel, 96, 188, 240–41
passports, 4, 79, 234; European, 1, 4, 5, 60, 164; nonrecognition of Somali, 60, 78–79, 85, 104, 106, 234–35; South African, 163, 164; UAE, 80–81, 96, 238; U.S., 4, 85–86, 106, 219, 234, 256n67; Western, 83, 85–86, 87, 101, 104–9, 233–34. *See also* citizenship; immigration policies; visas
patronage system, Somali, 41–42. *See also* nepotism, Somali
peddlers. *See* employment, Somali, in South Africa: peddling and hawking
Personal Responsibility and Work Opportunity Reconciliation Act of 1996 (PRWORA), 176–77
Pierre, Jemima, 211, 226
political asylum. *See* asylum seeking
politics, 14, 62, 68, 85–86, 229. *See also* Somalia, political turmoil in
Portes, Alejandro, 83

poverty: in South Africa, 5–7, 119, 125, 151, 154, 156, 157; in United States, 5–6, 109–10, 170, 177–80, 187, 209–10
Priven, Frances Fox, 179
public assistance. *See* welfare programs; welfare programs, U.S.
Puntland region (Somalia), 42, 43

qat (khat): chewing of, 249n34
Qatar, 63, 64, 252–53n11

race, 41, 167; and domestic work, 96–101; in South Africa, 18, 111–16, 123, 125–26, 134–35, 154, 157–58; in United States, 209–10, 238–39
racism, 102–3, 155–67, 199–200, 225, 226. *See also* blacks, South African: Somalis' distancing from; segregation; South Africa, racial polarization in
receiving countries, 8–9, 10, 15, 58. *See also* South Africa, Somalis in; United Arab Emirates, Somalis in; United States, Somalis in
Reception and Placement Programs (U.S.), 176
Refugee Act of 1980 (U.S.), 172, 173
refugee camps, 1, 175, 180–81, 182; in Kenya, 2, 9, 12, 43–49, 194, 231–32, 270n5. *See also* Dadaab refugee camps; detention centers
refugee-migrant binary: blurring of, 9–10, 60, 111. *See also* migrants; refugees
Refugee Resettlement Assistance (U.S.), 175
refugees: anthropological vs. sociological studies of, 10–11; strategies utilized by, 16–17, 25, 90–91; transnational lives of, 12, 213–14, 218, 234, 239, 240–41, 242; UAE does not recognize status of, 10, 69, 75; UN definition of, 173, 243–44n5; UNHCR resettlement role, 161–62; United Nations Refugee Convention of 1951, 60, 69, 114, 250n45; in United States, 172, 173, 175. *See also* asylum seeking
refugees, Somali, 20, 39, 87, 232; in South Africa, 4, 49–58, 114–15, 145–46, 162–63; stateless status of, 4–5, 17–18, 57; Tripartite Agreement on, 48; in United States, 6–9, 49–58, 170, 173–76, 186–207. *See also* Kenya: Somali refugees in; migrants, Somali; returnees, Somali; settlement process, Somali
religion: as force shaping migrant experience, 59–60; identity of, 112, 167, 222, 229; U.S. undermining of traditions, 189, 218–19, 222, 226, 238–39. *See also* Islam
remittances, 44, 56, 74, 178, 222; financial drain of, 87, 216–17, 240; husband's responsibility for, 4–5, 95, 215, 220–21, 222, 225, 228; from Jannaalayaal migrants, 2–3, 88, 89, 125; from South Africa, 5–6, 124, 137, 139; from United States, 170–71, 196, 213–18; by women workers, 92, 93, 100–101, 151
repatriation, 51, 257n13
resettlement. *See* settlement process, Somali
resources: mobilization of, 10–11, 14, 16–17, 214–15. *See also* tool kit, cultural; welfare programs; welfare programs, U.S.
returnees, Somali: to Africa, 6, 8, 221–22; gendered motivations for, 218–29; idealization of, 6, 8, 222–23, 236, 240;

limited options for, 13, 229; as refugee solution, 45, 48–49, 58; in UAE, 83–87, 103
Richmond, Anthony, 235
rights. *See* civil rights; human rights

Sangub, Mahamed Abdullahi, 171–72; *Qabyo*, 171
Saudi Arabia, 64, 65, 99, 135, 213; dream of becoming Jannaalayaal in, 43, 70
Scandinavia, 49, 185–86
security: migrants' search for, 149, 231, 232, 234–35, 241–42. *See also* insecurities, Somali
segregation, 62, 94, 121, 187. *See also* racism
September 11, 2001, terrorist attacks: border security following, 13–14, 20, 25, 52, 86, 232, 235, 241; discrimination against Somalis following, 86, 174, 199–200, 226. *See also* War on Terror
settlement process, Somali, 10–11, 12, 17; in Minnesota, 174; as refugee solution, 45, 58; in South Africa, 165–66; transnationalism of, 60, 170, 212, 214, 240–41; UNHCR's role in, 49, 51, 161–62, 173; in United States, 50–51, 53, 169–70, 170–71, 173–76, 223; in urban areas, 46–48, 58, 66, 235, 250n50
settlements, informal. *See* informal settlements
shaar gaduud: use of term, 138
Shabaab, al- (Somali terrorist group): affiliated with Westgate Mall attack, 48, 199; creating difficulties for Somali migration, 164, 200
Sharmarke, Abdirashid Ali, 35, 37

Sheik-Abdi, Abdi, 38
Shirdon, Abdi Farah, 42
Siad Barre, Mohamed: bombardment of northwestern Somali cities by, 40, 42, 43, 89; dictatorship of, 37–40; ouster of, 32–33, 40–41, 42
Smith, Andrew, 12
smugglers/smuggling: of boat people, 43; South African migration involving, 4, 49, 117–18, 125; UAE migration involving, 70, 79, 80, 94, 96–97; U.S. migration involving, 50, 52, 54–55; Western migration involving, 106, 107, 163–64
Social Security (SSI) (U.S.), 176, 180, 215
sociologists: migration studies by, 10–11
Somalia: class in, 55, 70, 193–94; literacy campaign in, 248n21; Mogadishu, 42–43, 44, 69, 70, 71, 72, 77, 97; population figures, 33, 247n6; sailors from, 258n20; and Tripartite Agreement on refugees, 48; welfare programs nonexistent in, 177, 180
Somalia, history of: colonial borders, 33–35, 42; democratic era, 35–37; diaspora, 42–58; dictatorship, 37–40; Ethiopian wars, 37, 38–39; postcolonial, 36; warlordism and fiefdoms, 40–42
Somalia, political turmoil in, 31–42; breakdown of central government, 35, 40–44, 54–55, 68–69, 71, 74–75, 78–79, 88, 92; citizens' uncertain legal status, 1, 17–18, 32–33, 59–60, 79, 83, 107, 108–9, 270n5; displacement caused by, 2, 3, 13–14, 42, 43–49, 70, 241; as failed state, 32–33, 42–58, 60, 86. *See also* diaspora, Somali;

marginalization: of Somalis, in United States; passports: nonrecognition of Somali
Somali Democratic Republic, 34
Somaliland, 33–34, 43
Somali National Movement, 39–40
Somalis: clothing, 21–22, 188–89, 192, 258n17; identity of, 69, 112; lack of legal status, 1, 4–5, 17–18, 32–33, 57, 59–60, 79, 107, 108–9; nomadic nature of, 35, 41, 178. *See also* Bantus; children and youth, Somali; gender norms, Somali; men, Somali; women, Somali
Somali Salvation Democratic Front (SSDF), 39
South Africa: citizenship, 60, 114, 162; constitution of 1996, 119; court system, 159–60; culture, 126, 134; education, 166; immigration policies, 18, 114–15, 125, 163; labor migrants in, 114, 129, 131; law enforcement, 131, 143, 155; minorities in, 119, 121, 123, 157, 159, 167; passports, 163, 164; postapartheid conditions, 129, 130, 140, 145, 155–56, 257n9; public assistance programs not available in, 177, 196; racial polarization in, 18, 111–16, 123, 125–26, 134–35, 154, 157–58; refugees' journeys to, 49–58; visas, 4, 232, 237, 238; welfare programs, 121, 177, 196; white-owned stores in, 257n7. *See also* Africa; apartheid; blacks, South African; economy, South African; townships, South African
South Africa, Somalis in, 3–6, 18, 122, 201, 211; affinity with Indian Muslims, 112, 116–22, 128, 148, 154, 158, 160–61, 170, 236–37; barriers to permanent settlement, 165–66; Bellville enclave (Cape Town), 20, 125, 132, 148, 152, 154, 161; family reunification, 162, 166; housing for, 125; integration into South African society, 127, 138, 192; Korsten enclave (Port Elizabeth), 20, 148, 154, 161; Mayfair enclave (Johannesburg), 20, 116, 120–21, 125, 147–49, 154, 161, 258n18; as middleman minority, 112, 135, 138, 140, 237, 239; migration by, 9, 15–16, 49–58, 115, 136, 232, 238; Mitchells Plain enclave (Cape Town), 145, 148, 154; refugees, 4, 114–15, 145–46, 162–63; sense of belonging, 116–21, 167, 229, 237; Uitenhage enclave (Port Elizabeth), 133, 134, 148, 149, 154; violence against, 5, 112, 143–47, 155–67, 237; welfare programs not available to, 121, 177, 196; women, 112, 128, 147–55, 166–67, 187, 193, 229. *See also* blacks, South African: Somalis' distancing from; businesses, Somali, in South Africa; employment, Somali, in South Africa
South Asians, 19, 200; as labor migrants in UAE, 18, 68, 82, 102, 103; Somalis treated differently from, 101, 236. *See also* Asians
Soviet Union: Somalia given military support by, 37, 38
spaza shops. *See* businesses, Somali, in South Africa: stores and spaza shops
Spickard, Paul: *Almost All Aliens*, 263n3
sponsorship: employers', 80–81, 81–82; family, 5, 53–55, 56–57, 88, 90–91. *See also* chain migration, Somali; kafeel system; visas, UAE: sponsorship for

state-building, 32, 33–34, 35. *See also* nation-states

statelessness: Somalis' condition of, 17–18, 59, 79. *See also* passports: nonrecognition of Somali; Somalia, political turmoil in

step-migration, Somali, 9, 32, 43, 232–33. *See also* chain migration, Somali

Sterns, Jessica, 200

street trading. *See* employment, Somali, in South Africa: peddling and hawking

structure(s): economic, 131, 187; ethnic and racial, 14, 126; family, 214; leadership, 42; power, 63, 238–39; public infrastructure, 38, 63, 64, 70–71; social, 242; tension between strategies and, 17; of welfare programs, 28

Supreme Revolutionary Council, 37

survival, refugees': economic, 133, 148, 196, 220; family, 28, 62, 177, 182, 197, 217; meeting basic needs of, 13, 32, 116; strategies of, 16–17, 25, 90–91

Swidler, Ann, 16–17

Syria, 87, 269n95

Tanzania: Somali migration through, 51, 55, 56, 118

Temporary Assistance to Needy Families (TANF), 176–77, 178–79

terrorist groups, Somali, 48–49, 164, 199–200. *See also* September 11, 2001, terrorist attacks; Westgate Mall attack

tool kit, cultural, 183, 235, 238; aligning with host countries, 58, 60, 101; malleability of, 112, 242; metaphor of, 16–17; return as a means of maintaining, 219, 222–23, 227. *See also* culture

townships, South African, 113–14, 237; also known as "locations," 140, 257n9, 260n46; Somali stores and spaza shops in, 131–55, 156. *See also* informal settlements: South African; insecurities, Somali: in South Africa

transformation, social, 16–17, 22

transitional federal governments (TFGs), 41–42

transnationalism, 12–14; anthropological vs. sociological studies of, 10–11; cultural logics of, 233–34; of entrepreneurs, 70, 71–72; kinship ties of, 87, 212, 213–18, 239; of migration, 18, 170–71, 221, 228–29, 241–42; mothering, 167; of refugee life, 12, 213–14, 218, 234, 239, 240–41, 242; of Somali settlement process, 60, 170, 212, 214, 240–41

Transparency International, 41, 46

travel documents. *See* passports; visas

tribes. *See* clans

Trucial States. *See* United Arab Emirates

Twin Cities, Somalis in. *See* Minneapolis, Minnesota, Somalis in

Ugaas: use of term, 6. *See also* clans: chiefs of

umma (community of believers), 59–60, 116–22, 237. *See also* communities, Somali

unemployment: in Kenya, 46; in South Africa, 126, 140, 151; in UAE, 65, 72; in United States, 200. *See also* employment, Somali, in South Africa; employment, Somali, in UAE; employment, Somali, in United States

United Arab Emirates (UAE): barriers to researching migration in, 19; cost of living in, 86, 87, 88, 89–90, 93–94, 151, 228; formation of, 63–64; Great Britain's interactions with, 62–63, 70; immigration policies in, 65–68, 69, 72; labor migrants in, 61–62, 64–68, 76–78, 91, 96, 101, 235–36; law enforcement, 46–48, 91–92, 102; map of, 64; minorities in, 18, 27, 65, 83, 84; oil wealth, 62, 63–66, 69; racism in, 102–3; sea trade, 61, 62–63, 69; as U.S. ally in War on Terror, 104; welfare programs, 65, 84, 177. *See also* Abu Dhabi; citizenship: UAE; Dubai; education: in UAE; health care: in UAE; language(s): in UAE

United Arab Emirates (UAE), Somalis in, 1–3; affinity with Muslims, 96, 103, 167; categories of, 70–71; class in, 72, 82, 84, 88; dream of becoming Jannaalayaal in, 43; economic opportunities, 82–101; education in, 82, 84, 87, 88, 90, 93; enclaves, 27, 83, 91, 102–3; housing for, 85, 254n55; India's trade with, 62–63, 71, 74, 101, 105; as labor migrants, 2–3, 10, 18, 60, 69, 70, 82, 92–95, 103; level of discrimination against, 102–3; migration to, 9, 15–16, 68–82, 83, 232; oil boom migrants, 87–92, 103; 1.5 generation, 70, 91, 103; passports, 80–81, 96, 238; population figures, 18, 61; post–civil war migrants, 92–95; relationship with Emiratis, 73, 77, 96–97, 102, 167, 236, 239–40; returnees from West in, 83–87; search for visas, 71–82; sense of belonging in, 59–60, 81–82, 84, 101–9, 143, 229, 236; social status of, 211; War on Terror's impact on, 103–4; welfare programs unavailable to, 84, 177; women, 80–81, 92–94, 95, 96–101, 187, 229. *See also* businesses, Somali, in UAE; employment, Somali, in UAE; entrepreneurs, Somali: in UAE

United Kingdom. *See* Great Britain

United Nations: Refugee Convention of 1951, 60, 69, 114, 250n45

United Nations High Commissioner for Refugees (UNHCR): definition of refugee, 173, 243–44n5; refugee camp oversight by, 44, 45–49, 115, 121, 175; report on Somali refugees, 43; resettlement programs, 49, 51, 161–62, 166, 173; and Tripartite Agreement, 48. *See also* refugees; refugees, Somali

United Somali Congress (USC), 40

United States, 38, 235, 241; economy in, 170, 186, 187, 200; education in, 186, 192–93, 194, 222, 241; Hmong refugees in, 174, 177, 179, 206, 207; immigration policies in, 18, 52–54, 72, 171–75, 187, 251n66; passports, 4, 85–86, 106, 219, 234, 256n67; poverty in, 84, 209–10, 265n28; refugee resettlement in, 51, 173–76; tensions between newcomers and marginalized groups, 156–57; Vietnamese migrants, 174, 186, 200, 226; visas, 4, 72, 232; War on Terror, 13–14, 104. *See also* citizenship, U.S.; minorities: in United States; welfare programs, U.S.

United States, Somalis in, 6–9; alienation felt by, 6–7, 178–79, 206, 228–29, 240–41; changing gender roles, 7, 170, 171, 180–86; cultural dissonance felt by, 218–20, 222–23, 236, 238–39; divergence and convergence of,

239–40; employment, 186–207; family reunification among, 49, 50–54, 169–70, 232, 251n66; migration by, 3, 8, 15–16, 169, 172–73, 179, 194–95, 211; as new earthly jannah, 106, 178, 225, 237; population figures, 18, 173, 174–75; poverty of, 170, 177–80, 206–7, 217, 219; refugees' journeys to, 49–58; smuggling into, 163–64; subsidized housing for, 183, 197, 207–12, 215. *See also* Columbus, Ohio, Somalis in; gender norms, Somali: in United States; Minneapolis, Minnesota, Somalis in; passports: U.S.; settlement process, Somali: in United States; visas: U.S.

urban centers: refugees self-settling in, 46–48, 58, 250n50

Venkatesh, Sudhir Alladi, 206

Vietnamese migrants: in United States, 174, 186, 200, 226. *See also* Hmong refugees

violence: between clans, 40–41, 42; sexual-based gender violence, 51, 97, 99–100, 147–48, 155, 270n96; in South Africa, 5, 112, 143–47, 155–67, 237

visas: Canadian, 4, 72; South African, 4, 232, 237, 238; U.S., 4, 7, 72, 232; Western, 163. *See also* citizenship; passports

visas, UAE: countries exempted from, 106, 234; difficulty securing, 65, 104, 232; family sponsorship for, 80, 95; for a fee, 103; as golden dirham, 72–73; loopholes in system, 76–78, 80–81; renewal of, 2, 70, 76, 88, 90, 94, 96–97, 235–36, 254n42; required to exit country, 106–7; search for, 71–82, 180; sponsorship for, 80–81, 81–82, 84; use of Somali passports to obtain, 78–79; working without, 93, 95, 97, 100, 107. *See also* citizenship: UAE; kafeel system; passports: UAE

voluntary agencies (volags), 174, 175–76

warlords, Somali, 25, 40–42, 44

War on Terror, 13–14, 163, 200, 234, 236, 238; impact on Somalis, 60, 103–4. *See also* September 11, 2001, terrorist attacks

welfare programs: in Canada, 178, 185–86; European, 5, 178; in South Africa, 121, 177, 196; in UAE, 65, 84, 177

welfare programs, U.S., 175–86; Clinton administrative reforms, 176–77, 179; combined with work, 196–98, 200–201; food stamps, 176, 183, 196, 197, 215; gender conflicts created by, 7, 193; income used for remittances, 215–16; women with children given priority, 170–71, 179–80, 180–86, 189–91, 196, 237–38, 239

West, the, Somalis in: desire to migrate to, 8, 43, 83, 112, 161, 218, 220; economic and political hegemony of, 85–86; family reunification, 56–57, 165; government assistance programs in, 121, 177–80; migrants' economic hardships, 84, 86, 170–71; passports, 83, 85–86, 101, 104–9, 233–34; resettling refugees in, 49, 87, 161–67, 214; visas, 163. *See also* citizenship, Western

Western Somaliland (Ogaden region), 33–34, 35, 36, 37

Western Somali Liberation Front (WSLF), 37, 38

INDEX 289

Westgate Mall attack (Nairobi, Kenya, September 21, 2013), 48, 58, 199–200
women, Somali: business owners, 128, 147–55; domestic workers, 80–81, 95, 96–101; dreams of return, 222, 223–29; factory/assembly line workers, 187, 195; family roles of, 94, 100–101; fertility rates of, 191–92; given priority for U.S. welfare eligibility, 170–71, 179–180, 180–86, 189–91, 196, 237–38, 239; lack of education, 179, 187, 189–90; in mosques, 258n21; as peddlers and hawkers, 148–50; in South Africa, 112, 128, 147–55, 166–67, 187, 193, 229; in UAE, 80–81, 92–94, 95, 96–101, 187, 193, 229; in United States, 179, 187–93, 198, 201–7, 220. *See also* violence: sexual-based gender violence

xenophobia: in South Africa, 155–67

Yemen, 2, 38, 43, 254n51
Yusuf, Abdinur Ali, 69

Zambia: Somali migration through, 55, 56, 118
Zimbabwe: migrants and refugees from, 114, 118, 126, 151, 156, 160; migration through, 55, 56

CAWO M. ABDI is assistant professor of sociology at the University of Minnesota and research associate in the Department of Sociology at the University of Pretoria.